ANCIENT ROME

in the Light

of Recent Discoveries

BRONZE STATUE OF A BOXER.

Discovered in Rome, 1885.

See Chapter XI.

ANCIENT ROME

in the Light

of Recent Discoveries

By

Rodolfo Lanciani

With One Hundred Illustrations

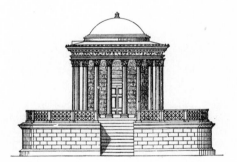

Benjamin Blom

New York

First published 1888
Reissued 1967, by Benjamin Blom, Inc., New York 10452
Library of Congress Catalog Card No. 67-13335

Printed in U.S.A. by
NOBLE OFFSET PRINTERS, INC.
NEW YORK 3, N. Y.

CONTENTS.

———✦———

iv   *CONTENTS.*

LIST OF ILLUSTRATIONS.

———•———

FULL–PAGE PLATES.

ILLUSTRATIONS IN THE TEXT.

PREFACE.

VERY few persons who have not seen Italy and its capital since 1870 are acquainted with the revolution which is being accomplished in Rome in the department of public works. From the official statistics which have been kindly supplied to me, it appears that between January 1, 1872, and December 31, 1885, 82 miles of new streets have been opened, paved, drained, and built; new quarters have sprung up which cover an area of 1,158 acres; 3,094 houses have been built or enlarged, with an addition of 95,260 rooms; 135 million lire (27 million dollars) have been spent in works of public utility and general improvement; and the population, which fourteen years ago numbered 244,000 souls, exceeds now the considerable figure of 379,000.

I have not quoted these statistics with the desire to create a sensation amongst those who still believe Rome to be the "city of death," and Italy a "mere geographical expression." I quote them simply on account of their connection with the progress of Roman archæology, because, since it is impossible to turn up in Rome a handful of earth without coming upon some unexpected find, it is easy to understand what an amount of discoveries must have been made by turning up *two hundred and seventy million* cubic feet of that land of promise.

I have not been able to ascertain the exact number of works of art and of antiquities brought to light by the gov-

ernment in the official excavations of the Forum, of the
palace of the Cæsars, of the baths, etc., or by private individuals in building their houses. However, as regards the
municipality of Rome, which owns about one third of the
ground within the walls, and of whose antiquarian wealth
I am, in a certain way, the happy treasurer, the following
works and objects have been stored in the Capitol since
1872: 705 amphoræ with important inscriptions; 2,360
terra cotta lamps; 1,824 inscriptions engraved on marble
or stone; 77 columns of rare marble; 313 pieces of columns; 157 marble capitals; 118 bases; 590 works of art
in terra cotta; 405 works of art in bronze; 711 gems, intaglios, cameos; 18 marble sarcophagi; 152 bas-reliefs;
192 marble statues in a good state of preservation; 21
marble figures of animals; 266 busts and heads; 54 pictures in polychrome mosaic; 47 objects of gold; 39 of
silver; 36,679 coins of gold, silver, and bronze; and an
almost incredible amount of smaller relics in terra cotta,
bone, glass, enamel, lead, ivory, iron, copper, and stucco.
These collections do not contain merely common or ordinary objects; they contain masterpieces in every branch
and department, — masterpieces which, in an age a little
less devoted to finance and politics, would have created a
deep sensation all over the world. Besides, the objects I
have named pertain to the material side of the question
only; the conquests of science are still greater. They
have thrown more light on the archæology of Rome than
had been thrown in a century before. There is an instance connected with one single branch of the science,
— the branch of epigraphy. The first part of volume vi.
of the "Corpus Inscriptionum Latinarum," published by
the Berlin Academy of Sciences, contains 3,925 ancient
inscriptions (of gods, emperors, magistrates, priests, and

military officers), discovered from the middle of the four-teenth century to 1876. From 1876 to the end of last year I have myself discovered and published more than one thousand; consequently in ten years' time the Roman soil has supplied epigraphy with one fourth as much as the total amount brought to light during the five preceding centuries.

It is impossible for me to mention, one by one, the scien-tific discoveries of special importance made under the au-spices of the city of Rome; if I did, this Preface would ex-ceed in length the volume it introduces. We have discov-ered a new archæological stratum, totally unknown before, — the stratum of prehistoric or traditional antiquities; we have discovered a necropolis older than the walls of Servius Tullius, containing more than 5,000 archaic specimens in bronze, amber, stone, and clay; we have brought to light more than 5,000 feet of the great *agger*, or embankment of Servius, and ascertained the site of fourteen gates; we have unearthed the remains of numberless houses and pal-aces, temples and shrines, roads and drains, parks and gar-dens, fora and porticoes, fountains and aqueducts, tombs and mausolea, to such an extent that whereas before 1872 science possessed only approximate attempts at an archæo-logical map of Rome, we have put at the disposal of stu-dents magnificent ones, covering an area of 3,967,200 square metres of the ancient city.

It would be of no use to deny that all these great con-quests in the artistic and scientific field have been obtained with a certain amount of loss and sacrifice. Persons ready to detect the mote in their neighbor's eye have filled the world with their lamentations over these partial losses and sacrifices. Pamphlets written on the subject, with but little impartiality, by eminent men, have been translated into many languages and largely circulated, with the intention of raising a crusade against the profane destroyers of the beautiful city of Rome. As is the case in all controversies not purely scientific, but mixed with personal, political, or religious feelings, the state of things has been exaggerated beyond measure. It appears to me that to satisfy our critics, whose love for art and archæology goes beyond the limits of practical good sense, it would have been desirable to have had Rome annihilated with the empire at the end of the fifth century, so that we might excavate it now with the same ease and with the same freedom with which we excavate Ostia and Pompeii. But we must remember that Rome has always lived, and lived at the expense of the past; every generation has, in a certain measure, absorbed or destroyed the works of the preceding one, and it is wonderful that so much should still be left of the works raised by the ancients, after a process of destruction and transformation which has been going on for fourteen centuries!

The history of the vicissitudes of Rome, from the point of view of the present controversy, must be divided into four periods. The first extends from the fall of the empire to the return of the popes from Avignon ; the second, the glorious period of the Italian Renaissance, during which the ruins of antiquity were most abominably treated, ends with the Seicento ; the third, which marks the destruction of mediæval remains, stops with the Napoleonic conquest of Italy ; during the fourth, from the empire of Napoleon to 1870, the first moves were at last made in the right direction of discovering and preserving ancient monuments.

The Romans of the Middle Ages were not excessively guilty as regards the destruction of ancient ruins, because the monuments crumbled more from sheer old age, from abandonment, from fires and earthquakes, than by the determinate action of men. In fact, the poverty and ignorance of the age made the raising of new structures either difficult or impossible; so that people took advantage, as well as they could, of the existing ruins when transforming them, or portions of them, into churches and convents and private dwellings. Thus the temple of Antoninus and Faustina became the church of S. Lorenzo; the temple of the Sacra Urbs, the church of SS. Cosma e Damiano; the Senate-House, the church of S. Adriano; the offices of the Senate-House, the church of Santa Martina. Thus, also, the basilica of Junius Bassus was dedicated to S. Andrea; the temple of Concord to SS. Sergius and Bacchus; the temple of Ceres to S. Maria in Cosmedin; the temple of Piety to S. Nicolas; that of Mater Matuta to S. Stefano; that of the Fortuna Virilis, to Santa Maria Egiziaca; the Macellum Magnum became the church of S. Stefano; the Pantheon and the temple of Minerva were dedicated to the Blessed Virgin; and so on indefinitely. Nearly one half of the thousand and more churches and shrines registered in Rome in the fourteenth century were indicated by the titles — in thermis, in porticu, in maximis, in archione, in formis, in palatio, in horreis, in marmorata, in paradiso, in lauro, in macello, in piscina. The example set by the clergy in appropriating the above descriptive terms was followed closely by the noblemen of the age: by the Savelli, who had intrenched themselves within the theatre of Marcellus, and within the temple of Libertas on the Aventine; by the Conti, whose famous tower near the Piazza delle Carrette rests on the ruins of the Templum Telluris; by the Frangipani, whose central fortress on the palace of the Cæsars was surrounded by detached works, erected on the Colosseum, on the arch of Titus, on the arch of Constantine, on the Janus of the Forum Boarium; by the Colonnas, masters of the mauso-

leum of Augustus and of the temple of the Sun on the
Quirinal ; by the Crescenzi, who sought refuge among the
great halls of the thermæ of Severus Alexander; by the
Orsini, whose headquarters were established in the theatre
of Pompey the Great; by the S. P. Q. R., masters of the
Tabularium, and so forth.   It is evident that such adap-
tations of ancient ruins for the use of churches, fortresses,
houses, indirectly contributed to their preservation.   At
any rate, when we hear of destructions accomplished in
the Middle Ages, we have, in many cases, the evidence of
their absolute necessity.   In the life of Hadrian I., the
" Liber Pontificalis " relates how the temple of Ceres in the
Forum Boarium was demolished to save the church of S.
Maria in Cosmedin from being crushed by the fall of the
overhanging ruins.   The same Pope Hadrian was obliged
to rebuild the church of SS. Sergius and Bacchus one hundred feet south of its original site, to save it from the
danger of being swept away by the fall of the temple of
Concord.

We must not forget, moreover, that the ruins of the ancient city were a permanent source of danger to the inhabitants of the mediæval city ; so much so that the destruction of some of those ruins must be considered to have been
in legitimate self-defence.   Those galleries tumbling into
pieces ; those crypts plunged in darkness ; those thermæ
lost in the wilderness of the abandoned quarters of the old
town ; those porticoes, many stories high, half concealed
under a thick growth of ivies and shrubs, were haunted by
outlaws, murderers, and brigands, who, sheltered as they
were, could defy from their inaccessible dens all the combined efforts of the police and of the baronial *gens-
d'armes*.   This state of things and this most curious rela-
tionship between ancient ruins and public security will be

better understood from one or two incidents which have taken place lately under our own eyes or under the eyes of the preceding generation.

Antonio Uggeri, the indefatigable explorer of Roman monuments under Pius VI., after relating how a great many skeletons of murdered men had been discovered in the excavations of the Colosseum, under the arcades of which they had been secretly buried, speaks of the following personal experience ("Antichità," vol. xxii.): "There is no doubt that the Colosseum has been for centuries the safest den of Roman outlaws. This is what happened to me there in 1790. I was engaged at that time in correcting some measurements which I had taken of the building on former occasions. I arrived on the spot one afternoon, an hour before sunset, climbed up, not without danger, taking advantage of the roughness of the walls, and entered the main corridor, on my way to the upper galleries. I had walked scarcely a hundred paces when, all of a sudden, a man sprang at me from behind a corner, — a man very tall, entirely naked, with rags around his head and ankles, black in the face, bearded, and absolutely repulsive to look at. He caught me by the waist, shook me violently, asking at the same time who I was, what business I had there, and other such questions. I answered, trembling, that I was an architect, and showed him my measure and my compass as an evidence of the purpose of my expedition among those ruins. In the mean while I heard a more gentle voice close by, begging him to leave me in peace; and, proceeding a few steps farther, I discovered the rest of the company under the vault of one of the staircases. It was composed of two more men and one woman (to whose interference I most likely owed my life), all three entirely naked, as the season was very warm. One of the men was standing;

the other was cooking something at the farther end of the passage. The poor woman crouched down to conceal her nudity as well as she could."

In case this adventure of 1790 should seem antiquated to the reader, I can instance a more recent and quite personal experience. In the year 1874, when the new Via Claudia was first opened between the Colosseum and the Navicella, I discovered a whole family nested in an underground corridor (thirty-six feet below the level of the temple of Claudius). The corridor or channel was but six feet wide, a few yards long, with a scanty supply of air and light. One of the family was lying dead on some straw; the others were praying and sobbing round the corpse. In 1877, when engaged in restoring the so-called Trophies of Marius (the fountain of the Aqua Julia), in the Piazza Vittorio Emmanuele, I discovered, likewise, a family who had been living for years inside the dry channel of the old aqueduct. A few months ago the hiding-place of a daring pickpocket was discovered right in the attic-room of the arch of Titus, together with many ancient marble heads and fragments, — a proof of his additional archæological instincts. If such things can happen in an epoch as civilized as ours, and under the eyes of a vigilant and acute police, we cannot wonder if in the Middle Ages the existence of ruins was considered in some cases inconsistent with public security.

I have said all this to prove that, in the long and sad history of the destruction of ancient Rome, the Middle Ages are perhaps the least guilty, — less guilty, at any rate, than the period of the Renaissance which followed. In spite of their enthusiastic love for ancient art and classic civilization, the great masters of the Renaissance treated our monuments and ruins with incredible contempt and brutality. The original cause of this state of things must be found, strange to say, in the increasing civilization of the age, in the softening and refining of former habits, in the development of public and private wealth, which was pushing popes, cardinals, patricians, bankers, and rich merchants to raise everywhere magnificent palaces and villas, churches and monasteries, aqueducts and fountains, harbors and bridges, castles and towers. All these constructions of the golden age, which justly form the pride of my city, and make it unique and enviable by the whole world, were built, stone by stone, with materials stolen from ancient ruins. In the course of the present book I shall have occasion to speak at length on this subject, proving that the cinquecento excavations did more harm to the monuments of imperial, republican, and kingly Rome than the ten centuries of preceding barbarism. I do not say these things to cast reproach upon the memory of men — popes, princes, artists — who so powerfully contributed to the embellishment of Rome, and who in place of the edifices destroyed by them left to us other creations which leave nothing to envy in the ancient ones. I make these remarks only to confirm what was said at the outset, namely, that the process of destruction and transformation is as old as the history of Rome itself, and that this state of things is so true and so in accordance with the nature of the place and its inhabitants that, to prevent so far as was possible further damages to our ruins, the famous *legge Pacca* was promulgated, a law worthy the brutality of the Middle Ages, which partially attained its end, thanks to its clauses of unheard-of violence.

The next period, which runs from the middle of the seventeenth century to the end of the eighteenth, ranks also among the saddest in our history, because it marks the almost complete destruction of mediæval buildings.

Under the pretence of restorations and embellishments, the
authorities laid their hands upon the most noted and the
most venerable churches of the city, which had until then
preserved their beautiful basilical type in all its simplicity,
purity, and majesty.   Alfonzo Sotomayor in 1665, Pier da
Cortona under Urban VIII., and Borromini under Alexander VII. disfigured the twin churches of S. Adriano and
S. Martina.   Onorio Longhi destroyed in 1651 the church
of S. Ambrogio and its marvellous frescoes by Pierino del
Vaga, to build in its place the tasteless structure of S.
Carlo al Corso.   The old church of S. Alessio was shame-
fully modernized by Tommaso de Marchis in 1750, and so
were those of S. Anastasia in 1722 by Carlo Gimach, of S.
Apollinare by Ferdinando Fuga, of SS. Apostoli by Fran-
cesco Fontana, of SS. Cosma e Damiano by Aririgucci.
The basilica of S. Croce in Gerusalemme, profaned and
reduced to its present form in 1744 by Passalacqua and
Gregorini, is classified by Milizia among the works of nefarious architects.   The same title of nefarious is given by
Fea to Paolo Posi, who under the pontificate of Benedict
XIV. profaned the attic of the Pantheon, substituting chi-
aroscuro daubs for the exquisite marble incrustations of
Septimius Severus.   And we must acknowledge that the
same criticism ought to be applied — from the point of
view of church architecture — to Borromini for the disfig-
urement of the Lateran, to Antonio Canevari for that of
SS. Giovanni e Paolo, to Francesco Ferrari for that of S.
Gregorio on the Cœlian, and so forth.

These churches, before the shameful restorations, were
generally divided into three naves by means of colonnades,
the shafts of which had been removed from some neighboring classic edifice ; their pavements were inlaid with marble
slabs, for the greater part inscribed with pagan historical

inscriptions or with epitaphs, or else worked in alto or basso rilievo, with patches of Cosmati tessellated work here and there. The walls of the central nave, supported by the two parallel rows of columns, were still covered with paintings and frescoes of the Middle Ages or of the earliest Renaissance, and were perforated by narrow, oblong Lombardesque windows, through which a thread of subdued light penetrated, enough to keep the sanctuary in a dreamy twilight, which invited the faithful to meditation and prayer. The roof was supported by beams of cedar wood; the façade was ornamented with a portico of spiral or fluted columns, with bases and capitals of various styles and workmanship; the doorposts of the only entrance rested upon the backs of lions, modelled by Vassalletus; the upper façade, above the portico, was covered with frescoes and mosaics.

The system followed in restoring these churches was everywhere uniform. The columns of the nave were walled up, and concealed in thick pilasters of whitewashed masonry; the inscribed or sculptured marble slabs and the mosaic pavements were taken up, and replaced by brick floors; the windows were enlarged out of all proportion, and assumed a rectangular form, so that floods of light might enter and illuminate every remote, peaceful recess of the sacred place. For the beautiful roofs made of cedar wood, vaults or *lacunaria* were substituted. The number of entrance-doors was trebled; the simple but precious frescoes of the fourteenth century were whitewashed, and the fresh surface was covered with the insignificant productions of Francesco Cozza, Gerolama Troppa, Giacinto Brandi, Michelangelo Cerruti, Pasquale Marini, Biagio Puccini, and other painters equally obscure. All these profanations could be accomplished, not only without opposition, but amid general applause, because such was the spirit and the perverted taste of the age.

It is enough to quote the example of G. B. Piranesi, architect, archæologist, engraver, educated under the influence and the inspiration of ancient art, worshipper of ancient masterpieces of architecture, who, when asked in 1765 by Cardinal Rezzonico to restore the church of S. Maria del Priorato di Malta on the Aventine, created such an *ensemble* of monstrosities — inside and outside the church — that it would be difficult to find its parallel anywhere in the world. We must remember, however, that the artists who took such an active and shameful part in the crusade against our mediæval churches and cloisters were the very ones who embellished Rome with such beautiful creations as the Trevi fountain, the Palazzo della Consulta, the Curia Innocenziana, the Corsini chapel in the Lateran, the churches of S. Agnese, of S. Andrea al Quirinale, of S. Carlo a' Catinari, the palazzi Rinuccini, Corsini, Altieri, Pamphili, Falconieri, Madama, etc.

Very few words need be spent on the fourth period, — from the end of the last century to 1870, — because the beneficial and munificent spirit shown towards our monuments by Pius VI., Pius VII., Count de Tournon, the Napoleonic prefect of the "département du Tibre," of Gregory XVI., and Pius IX. is known to every one, as we know the grave faults committed at the same time, and the damages inflicted without any apparent reason upon many works of art.

Pius VI. founded, in the Vatican, the gallery of inscriptions, the cabinet of masks, the hall of the Muses, the Rotunda, the halls of the Greek Cross and of the Biga. Pius VII founded the Braccio Nuovo and the Chiaramonti museum. Under the wise administration of Count de Tournon not less than one million dollars were spent in works of public utility, and in excavating and laying bare to archæological investigation such monuments as the temples of Vespasian, of Castor and Pollux, of Antoninus and Faustina, of Venus and Rome, of the Mater Matuta, of the Fortuna Virilis, the basilica of Constantine, the Colosseum, the Golden House of Nero, the Janus of the Forum Boarium, the Basilica Ulpia, the Forum of Trajan, etc. All these works, begun by Tournon, were most successfully brought to perfection by Pius VII. Gregory XVI., devoid as he was of classic instruction and refinement, left to us three incomparable new museums, the Egyptian, the Etruscan, and the Lateran. Under the rule of Pius IX. the monuments of the city, the museums, the galleries, were the object of constant and liberal care.

As for the damage done to ancient or Renaissance monuments during the same period, a small portion of it has been described by Pellegrini, in the Mémoire which was forbidden publication in Rome by the papal authorities of the time.

Coming now to our own times, and the controversy lately raised on the so-called destruction of Rome, I must acknowledge that the sensation we felt when the controversy was opened was one of disgust rather than of sorrow. These pretended revelations of vandalism, these condemnations of operations characterized at first as destruction of Rome, later on as simple transformation or disfigurement, were levelled at men who for the last seventeen years have been constantly on the watch to defend inch by inch the archæological ground against the princes of finance and speculation, against engineers and contractors, against the daily press. Considering, however, the state of things more calmly, we must be grateful to the authors of the controversy, not only because we believe them to have been inspired alone by the pure love they feel for art and archæology, but also because they have given us a solemn occasion for discussing the subject, and making the light of truth shine forth in its full splendor. When at the end of 1870 the Italian government turned its attention towards the archæological interest of the city, the valley of the Forum was still the Campo Vaccino of past ages. With the exception of the column of Phocas, excavated by the Duchess of Devonshire, of a narrow ledge of the Basilica Julia, and a portion of the temple of Castor and Pollux, excavated by Tournon, all that classic group lay buried under an embankment thirty-three feet high. If in 1870 any one had spoken to us of the probability of an imminent and complete excavation of the Forum, from end to end, we should have denied the possibility of such an enterprise being accomplished by a single generation. But now the golden dream has become a reality. To-day, for the first time since the fall of the empire, we are able to walk over the bare pavement of the Sacra Via, from its beginning near the Colosseum to its end near the temple of Jupiter Capitolinus, admiring on either side of the wonderful road the most glorious monuments of the republic and of the empire. To the discovery and excavation of this group we must add the excavation of the baths of Caracalla, of the Stadium of Domitian, of the greater portion of the palace of the Cæsars; the isolation of Agrippa's Pantheon, and of the so-called Nymphæum of Minerva Medica; and the transfer from private to public domain of the whole Palatine hill, the lands covering the baths of Titus and Caracalla, the necropolis on the Via Latina, the tombs of the Scipios, Ostia, and the villa of Hadrian.

As regards the art-treasures collected since 1870, it is enough to name the two bronze athletes lately discovered on the slope of the Quirinal, the bronze Bacchus of the Tiber, the Juno of the Palatine, the bas-reliefs of the Forum, and the four hundred and seventy-nine statues and busts brought together by the municipality. To obtain these results, the state and the municipality have spent about one million dollars, and excavated and removed miles away in all two hundred and eighty-six million cubic feet of earth. What state, what city, in the world can boast of having done in so short a time the hundredth part of what has been accomplished in Rome?

We must not forget that whereas in former times archæological discoveries were made known to a limited number of privileged experts, sometimes years after they had taken place, now the "Bullettino della Commissione archeologica comunale di Roma" describes every month all the latest discoveries,[1] thus enabling specialists scattered all over the world to share the privilege of those residing in Rome.

I have spoken hitherto almost exclusively of ancient monuments and works of art, to keep myself within the radius of my own studies and within the boundaries of my own province. If the action of the state and of the city authorities has not proved of equal benefit in preserving mediæval buildings, it is only because mediæval buildings are exceedingly scarce in Rome. Still something has been, and more will be, done. The house of the Anguillara, for instance, with its picturesque tower and surroundings, has already been purchased by the city, with the intention of having it turned into a mediæval museum. The Torre delle Milizie has also been rescued from private hands, as well as the Tower of

[1] The *Bullettino della Commissione archeologica comunale di Roma* was established December, 1872, first as a quarterly, later on as a monthly publication. Issued on the first day of each month, it describes the archæological novelties up to the twenty-fifth day of the preceding one. It is considered the most interesting "magazine" of its kind, especially on account of its beautiful illustrations.

S. Martino a' Monti and the fortified convent of SS. Quattro Coronati.

As I have remarked above, it would be useless to deny that all these important conquests in the historical, archæological, and artistic field have been accompanied and followed by a certain amount of loss and sacrifice. It is useless to deny that the picturesqueness and the main characteristics of the Rome of the popes are now a matter of the past. Our churches, our monasteries, our monuments, are still left undisturbed, — in fact they are better taken care of : but we miss their old surroundings ; we miss the aged ilexes, forming as it were the frame of the picture, their deep green giving by contrast that vigor and brilliancy to the golden hue which old age lends to ruins in southern climates ; we miss the exquisite background of the Alban hills, and the snow-capped summits of the Apennine range ; we miss that sense of quiet and peaceful enjoyment which pervaded the whole scene. It is impossible to imagine anything more commonplace, and out of keeping, and shabby, and tasteless, than the new quarters which encircle the city of 1870. An excuse for this wretched state of things can be found in the rapidity with which these new quarters have sprung out of the ground, and also in the necessity of giving a hasty shelter to the new population of nearly two hundred thousand immigrants. The lovely districts crossed by the Via Salaria and the Via Nomentana, formerly studded with patrician villas and gardens, overlooking the Campagna, the valley of the Anio, the Sabine and Volscian mountains, have been transformed into an ugly city of five-storied antiæsthetic houses, looking more like barracks and barns than like dwellings for the cultivated inhabitants of the metropolis of a great kingdom. The same practice has been followed in building on the Esquiline, the Viminal, and the Quirinal hills, the plains of Testaccio and of Castello, and the outskirts of the city outside the gates S. Lorenzo, Maggiore, S. Giovanni, Angelica, and Portese.

As I wrote in the " Athenæum " of December 10, 1887, Rome, seen from one of the neighboring heights, — from the Monte Cavo for instance, — is no more the Rome of our dreams, of a beautiful brownish hue, surrounded by dense masses of foliage : it is an immense white dazzling spot, some six miles in diameter, bordering directly on the wilderness of the Campagna. In other words, Rome is assuming the look of a modern capital, with all its comforts and disadvantages, — perhaps with more disadvantages than comforts. The thought that, to make room for the new quarters, all but two of our villas have been mercilessly sacrificed, makes us hate the very name and sight of new quarters ! It is difficult to decide who is to blame for the present state of things. The city authorities have been taken by surprise : they never dreamt that the population would double in fifteen years; that Italian and foreign speculation was ready to throw hundreds of millions on the Roman market ; and lastly, that the result of this sudden influx of " ready money" would be the raising of the value of land from a few centimes the square metre to more than one thousand francs. In my opinion, the blame must be cast especially on the Roman aristocracy, on our noble land-owners unworthy the great names, which to our misfortune they have inherited ; because no sooner did this degenerate race discern the possibility of raising a little money on the magnificent villas which their forefathers had built and laid out for the comfort, health, and welfare of their fellow-citizens, than they did not hesitate one second to sell by the yard, as it were, the glory and pride of their families. We have seen three of them sell the very gardens which surrounded their city

mansions, allowing these mansions to be contaminated by
the contact of ignoble tenement houses. We have seen one
of them sell, piece by piece, even his collections of works of
art and of family souvenirs and documents and relics. We
have seen every single one of our patrician villas — the
Patrizi, the Sciarra, the Massimo, the Lucernari, the Mira-
fiori, the Wolkonsky, the Giustiniani, the Torlonias, the
Campana, the San Faustino — destroyed, their casinos dismantled, and their beautiful old trees burnt into charcoal ;
the destruction of the Villa Borghese has been stopped, for
the moment, by a more or less just decree of court. In one
case only, a nobleman *de la vieille roche* resisted up to his
last breath the temptation of selling his villa. His burial
service was scarcely over, when the opportunity was seized,
and what he had before strenuously prevented, as a shame
to the family, was accomplished by his princely sons and
daughters in less than a week, and the site of the villa, the
most magnificent one Rome possessed within its walls, is
already covered with tenement houses.

It is impossible to give an idea of the cruel persistence
with which foliage, vegetation, trees, everything which is
green, are persecuted in and around Rome. Public admin-
istrations, state, municipality, and private individuals seem
to vie with each other in taking the lead of the crusade
against the few samples of vegetable life which the *auri
sacra fames* of the Roman aristocracy has left standing.
When the municipality took possession of the Villa Corsini
on the Janiculum, to transform it into a public promenade,
they began their work by cutting down the great oaks
planted by Queen Christine of Sweden, under the pretence
that they interfered with the view. When the Italian authorities reorganized the department of public instruction
in Rome, they gave up the lovely botanical gardens on the

Lungara, under pretence of finding a better site for the new ones. The site has not yet been found. The Vatican authorities, to make room for a monumental column of the Council of 1870 have simply obliterated the beautiful Giardino della Pigna. No wonder that private citizens do not hesitate to follow such noble examples. No wonder that we already begin to feel the effects of this wholesale destruction, by an increase of two degrees in the average temperature in summer, and by a decrease in the average proportion of the oxygen of our atmosphere. Let us hope that the projects prepared and sanctioned by the city government for the establishment of new parks may soon be carried into execution. There will be three of them: One on the Monti Parioli, bordered by the Tiber, the Anio, and the Via Salaria and Flaminia, the ground for which — nearly five hundred acres — has already been purchased; the second on the ridge and on the slopes of the Janiculum, half of which is already opened for the recreation of the public; the last, approved by law of Parliament on July 14, 1887, will be, without exception, the finest park in the world, provided political or financial difficulties do not interfere with its construction. This *Passeggiata Archeologica*, as the movers of the bill, Professors Baccelli and Bonghi have named it, comprises the palace of the Cæsars, the valleys of the Forum and of the Colosseum, the baths of Titus, half the Cœlian hill, with the temple of Claudius, the picturesque groups of S. Gregorio, SS. Giovanni e Paolo, S. Stefano Rotondo, the Villa Mattei, the *vallis Egeriæ*, etc., the baths of Caracalla, the ancient necropolis between the Via Appia and the Via Latina, half of the Aventine hill, the Circus Maximus, the Forum Boarium, and the mediæval fortress of S. Balbina.

To conclude this long Preface I must observe that as in

all human controversies, so in this one concerning the
transformation of Rome, there are many arguments in favor
and many against. The impartial judge must put in each
plate of the scales what has been gained and what has
been lost, and must weigh the matter not from one single
point of personal view, but from the general point of view
of public health, cleanliness, comfort, art, science, history,
and archæology. Our judgment must start from the con·
sideration that works of improvement, of enlargement, of
transformation are *absolutely* necessary in Rome. We all
remember how difficult it was to move or drive safely about,
under the old rule, on account of the narrow and winding
character of the streets. Now that the population is fast
approaching a half million, how could we live and move in
the same space as before, without running serious risks,
even risks of life? There were quarters, like the Ghetto
and the Regola, the picturesqueness of which was the direct
produce of filth, and of a half-savage state of moral and
material life. There were the banks of the Tiber, — the
main sewer of the city, — the poisonous effluvia of which,
at low water, affected all the bordering districts. Can we
honestly blame the city government for their efforts to improve this shameful state of things? Can we blame them
for the embankment of the river, for the destruction of the
Ghetto and of the Regola, for the widening and straighten-
ing of the principal thoroughfares, especially as we know
that, in consequence of these works, the health of the city
has improved wonderfully?

My opinion is that, since the works began, we have
gained far more than we have lost: it appears to me that
those who have so strongly denounced the proceedings of
the municipality of Rome act like the miser, who, forgetful
of the treasure already secured, gets into a fit of despair

over any small gain which escapes his grip. We must remember, finally, that in every great undertaking there is a period of transition, which is exceedingly disagreeable. Let us reserve our final judgment until the period of transition is over, and the undertaking accomplished. At any rate, if there is a class of people that has no right to complain, it is the archæological brotherhood ; because never before has such a field been thrown open to their investigation, never has the Roman soil yielded such a magnificent archæological harvest, as within the last few years.

I desire to express my obligations to Mr. Edward Robinson of the Museum of Fine Arts, Boston, for the kind service which he has rendered me in superintending the preparation of this volume during the process of its manufacture. The distance at which I have been from the publishers and printers has been greatly lessened by his most generous interest in the work.

RODOLFO LANCIANI.

ANCIENT ROME

in the Light

of Recent Discoveries

ANCIENT ROME IN THE LIGHT OF RECENT DISCOVERIES.

CHAPTER I.

THE RENAISSANCE OF ARCHÆOLOGICAL STUDIES.

VERY few students are aware that Cola di Rienzo, the Roman tribune of the fourteenth century, is the real founder of the modern archæological school; and that to him must be adjudged the credit as regards the renaissance of classical studies, which has been almost exclusively bestowed on Dante Alighieri and Francesco Petrarca. They do not deserve it. Dante, " savio gentil che tutto seppe; " Dante, who collected in his wonderful " Divina Commedia " all the learning of his age, and in his wanderings through Italy and Southern France had ample opportunities of admiring the most splendid creations of Roman architecture, once only alludes to antique monuments as a subject of comparison : —

> " Sì com' ad Arli ove 'l Rodano stagna
> Sì com' a Pola presso del Quarnaro
>
> .   .   .   .
>
> Fanno i sepolcri tutto 'l loco varo." [1]
>
> *Inferno*, ix. 112–115.

[1] Even as at Arles, where stagnant grows the Rhone,
   Even as at Pola, near to the Quarnaro,

   .   .   .   .

   The sepulchres make all the place uneven.
                                    LONGFELLOW'S *Translation.*

This is a similitude derived from his recollections of the Roman cemeteries of Arles and Pola, the sarcophagi of which, white as fresh snow, were reflected in the blue waters of the Rhone and of the Gulf of Quarnaro.   But we should look in vain in his cantos for a souvenir of the amphitheatres of the same cities of Arles and Pola, which have come down to the present age in a good state of preservation, and which he must have seen in all their magnificence ; neither does he mention the Verona amphitheatre, on the steps of which he had so often sat in deep meditation, lamenting, —

> " Com' è duro calle
> lo scendere e 'l salir per l' altrui scale."

Not less silent and indifferent does his Muse remain at the sight of the ruins of Rome.   One episode only she drew, not from Church traditions, as it is commonly believed, but from a genuine antique monument, the remains and the memory of which have long since disappeared.   I refer to those fascinating lines in which he describes the meeting of the poor widow with the Emperor Trajan. I quote the passage in Italian, that the full harmony of the verses may be enjoyed, — a harmony which can scarcely be preserved in a translation : —

> " Quiv' era storïata l' alta gloria
> Del roman prince, lo cui gran valore
> Mosse Gregorio alla sua gran vittoria.
>   Io dico di Traiano imperatore :
> Ed una vedovella gli era al freno,
> Di lagrime atteggiata e di dolore.
>   Dintorno a lui parea calcato e pieno
> Di cavalieri : e l' aquile dell' oro
> Sovr' esso in vista al vento si movieno.
>   La miserella infra tutti costoro
> Pareva dir : Signor, fammi vendetta
> Del mio figliuol, ch' è morto, ond' io m' accoro.

Ed egli a lei rispondere : Ora aspetta
Tanto, ch' io torni.   Ed ella : Signor mio,
Come persona in cui dolor s' affretta —
   Se tu non torni ? Ed ei : Chi fia dov' io,
La ti farà.   Ed ella : L' altrui bene
A te che fia, se 'l tuo metti in obblio?
   Ond' elli : Or ti conforta : chè conviene,
Ch' io solva il mio dovere anzi ch' io muova :
Giustizia il vuole, e Pietà mi ritiene."

Purgatorio, x. 73–93.[1]

The bas-relief described by Dante as representing this lovely episode is not imaginary, but real ; and it does not belong to Purgatory, but to this world.   It was sculptured on one of the panels of a triumphal arch, which stood in the centre of the great square in front of Agrippa's Pantheon.   The bas-relief, as is often the case with this class of commemorative monuments, represented and personified a conquered Nation kneeling and begging for mercy before

[1] There the high glory of the Roman Prince
      Was chronicled, whose great beneficence
      Moved Gregory to his great victory ;
   'T is of the Emperor Trajan that I speak ;
      And a poor widow at his bridal stood,
      In attitude of weeping and of grief.
   Around about him seemed it thronged and full
      Of cavaliers, and the eagles in the gold
      Above them visibly in the wind were moving.
   The wretched woman in the midst of these
      Seemed to be saying : "Give me vengeance, Lord,
      For my dead son, for whom my heart is breaking."
   And he to answer her : "Now wait until
      I shall return."   And she : "My lord," like one
      In whom grief is impatient, "shouldst thou not
   Return ? "   And he : "Who shall be where I am
      Will give it thee."   And she : "Good deed of others,
      What boots it thee, if thou neglect thine own ? "
   Whence he : "Now comfort thee, for it behoves me
      That I discharge my duty ere I move ;
      Justice so wills, and pity doth retain me."

LONGFELLOW'S *Translation.*

the Roman invader.   The simple and inerudite imagination
of the Middle Ages gave a different meaning to this plain
representation, so common on antique coins and bas-reliefs;
it was supposed to commemorate the well-known legend of
Trajan's soul rescued from damnation at the request of S.
Gregory the Great, — a legend which is still believed by
the Roumanians, who worship Trajan as their national hero
and national saint.   The triumphal arch opposite the Pantheon was accordingly called the Arch of Piety; a hospital close by was called the Hospital of Piety; and the
name is still attached to a little church not far from
the Pantheon, called the Madonna della Pietà.   The arch
was destroyed to the level of the foundations by Pope
Alexander VII., Chigi, in order that its marbles might
be employed in his restoration of the portico of the Pantheon itself.

It would be useless to deny or excuse the ignorance of
Dante in this branch of human learning, and it would be
equally unjust to lessen our admiration for him on account
of that ignorance.   The science of archæology did not
exist in his age, and he cannot be blamed if he was ignorant of what did not exist.   Many years had to elapse
before the dawn of the new day should lighten the darkness of mediæval science.   Even the most powerful intel-
lects are obliged by the law of nature to proceed by slow
degrees, and not by leaps.   In the literary education of all
nations the poetic faculties are the first to germinate and
blossom; last of all comes the culture of the critic.   And
archæology, founded as it is upon accurate investigation,
upon the comparison of antique monuments with one another, and with documentary evidence, written and engraved, belongs to the period of criticism.

Dante confined himself to the study of the few documents

which were known in his age; he increased their number, and his work was carried still further by Francesco Petrarca, to whom we are indebted for many classical texts, discovered in various monastic libraries in the shape of manuscripts and palimpsests. Still, in spite of his love and admiration for ancient authors, Petrarch no more than Dante deserves the praise bestowed on him by Tiraboschi, of having been the first student of archæology in modern times. We know that at great expense and labor he had formed a small collection of Roman imperial coins, which he offered as a very rare present to Charles IV., but we doubt whether he could appreciate their historical or chronological value. At any· rate, the letters on ancient and mediæval Rome which Petrarch wrote are, from an archæological point of view, monuments of ignorance. He calls the baths of Caracalla *palatium Antonini ;* the fountain of the Aqua Julia, *cymbrum Marii ;* the pantheon of Agrippa, *templum Cybelis.* He refers to the column of Trajan as the tomb of that emperor ; and the pyramid of Caius Cestius as the *mausoleum of Remus,* brother of Romulus, although the title and nature of each of these monuments were carved in huge letters on its front. To explain Petrarch's negligence, Poggio Bracciolini has supposed that the inscriptions were concealed from him by plants growing in the joints of the marble blocks. This excuse is excessively poor and has in fact no foundation, inasmuch as these inscriptions were seen and copied by Petrarch's contemporary and friend, Cola di Rienzo.

According to his biographer, who wrote in the vernacular of his age, — producing a document most precious as showing the transition from the Latin into the Italian language, — Cola di Rienzo, born in 1313, became in early youth a strong admirer of the Roman classical authors, especially of

Livy, Sallust, and Valerius Maximus. "Every day," says his biographer, "he would walk among the ruins, scrutinizing every piece of sculptured marble. None could read and decipher inscriptions better than he." Yet in spite of his enthusiasm for the antique world and its epigraphic records, in spite of the admiration for Roman grandeur which stirred his soul, Cola di Rienzo cannot be cited, as his biographer claims, as a model of scientific accuracy. His Latin epistles are written more in the style of the Bible than in the style of Sallust; and as regards his power of deciphering and expounding ancient inscriptions, the only evidence we possess does not speak highly in his favor.[1]

Famous among ancient epigraphic documents is the bronze tablet, now in the Capitoline Museum, containing the *lex Regia*; that is, a copy, engraved in bronze, of the decree by which the S. P. Q. R. conferred on Flavius Vespasian imperial power, and the power of life and death. This tablet had been employed by Pope Boniface VIII. in the construction of an altar in S. John Lateran, and it was set in the wall so awkwardly that it was almost impossible to read it. Cola, in 1346, caused it to be removed from its obscure hiding-place, and set up in the middle of the basilica. There, showing it to his countrymen, he was wont to speak fiery words on the rights of the people to select their own form of government. So far, so good. But when he begins to explain the text of the document he loses his way and treads upon treacherous ground. The paragraph of the law concerning the *pomœrium*, that is to say, the right bestowed upon Vespasian to enlarge the boundaries of the city of Rome, is interpreted by Cola as if *pomœrium* meant *pomarium*, or apple-orchard; as if

---

[1] A complete edition of Cola's epistles will shortly be published by A. Gabrielli, under the auspices of the Historical Society of Rome.

ROME IN THE XIVth CENTURY.

Miniature in the Duc de Berry's "Livre d'Heures."

From Müntz, Les Antiquités de la Ville de Rome.

this paragraph spoke of Italy as the garden of the Roman Empire. I am sorry to say that this interpretation, absurd as it is, was not his own, but was traditional in the Ghibelline party. Dante himself had already styled Italy the *giardin dell' impero*.

These unsuccessful attempts to explain ancient texts do not lessen the title of Cola to our gratitude ; we are indebted to him for the very first collection of Latin epitaphs that was compiled according to the principles of modern science. In Prince Chigi's library at Rome, in the Medicean Library at Florence, and in the Public Library at Utrecht, three manuscript copies of an epigraphic collection were discovered many years ago, the authorship of which was attributed, first, to Nicola Signorili, secretary of the Roman Senate, under Pope Martin V. Further researches made in the National Library at Naples led to the discovery of a much older copy of the same book, dating from the pontificate of Urban VI. ; that is to say, written at least seventy-five years earlier. After long and patient investigation, the original copy has been finally discovered in the library of the abbey of S. Nicola dell' Arena at Catania. There is no doubt that it is the work of Cola di Rienzo. Its materials were collected, evidently, between 1344 and 1347. At that period, nobody but Cola could read and copy ancient marbles ; the book is consequently his. We shall henceforth admire the fierce tribune, not only as a great politician, leader, and agitator, but also as an archæologist, great for his age.

We must now pass to the time of the return of the popes from Avignon to Rome, which marks the beginning of the Renaissance, — the beginning, that is, of the most glorious period in the history of my own nation. At this period, mediæval Italy had disappeared. A new element, the genius of the ancient world, had risen in its glory, and had fascinated the higher classes of society, the heads of the various states into which the Peninsula was politically divided, the aristocracy, the fashionable and literary circles, and, in a more modest measure, the members of the clergy and of monastic orders. That mighty genius took possession at once of the field of art and science, modified the manners and the education of the higher classes, and even shook, for the time being, the very foundations of the Christian faith. At the head of the movement marched a handful of scientific men, philologists rather than archæologists, better known under the name of the Humanists. They became professors in the universities, they won confidential positions in princely houses as private secretaries, they attached themselves especially to the princes of the Church. Their engagements lasted only for a short period, sometimes for six months only: thus they were able to move without intermission from town to town, from court to court, from college to college, multiplying, as it were, from one end to the other of the Peninsula, and sowing everywhere the seed which was to bring forth such magnificent harvests.

The study of the Greek language and literature was the most fashionable of all studies: hence the fifteenth century has been called the Golden Age of Hellenism. The beginning of the following century saw the first decline of this pursuit; under the Popes of the Medici family, Greek had already left public life, to confine itself again within the precincts of cloisters and schools, which became, and are now, I regret to say, its last insecure shelter. In order to obtain able masters from the East, especially from Byzantine schools, fabulous prices were offered and paid to those professors who were willing to change their country; but the capture of Constantinople, May 29, 1453, very soon dried up this rich source. These circumstances enable us to understand why, at the beginning of the fifteenth century, men of letters and women of the upper classes could easily converse in Greek ; whereas, fifty years later, the same language was no longer spoken, but only read, and was totally forgotten at the beginning of the sixteenth century.

It is difficult to form an idea of such a powerful movement towards classical studies ; more difficult to investigate its causes. We can explain something by a reference to Fashion, that despotic and capricious goddess ; but this will not explain all. Captivated by hitherto unknown fascinations, eager to tear aside the veil which concealed its mysteries, the Humanists deified and idolized archæology, and congregated around its temple to partake of the treasures of science which had been kept there in safe concealment since the fall of the Roman Commonwealth, more than nine centuries before. Many conceived the hope or labored under the illusion that pagan science would heal the wounds of society ; some followed the movement out of pure love of fascinating inquiries, others from curiosity ; the *profanum vulgus* felt the contagion of example and fashion ; the higher classes hoped to find in ancient philosophy the consolations which, to their own misfortune, they had ceased to expect from faith.

Paganism not only penetrated the domain of science, but conquered also the field of fine arts, although this last was exclusively and absolutely consecrated to the service of the Church. The evidence of this fact is to be found everywhere in Italy, in churches as well as in public edifices of Rome, Florence, and Venice. Those genii who surround the Blessed Virgin, holding on high the torch of life ; those winged classic youths who are meant to represent angels ; those nymphs whose part it is to represent the holy women of Christendom, and whose immodest forms were not considered out of place in a church, — are all nothing but a revival of paganism and pagan art. Every one knows that Daniele da Volterra was surnamed "il Braghettone," or breeches-maker, because he contrived to cover the most crude nudities of Michael Angelo's "Last Judgment," and that the reclining statue of Giulia Farnese, near S. Peter's chair in the Vatican, the masterpiece of Guglielmo della Porta, was clothed by Bernini with clothes of painted lead. Giorgio Vasari asserts that Perugino could never be induced to believe in the immortality of the soul, although he had devoted all his life to painting saints and madonnas.

I must quote here an incident from the life of the great Humanist of the fifteenth century, Pomponius Lætus, because, owing to a recent discovery made in the catacombs of S. Calixtus, on the Appian Way, we are able to solve for the first time a mystery connected with the pagan tendencies of the Renaissance. Pomponio Leto founded in Rome an academy for classic studies, to which the most celebrated literary men of the period belonged: Cardinal Platina, the historian of the Church; Giovanni Antonio Campano, Bishop of Teramo; Pietro Sabino, professor of epigraphy in the University of Rome; Marco Antonio Sabellico, Pietro Pallini, and many others. All these illustrious members of the Roman Academy, either because they had exchanged their Christian names for names of pagan heroes, or else on account of their extravagant worship of ancient philosophy and civilization, were stigmatized by so-called public opinion as apostates from the faith, as worshippers of false gods, as conspirators against the authority and the life of the Pope. Imprisoned and chained in the Castle of S. Angelo by order of Paul II., a religious and political action was brought against them upon the charge of conspiracy to secure the supreme pontificate of Rome for their master and president, Pomponio Leto. Cardinal Platina vindicated the innocence of his colleagues, and Pomponio himself addressed to the court of Castle S. Angelo a vigorous speech, the original of which is preserved in the Vatican archives. The lack of positive evidence and the intervention of influential friends caused them to be set free; so that the Academy was able to return to its work, amidst the applause and with the help of cardinals and prelates of the Roman Church.

It is, no doubt, exceedingly remarkable that the evidence against these men, sought in vain by Paul II. and his judges, should have come to light only a few years ago, and in a place entirely unsuspected. In the course of the excavations carried on by my illustrious master, Commendatore G. B. de Rossi, in the catacombs of Callixtus, a *cubiculum*, or crypt, was discovered, May 12, 1852, in the remotest part of that subterranean labyrinth which had been used by Pomponio's brotherhood as a secret place of meeting. On the white plaster of the ceiling the following inscription had been written with the smoke of a tallow candle : " January 16, 1475. Pantagathus, Mammeius, Papyrius, Minicinus, Æmilius, Minucius, all of them admirers and investigators of antiquities, and the delight of the Roman dissolute women, [have met here] under the reign of Pomponius, supreme pontiff." Many other records of the same nature have been since discovered in the catacombs of SS. Pietro e Marcellino and of Prætextatus, in which records Pantagathus (Cardinal Platina ?) is styled *sacerdos academiæ Romanæ*, and Pomponius again sovereign pontiff.

It is evident that such a priesthood and such a pontificate have nothing to do with the Christian hierarchy ; on the other hand, it is difficult to determine whether we have to deal with a more or less absurd pedantry, or with a solemn apostasy from the Christian faith by a handful of dissolute conspirators. One thing only is certain : that Pomponio and his colleagues were very wise in confiding their secret to the deepest and most impenetrable recesses of the Roman catacombs. One line, one word alone, of the records which have been discovered by us four centuries later, made known in proper time to the court of Castle S. Angelo, would have brought their heads under the sword of the public executioner.

In view of the failure to prove the case against Pomponio, it is no wonder that of all the popes of the fifteenth century, the promoter of the trial, Paul II. (Pietro Barbo of Venice), the builder of the Palazzo di Venezia in Rome, should have been the one most violently attacked by the Humanists and the rising archæological school, as an enemy of the grand movement of the Renaissance. Nevertheless, documents discovered by Eugène Müntz and Constantino Corvisieri prove that Paul II., without being a Humanist in the true sense of the word, loved antiquity and its masterpieces with a passionate love, and did his best to favor the development of classical instruction. He reorganized the University of Rome, and actually struck a medal for the occasion, with the legend LÆTITIA SCHOLASTICA ; he helped the introduction of printing ; granted fifty ducats to the old archæologist Flavio Biondo, and four hundred to Filelfo. The triumphal arches of Titus and Septimius Severus, the two colossal groups on the Quirinal, and the equestrian statue of Marcus Aurelius were restored at his expense ; he caused the porphyry sarcophagus of S. Constantia (now in the Hall of the Greek Cross) and a basin of green serpentine to be artistically set up in the Piazza di S. Marco ; removing the first from the mausoleum of Costantia, near the second milestone of the Via Nomentana, the second from the baths of Titus, near the Colosseum. He undertook with enthusiasm one of the favorite plans of Nicolas V., the removal and reërection of Caligula's obelisk in front of S. Peter's. The work of transportation had actually been begun under the skilful leadership of Master Aristotiles, but was soon after given up on account of the sudden death of the Pope.

This gifted man was born a collector: from his early youth he devoted himself to searching all over Italy for antique gems and coins, and Byzantine stuffs and jewelry; disputing the possession of every piece with his competitors Charles de' Medici and Lorenzo il Magnifico. The passion for antique and precious works did not abate with his election to the pontifical throne. There came a moment when his mania rose to almost heroic proportions. He did not scruple to lay hands on miraculous images of the Blessed Virgin, if they were remarkable or curious from an artistic point of view, such, for instance, as the one preserved in the church of S. Maria in Campitelli, made in *opus sectile,* that is to say, in a kind of Florentine mosaic of precious stones. He had at one time a plan for removing to his palace the library of the Benedictine Abbey of Monte Cassino; he offered to build at his own cost, for the township of Toulouse, a bridge across the Garonne, in exchange for a single cameo. As regards his personal appearance, he was in the habit of dressing with unheard-of magnificence. He was so conscious of his own beauty and majestic size and form, that on the day he was elected Pope he actually took the name of Formosus II., "the handsome," a name which the unanimous protest of the Sacred College obliged him to exchange for the more religious one of Paul. No consideration of expense could deter him from acquiring for his personal adornment any extraordinary piece of jewelry which might be brought to his notice. A single one of his tiaras cost him the enormous sum of 120,000 ducats of gold (more than six millions of francs); he justified this excess of luxury by remarking that the tiara of his uncle, Eugenius IV., had cost 38,000 gold ducats, the "ransom of a king."

The museum in his Palazzo di S. Marco or di Venezia comprised forty-seven works in bronze; two hundred and twenty-seven cameos; three hundred and twenty-five intaglios, mostly portraits of emperors and empresses; ninety-seven gold coins and one thousand silver ones (among which two were forged); ten Byzantine cameos, a respectable number, if we consider that the "cabinet des médailles" in Paris and the "cabinet impérial" in Vienna contain only an equal number of these rare productions of Eastern glyptic art; twenty-five Byzantine mosaic pictures, more than all the European museums put together now possess; two pictures in stained glass; many ivory carvings; and many antique embroideries in silk and gold. As regards the works of the Renaissance goldsmiths and the silver plate, the figures of the inventory are simply astonishing. Pearls, turquoises, jacinths, emeralds, amethysts, diamonds, mostly mounted in rings and signets, are numbered by thousands. As for silver plate, I shall mention only two wine-jugs of exquisite workmanship, each weighing one hundred and ten pounds.

What has become of all these treasures? There is no doubt that many pieces have been transferred to the "Sala delle Pietre Dure," in the Uffizi at Florence, from bequests and legacies of the Medici family. But this is almost nothing in comparison with what seems to be lost. Eugène Müntz has been able to trace the existence of one set only, from the museum of Paul II., a set of superb nielli, which belonged originally to an evangeliarium offered to Paul II. by Cardinal la Balue. In 1831, half of these nielli were in the possession of the Duke of Hamilton, half in the Galerie Manfrin in Paris. I do not know where they are now.

In view of such exceptional services rendered to classic antiquities by Paul II., who can honestly condemn him for one isolated act of vandalism, the quarrying of blocks of marble and travertine from the Colosseum? In the fifteenth century, — it is useless to deny it, — the Flavian amphitheatre was considered by everybody, whether Humanists or illiterate, as a mere quarry of stone for building purposes. Nicholas V., Pius II., in spite of their laws of protection of ancient buildings, knocked down arcade after arcade, without the slightest scruple. To reproach Paul II. for having followed their example would be historically unjust, since the Colosseum paid the ransom of so many other antique edifices, which were protected, restored, saved from destruction, by him. Let us reserve the severity of our judgment for those who, in a more civilized and appreciative age, have destroyed without a moment's hesitation the finest monuments of Rome : for Sixtus V., who at the end of the sixteenth century destroyed the Septizonium of Septimius Severus ; for Paul V., Borghese, who employed the marbles of Minerva's temple in the Forum Transitorium to build the Borghese Chapel in Santa Maria Maggiore and the fountain of the Aqua Paola on the Janiculum ; for Alexander VII., Chigi, who demolished in 1662 the triumphal arch of Marcus Aurelius on the Corso. The responsibility of Paul II. is very light indeed in comparison with the responsibility of others.

The brief account I have given of the museum collected

by him in the Palazzo di Venezia (a palace the architecture of which has been wrongly attributed to Giuliano da Maiano and Baccio Pontelli, whereas it was designed and partly executed by Meo del Caprino and Giacomo di Pietrasanta) leads me to mention another subject, of which little is known even to the initiated, — the subject of the collections of early Italian art and antiquities, in the Renaissance, from its beginning to the end of the fifteenth century. In the Middle Ages, one class only of antiquities seems to have been cared for, that of engraved stones, and, as a rule, of any objects the *materia prima* of which is precious.

Engraved stones, even when representing profane and immoral subjects, were employed in the ornamentation of Church implements, such as chalices, evangeliaria, pontifical robes, rings, and tiaras. It was not Italian noblemen or prelates only who had a passion for accumulating this class of valuables. Charles V., king of France, owned in 1380 fifty-two cameos ; Charles VI., in 1399, one hundred and one. In 1343, Philippe le Bel is said to have sent to the Pope " un Joel appelé le camahieu." Boniface VIII., of the Caetani family, the illustrious contemporary of Dante and Giotto, possessed from forty to fifty cameos; the catalogue of them, dated 1295, discovered in the Bibliothèque Nationale, Paris, is remarkable because one of the reliefs is described in it as representing Hercules, an identification really wonderful for such an age. But I can give an instance, far earlier than this, of a real appreciation of antiquities. I speak of the picturesque mediæval house in Rome near the temple of Fortuna Virilis and near the Ponte Rotto, miscalled sometimes the " house of Cola di Rienzo," sometimes " the house of Pilate." The building was erected, in fact, by Nicolaus Crescentius, son of the tribune Crescentius, and was built mostly of the fragments of ancient marble edifices and bas-reliefs, in order — as the inscription testifies — that his contemporaries might appreciate the artistic skill of their ancestors. Arnaldo da Brescia, the reformer of the twelfth

The House of Crescentius.

century, proclaimed in 1150 the necessity for rebuilding the Capitol. I have spoken above of the modest set of Roman coins offered by Francesco Petrarca to the Emperor Charles IV. at Mantua, in 1354. This set was by no means the first collected in Italy; Petrarch had been pre-ceded by another numismatist, Oliviero Forza, or Forzetta, a wealthy citizen of Treviso, who must be considered, if not the originator, certainly one of the first promoters of the new tendencies, and of the new artistic and archæological tastes. His inventory, written by himself, speaks so seriously and freely of medals, coins, bronzes, marbles, engraved stones, and manuscript books that one would think it written fully two or three centuries later.

At the beginning of the fourteenth century, Florence, which had preceded so many other Italian towns in the reform of literature and art, showed hospitality within its walls to the most remarkable collections of the time. Architects, sculptors, antiquarians, worked harmoniously and simultaneously towards the development of refined tastes. The names of the three greatest Italian masters of the fifteenth century — Filippo Brunellesco, the creator of the dome of the cathedral of Santa Maria del Fiore ; Donatello (Donato Bardi), the inimitable sculptor of the S. George on the façade of the church of Or S. Michele ; and Lorenzo Ghiberti, the designer and caster of those bronze doors of the Baptistery which Michaelangelo considered worthy of being the doors of Paradise — are strictly connected with this archæological revival. Brunellesco and Donatello, during their visit to Rome in 1407, spent all their time and leisure in measuring ancient buildings and in excavating ruins ; so much so that they were nicknamed by the populace of Rome *quelli del tesoro,* " searchers for hidden treasures." On his return to Florence, Donatello inspired his protector, Cosimo de' Medici, with his love and passion for antiques, and restored with his own masterly hand the statues which ornamented the mansion of the noble patrician. Lorenzo Ghiberti felt even a deeper sense of admiration for ancient statuary and gems. The commentaries published by Lemonnier in the first volume of his Florentine edition of Vasari, speak eloquently of his admiration for a statue of the Hermaphrodite discovered in Rome under his eyes, for a statue by Lysippus (?) discovered at Siena, for an

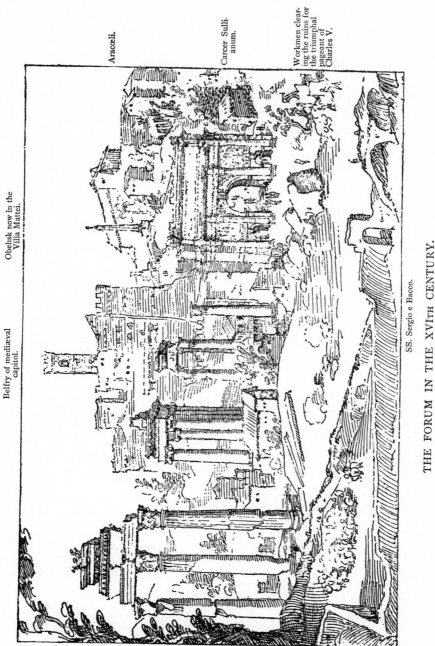

Belfry of mediæval capitol.

Obelisk now in the Villa Mattei.

Araceli.

Carcer Sullianum.

Workmen clearing the ruins for the triumphal pageant of Charles V.

SS. Sergio e Bacco.

THE FORUM IN THE XVITH CENTURY.

From a drawing by Martin Heemskerk, now in the Berlin Museum.

engraved stone belonging to Niccolò Niccoli, and so forth. To him was entrusted the delightful task of mounting in gold the famous cornelian of Giovanni de' Medici, representing Apollo and Marsyas, and it is touching to see with what sincere enthusiasm he speaks of a stone and of an engraving the subject of which is a mystery to him.

Poggio Bracciolini, of Florence, born in 1380, has left interesting records of the ancient marbles which he collected during his travels in central and southern Italy. He speaks of a room in his museum entirely filled with busts, all noseless save one ; a particular which shows that the disfigurement of statues and heads is the work of the Romans of the decadence, and not the work of the Middle Ages, as commonly supposed. I must quote here a fragment of a letter written by Poggio to one of his learned friends, because he speaks of his acquisitions, and of his hopes and fears as a collector, with such good sense and enthusiasm that one would be ready to believe the letter written in our own days by Marchese Campana or Alessandro Castellani. Poggio's letter makes evident, also, the fact, almost incredible, that, at the very beginning of the Renaissance, works of art were collected by passionate admirers, even from the shores of Asia Minor and from the islands of the Greek archipelago. " I received yesterday a letter from Chios, in which my correspondent, Master Francis, of Pistoja, announces that he has secured for me three marble heads, one of Juno, one of Minerva, one of Bacchus, the work of Polycletus and Praxiteles (as he says), which he expects to ship at once to Gaeta. I cannot vouch for the accuracy of the alleged authorship of these three marbles. Modern Greeks, as you know, like large talk, and in this instance I suspect them to have mentioned those grand names to justify an exorbitant demand. I hope I am giving voice to a false suspicion. My correspondent says that he bought the heads from a certain Caloiro, who, not many months ago, discovered in the deepest recess of a grotto in the same island of Chios about one hundred marble statues, of marvelous beauty and preservation. Do you not share my wish, in hearing of these wonders, to be able to spread wings and fly to Chios ? "

The most successful and liberal Florentine collector of his age was, beyond doubt, Niccolò Niccoli, a simple citizen, who without having large means at his disposal, by skill and perseverance, and with the help of such friends as Ambrogio Traversari, of Camaldoli, and Leonardo d' Arezzo, got together a library and a museum which formed the pride of his native town. Here is an instance of the sureness and perspicacity of his *coup d'œil* in artistic matters, which is described in the life of Niccolò. In walking through the streets of Florence, Niccolò spied, one day, a child, from whose neck a chalcedony, most exquisitely engraved, was suspended. He coaxed the boy to come and speak with him ; asked the name of his father, and in what place they lived. The next day he offered five florins in exchange for the stone. The good man, having never in his lifetime seen five florins at once, was enchanted with the bargain, and Niccolò became thus the happy possessor of the masterpiece. However, it did not remain long in his hands. During the pontificate of Eugene IV., the Pope's vicar, having heard of the famous stone, sent for Niccolò, in passing through Florence, and offered him two hundred gold ducats, which Niccolò, not without hesitation and sorrow, decided to accept. After the death of the vicar, the stone was bought by Paul II., and fell ultimately into the hands of Lorenzo de' Medici.

As for Rome herself, she can boast of having had a

museum, not of small objects, however precious, but a museum containing the grandest productions of ancient art, at least since the time of Charlemagne and the ninth century of our era. The museum was kept in and near the Pope's palace at the Lateran, and comprised, first, the equestrian bronze statue of Marcus Aurelius, now on the Capitol, commonly asserted to have been found between the Scala Santa and S. Croce in Gerusalemme. It was never found, because it was never lost: it was constantly kept, after the fall of the Empire, near the Pope's residence at the Lateran, until Paul III., Farnese, caused it to be removed to the Piazza del Campidoglio. Besides this colossal bronze, the Lateran museum contained the celebrated Wolf, which is wrongly asserted to have been found in the seventeenth century near the

The Wolf in the Fifteenth Century. From the *Mirabilia Urbis Romæ*, Rome, 1499.

church of S. Teodoro; the colossal head of Domitian, now in the courtyard of the Palazzo dei Conservatori, wrongly asserted to have been found in the fifteenth century near the basilica of Constantine; and the lex Regia, or decree by which the Senate and people of Rome elected Vespasian as their emperor, a document which I have already mentioned in speaking of Cola di Rienzo. All these bronzes were removed to the Capitol from the Lateran by Sixtus IV. The founding of the Capitoline museum, considering the conditions of the age and the elementary state of general culture, is one of the greatest glories of Pope Sixtus IV., Riario della Rovere, and exonerates him in a certain measure for many acts of wanton destruction of ancient buildings which took place under his pontificate. The museum, solemnly inaugurated on December 14, 1471, was the very first thrown open to the public after the fall of the Empire. It contained the boy extracting a thorn from his foot; the Hercules of gilt bronze discovered in the Forum Boarium; all the bronzes of the Lateran; the Camillus, which was then called, I know not why, the " Zingara," or Gypsy; a marble group of a lion devouring a horse, discovered in the bed of the river Almo; the cinerary urn of Agrippina the elder, wife of Germanicus and mother of Caligula, which urn had been transformed in the Middle Ages into a standard measure for grain, *rubiatella di grano ;* the bust of Brutus, and the marble statue of Charles d'Anjou. It is to be regretted that this venerable nucleus of the Capitoline collections, a truly national glory, should have been dispersed all over the municipal palaces of Rome, without any regard for the mutual connection of the various pieces in the history of art and science, or for the memory of the founder of the museum, Sixtus IV., whose name is dear to all who appreciate taste, refinement, and liberality. The Riario della Rovere family is certainly one of the most sympathetic, I might say attractive, families of the Renaissance: even the defects and the errors of some of its members have their bright side, and can be excused on account of their very magnitude. Take, for instance, the Pope himself: after blaming the memory of his predecessor, Paul II., for his extravagant luxury, Sixtus IV., near the very end of his life, orders a tiara, worth 110,000 gold ducats. As for his nephew, Pietro Riario,

THE CAPITOL IN THE XVIth CENTURY.

From Kock's Operum Antiqq. Romanor. Reliquiae, 1562.

whom he had named Cardinal of S. Sisto when only twenty-six years old, with a yearly income of 60,000 ducats, corresponding to $600,000, he was capable of spending and squandering during the two years of his cardinalship not less than $2,800,000. We may have instances in our own times of more colossal expenditures; but who among these modern spendthrifts could boast of having left to mankind such souvenirs as those left by the Riarios? — the Palazzo della Cancelleria, the porch and convent of SS. Apostoli, the cloister of S. Agnese fuori le mura, and many similar masterpieces of the Renaissance.

I ought now to mention the illustrious group of the cinquecento masters, at once artists and archæologists, whose researches, descriptions, measurements, and drawings of the ancient buildings of Rome rank among the finest documents which our favorite science possesses. These documents, which are numbered by thousands, each more precious than the other, were not known until a few years ago. Abeken, the editors of the Florentine edition of Giorgio Vasari, and Baron Heinrich de Geymüller had occasionally mentioned, or actually published, some samples of the collection; but from these fragmentary indications we had conceived the idea that the drawings of the cinquecento masters would be more useful to illustrate contemporary than antique art. As an instance of the generosity with which archæology repays from time to time the devotion and the zeal of its students, as an instance of the healthy joys and emotions which the study of the ancient world is capable of affording to the initiated, I beg to be allowed to relate a personal experience. In spite of more than twenty years of uninterrupted research, both in the active and the speculative field, many of our Roman ruins were still an enigma to me, their origin, their

design, their history, being absolutely unknown. How many
hours have I spent before and around such antique buildings as those transformed into the church of S. Adriano,
of SS. Cosma and Damiano, of S. Stefano delle Carozze,
and others, trying, like Œdipus, to solve the mystery of
the Sphinx, to snatch the secret which seemed to have
been buried under those ruins with the fall of the Empire!
After giving up all hope of success, having in fact classified
these buildings as "nameless," I happened one day to
enter the department of drawings and engravings in the
Galleria degli Uffizi at Florence, under the kind guidance
of their keeper, Signor Nerino Ferri. The original and un-
published architectural sketches of Florentine cinquecento
artists were shown to me as a simple matter of curiosity. I
could not possibly describe what I felt at that moment, when
I saw (at once) the solution of nearly every topographical
problem pass slowly before my eyes, in the shape of sketches
taken on the spot when those monuments were first excavated, three or four centuries ago, and taken by such men,
artists, and archæologists as the eight Sangallos, Baldassare
and Sallustio Peruzzi, Raphael Sanzio, the two Albertis,
Bramante, Sansovino, Giovanni Antonio Dosio, De Marchis,
and so on. I do not think that the naturalist who discovers
a new species of coleoptera, the chemist who discovers a
new chemical element, the astronomer who discovers a new
asteroid, can feel what the archæologist feels under the
blessed influence of such important and utterly unexpected
discoveries. When my master, Commendatore de Rossi, discovered in the Biblioteca Marciana at Venice the famous
codex of Pietro Sabino, he spent thirty-six hours in devouring, as it were, the volume, with no consideration whatever
for food or rest, and did not leave his long-sought-for prey
until he actually fainted from exhaustion. Archæology is a

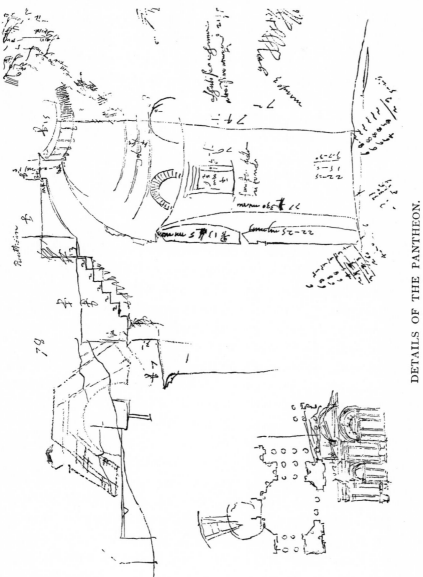

DETAILS OF THE PANTHEON.

Sketched by Antonio da Sangallo, Jun. (1482–1546.)

science which, different from others, begins at once to repay
the zeal of the student with deep moral satisfaction without
obliging him to serve a dull, tiresome apprenticeship.   It is
a science so noble and fascinating that it helps wonderfully
to form the character of intelligent youths ; and so protean
in form, in its various aspects and branches, that it can suit
any taste, any inclination.   It is true that its study requires
the spirit of enterprise, plenty of means, a subtle mind, and
constancy of application.   To the young men of America,
however, to whom these pages are especially dedicated,
these elements have been supplied even more liberally than
is the case, perhaps, with other nations.   The first movements the present generation has made in the archæological
field, such as the exploration of Assos, the contribution to
the investigations at Naukratis, the institution of the school
at Athens, the establishment of first-class scientific journals,
and the like, prove that American students bring to the
antiquarian field the same amount of successful enterprise
which has made them take the lead in many other fields of
science.   Let me express the hope that the account of our
recent discoveries in Rome which is given in the following
chapters will confirm, and even increase, their fancy for
these noble and useful pursuits, and entice a greater number of bright young men into the ranks of our sympathetic brotherhood.

CHAPTER II.

IN the preface to his beautiful volume, "Ancient Rome in 1885," Professor Henry Middleton announces the discovery of an Etruscan city "of great size and importance," said to have existed even "before the legendary regal period, on one of the largest hills" of Rome. This announcement has been made popular and more widely known by the comments published in English literary papers and reviews, especially by an elaborate criticism in the "Athenæum" of February 6, 1886. The interest raised among students and amateurs by such an extraordinary statement can be easily understood. The existence of an Etruscan settlement on the ground afterwards occupied by the Eternal City would not only give "a serious blow to the long-established tradition of the early supremacy of the Latin race" on the region of the seven hills, but would also upset the notions established by the modern school regarding the origin and early history of Rome. As I have had officially the charge of scientific investigations in the area of the new quarters of the town, on the Esquiline and Viminal hills, in which the alleged discovery would have taken place, and as I have brought to light, as it were with my own hands, the many thousand objects belonging to the archaic cemeteries of those same hills, upon the nature of which this new theory of a pre-Roman Etruscan city is based, I may be allowed, I hope, to express my opinion on the subject, *en pleine connaissance de cause.*

To begin at once with the conclusion, I say that nothing has been found within the last sixteen years, either in the new or in the old quarters of Rome, which can give any foundation to Professor Middleton's theory. What has been ascertained confirms fully and corroborates with additional evidence the conclusion at which modern science, palæo-ethnology as well as history, had already arrived, namely, that Rome was founded by a colony of shepherds from the Alban hills, on ground which had never been occupied permanently before.

Many among my readers will recollect with delight the

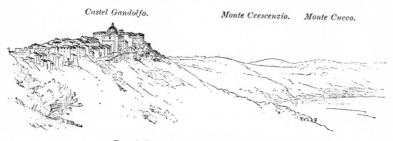

Castel Gandolfo.   Monte Crescenzio.   Monte Cucco.

Castel Gandolfo and the Alban Hills.

drive taken from Frascati to Castel Gandolfo and Albano, following the rim of the volcanic crater, which age has transformed into a lake, the Lago di Castello, one of the loveliest sheets of water in the world. On one side of the road, the precipitous cliffs descend almost perpendicularly far below the level of the deep greenish water; on the other side, the mountain slopes more gently toward the ancient Appian Way and toward the blue Tyrrhenian, undulating in rich pasture lands which are called the " Pascolare di Castello." It was precisely here, in the Pascolare di Castello, that in the early spring of 1817 a discovery took place, which, despised and neglected at the time, is now considered to be the most important ever made in connection with the foundation and early history of Rome.　Some peasants of the neighborhood, having decided to plant new vineyards on the Monte Cucco and Monte Crescenzio, the highest hills of the Pascolare, cut a trench many yards long and four feet wide, to investigate the nature of the ground, and determine whether it would prove adapted to the cultivation of the grape.

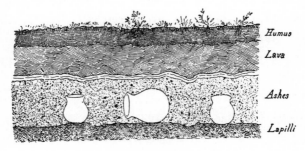

Humus

Lava

Ashes

Lapilli

Section of Trench.

First of all comes a stratum of modern vegetable soil, *humus,* fourteen inches thick; in the second place, a stratum, thirty-six inches thick, of the hardest kind of peperino, which is a volcanic stone produced by the mixture of greenish ashes with hot water; in the third place, an exceedingly narrow line of fossil vegetation.　Then follows a bed, about fifty inches thick, of yellowish volcanic ashes; and underneath, other more or less compact volcanic matters, such as lapilli, tufa, and again ashes and peperino. Taking into consideration only the four upper strata, it is evident that after the eruption of yellowish ashes a long period of comparative tranquillity must have elapsed, during which plants and grass could grow and vegetate abundantly on the surface of the ashes.　Then another eruption of lava followed, which was evidently the last of its kind in this district of the Pascolare, but not the last in the history of the

Alban craters. The discovery above alluded to took place in the bed of yellowish ashes immediately under the lava. Here began to appear to the astonished eyes of the peasants hand‑made and sun‑dried jars, of an exceedingly rough kind of terra cotta, each one containing one of those vases shaped like a prehistoric hut, which have been accordingly called by Sir John Lubbock *hut‑urns*. Each hut‑urn contained the remains of an incinerated body, with fib‑ulæ and other objects in am‑ber and bronze, and it was surrounded by vases and utensils of every shape and description.

Hut-Urn, in the Vatican Museum.

As soon as the news of the find spread, it was met at first with incredulity; the superstition of the peasant was also aroused, as if the evil spirit himself, or a supernatural power, had accomplished the deed of concealing treasures in the thickness of a virgin rock. But when the news reached the ears of the authorities and of scientific men, a legal *compte-rendu* of the discovery was drawn by the hand of a public notary, and Alessandro Visconti was asked to illustrate it from an archæological point of view. In Visconti's pamphlet, *Sopra alcuni vasi sepolcrali rinve-nuti nelle vicinanze dell' antica Alba Longa*, the true ex-planation of the mystery, wonderful to say, is given at once. He describes the jars as cinerary urns buried by vol-canic eruptions, but fails to trace any connection between this fossil cemetery and Alba Longa and Rome.

Tambroni, who wrote a *Lettera intorno alle urne cinerarie dissotterrate nel Pascolare di Castel Gandolfo*, suggested the idea that the cemetery belonged to barbaric warriors of the fifth century of our era ; the learned Duc de Blacas came back to Visconti's opinion, modifying it according to his own judgment ; and finally, Giuseppe Ponzi, the late leader of Italian geologists, decided that the vases had not been buried by the lava eruptions, but had been introduced under the lava bed from a Roman road which crosses the Pascolare close by.

The controversy was finally settled in May, 1867, fifty years after its origin, by a committee composed among others of Professors Ponzi, De Rossi, and Pigorini. They broke the crust of lava in many places, and succeeded in discovering jars and smaller pottery under the same conditions as those described by Alessandro Visconti.[1] The scientific results of the inquiry were far more important. It was determined that traces of the work of man are to be found all over the northwest spurs of the Alban hills, and around the craters of Castello, Valle Marciana, and other volcanoes ; in the second place, it was ascertained that the grass which grew in the period between the last two (ash and peperino) eruptions was the *lolium perenne*, the shape of the leaves and stems being still visible against the lower surface of the peperino ; in the third place, that the district inhabited by the population to which the cinerary urns belong stretched between the famous *caput aquæ Ferentinæ*, in the Parco Colonna at Marino, and the cliffs of Palazzolo, the supposed site of Alba Longa, remains of square huts with hard blackened floor, traces of coal and domestic utensils, having been found, especially in the neighborhood of springs of pure drinkable water. In the fourth place, it was ascertained that

---

[1] I myself successfully tried the same experiment in the summer of 1886.

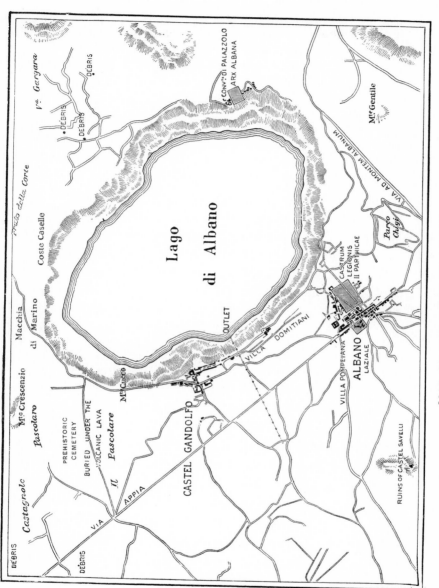

MAP OF THE LAKE OF ALBANO.

the inhabitants of the slopes of the Alban volcanoes carried on a brisk traffic with their more civilized neighbors, the Etruscans; many specimens of Etruscan or Italo-Greek pottery, of a beautiful archaic pattern, having been found scattered on the floor, not only of tombs, but also of the square huts. It follows, evidently, from these facts, not only that the Alban shepherds, of a well-to-do sort, imported foreign earthenware, but also that local manufacturers tried to imitate the shape and the style of the imported specimens by moulding their rough cups and flasks with a certain degree of approximation. Finally, it was determined that, although the use of iron may have been known in this district before the total extinction of the craters, no iron is to be found inside or near the cinerary urns above described. The tombs consequently belong to the prehistoric age of bronze.

What are the consequences to be drawn from the discovery of this geological Pompeii on the Alban hills? Let us compare the data concerning the history of the Latin volcanoes with the earliest traditional accounts of Alba Longa and Rome. If we could trust Dionysius of Halicarnassus, who describes Alba Longa as lying between the foot of Monte Cavo and the lake, near the modern Palazzolo, we ought to place the extinction of the Castello craters at a very remote period, before the first appearance of mankind in Central Italy. It is impossible, in fact, to suppose that men would willingly and permanently settle within a few thousand feet from the mouth of a very active volcano. But students familiar with Dionysius will easily recognize that he describes the site of Alba as it appeared in his own age, not as it was in prehistoric times. One crater only was in full activity during and after the foundation of Alba, the crater of Monte Pila; its position, however, is such that a town at Palazzolo is absolutely out of reach of a direct lava eruption, although it may have been exposed to indirect havoc and danger from earthquakes and showers of ashes. Alba Longa was much safer than Nicolosi is now on Mount Etna, or S. Sebastiano on Mount Vesuvius. (See the accompanying map.) There is no possibility of denying the continuation of volcanic action long after the foundation of Alba Longa and Rome, during the period of the kings. Livy speaks so often, so minutely, and so exactly of eruptions, of showers of pumice-stones and ashes, of *boati*, or subterranean thundering noises, that it is impossible to resist his overwhelming evidence. The historian describes the eruptions with the phrase, *In monte Albano lapidibus· pluit* — A rain of stones fell on the Alban hills. Sometimes he adds fuller particulars; *In monte Albano biduum continenter lapidibus pluit* — For two consecutive days and without intermission the shower of pumice-stones lasted. He picturesquely calls the " boati " *vox ingens e luco et e summo montis cacumine* — a supernatural voice from the woods which clothe the summit of the mountain. Is it possible to suppose that so many characteristic circumstances should be a creation or a fiction of the historian's fancy? His accounts are proved absolutely correct by a decisive argument. In the early religion of Rome, there was a special ceremony to be performed, according to a prescribed ritual, every time an eruption was announced from the Alban hills: *Quoties idem prodigium in monte Albano nunciaretur, feriæ per novem dies agerentur.* This religious practice shows how frequent and common phenomena of a volcanic nature were in Latium during the first centuries of Roman history.

I have now to bring evidence on three different points, to which allusion has briefly been made above. I have to demonstrate, first, that Rome was built by colonists from Alba Longa; secondly, that these colonists were simple shepherds; thirdly, that the foundation of Rome dates from the age of bronze, and was caused by the necessity felt by the Alban shepherds to escape from the threatening neighborhood of the volcano.

From these facts, duly verified and established, will follow the consequence that the Etruscans had nothing to do with the foundation of Rome, and that the theory proposed by Professor Middleton is not based upon the evidence of recent discoveries.

As regards the first point, we have in our favor early Roman traditions and the unanimity of early annalists and historians; although, of course, their evidence must be accepted with caution and with a certain degree of skepticism. Let me repeat what Livy remarks in the magnificent preface to his history: " Whatever tradition reports regarding the origin of Rome is to be taken rather as a poetical legend than as true history. We cannot condemn our ancestors, if, by mingling human and supernatural events, they gave an almost divine origin to their city. At any rate, if there is a people in the world which may claim and boast a direct descent from the gods, and can actually call Mars its founder and forefather, it is certainly the people of Rome, which, exchanging the shepherd's staff for the warrior's sword, has subjected the entire world to its rule."

It would, of course, be impossible to discuss in the compass of a single chapter the general question of the credibility of early Roman history. We are already far, thank Heaven, from the period in which it was fashionable to follow the exaggerations of that famous hypercritical school which denied every event in Roman history previous to the second Punic war. Late discoveries have brought forth such a crushing mass of evidence in favor of ancient writers, and in support of their reports concerning the kingly period, that every detail seems to be confirmed by monumental remains. In our younger days, when we were stepping for the first time over the threshold of an archæological school, we used to scorn the idea that a real Romulus had existed, and that such was the name of the builder of Rome. Philological researches have shown that the name of Romulus is a genuine one, and that it belongs to the builder of Rome, as we shall presently see. There is no doubt that the general spirit of modern criticism has been unreasonably skeptical and unduly captious with respect to early Roman history ; any further attempt to diminish or to lessen the value of its traditional sources must henceforth be absolutely unsuccessful. What does tradition say, under the guise of poetical myth and legend, of the meeting of Rhea Sylvia with Mars, and of the exposure of the twin infants on the banks of the Tiber, at the foot of the Palatine hill? Nothing, except that the leader of the new group of settlers on the banks of the Tiber was a man from Alba, and a man of high birth, connected with the royal house of the Sylvii. The various and sometimes absurd versions of the event agree always on these two points, and we cannot be blamed if we accept them as historical truth.

The legend of Rhea Sylvia, the vestal virgin, the daughter of the kings, led into temptation by Mars, inspired many artists, whose masterpieces have come down to us intact. I shall mention one only, of comparatively recent discovery, a marble altar found at Ostia, in the office of the corporation of the Sacomarii, on the west side of the Area Cereris (the square surrounding the temple of Ceres). On the opposite page is a sketch of this lovely piece, which dates from the time of Hadrian.

For the second point ascertained in connection with the building of Rome, namely, that the colonists from Alba Longa, the settlers on the Palatine were simple shepherds,

Marble Altar found at Ostia.

we have to resort to philological arguments, which, however, are so powerful and convincing that not a trace of doubt will be left on the mind of the reader.

The oldest and most venerable sanctuary of kingly Rome was the Lupercal, a grotto consecrated by the emigrants from Alba to Faun, called *Lupercus;* that is to say, the

" driver-away of wolves " and the protector of herds. This
grotto, through which an icy crystalline spring flowed into
the green field below, opened under the northwest spur of
the Palatine. On February 15, it was the centre of great
rejoicings and of religious ceremonies called the Lupercalia,
during which the head shepherds, clothed with skins, used
to run around the precincts of their Palatine village, asking
the protection of Faunus Lupercus on their flocks of sheep.
These Lupercalia show clearly what was the condition of
the founders of Rome : they were shepherds. I may remark also that this worship of Lupercus was so deeply
rooted in Rome that it was .the very last to die out, in the
fight between Christianity and pagan superstition. Traces
of it have been found as late as the end of the fifth century
of the Christian era, under the pontificate of Pope Gelasius.
It is evident from what I have said that the pasture
grounds on the Alban hills having become inadequate to
support the increased number of flocks, or having become
insecure in consequence of violent volcanic eruptions, which
followed a long period of calm, a certain number of owners
of cattle assembled, and decided to migrate into a richer,
larger, and more secure district. The luxuriant plains
which stretched from the foot of the hill to the shore
of the blue Tyrrhenian naturally attracted their attention.
The migration began by exceedingly slow stages ; the shepherds advanced through the green fields until a mighty
river stopped their journey, and obliged them to settle on its
banks. Here they found a hill surrounded by almost inaccessible perpendicular cliffs, and protected besides by a
circuit of deep marshes ; here they found springs of pure
water in a grotto which they dedicated at once to Faun, the
god of the shepherds ; here, accordingly, they settled and
built a village, or rather a huge sheepfold. Such was the

origin of Rome; such has been the origin of many other prehistoric settlements, which in process of time have taken a prominent place in the history of the world. Thus the central village of the Edomites, in the plains of the Haûran, was named *Bozrah*, and Bozrah means a " fortified sheepfold." The hill on the banks of the Tiber, which harbored the Alban emigrants and their flocks, was named the Palatium or Palatinus mons. The root of this name is Pales, the goddess of shepherds, the *pastorum dea*, whose feast, called Paliliæ, fell on April the 21st. Such was the importance of Pales for the primitive inhabitants of the Palatine that the date of her festival, the 21st of April, has been universally accepted and recognized for the last twenty-five centuries as the date of the foundation of Rome itself, and we modern Romans are proud to keep it as a great national day, since very few celebrations are, like ours, two thousand six hundred and forty years old.

The fortified sheepfold or inclosure on the Palatine had a gate named Mugonia; the root of the name is *mugire*, the mooing of cattle. In the worship of their gods, the men of the Palatine used milk for the sacred libations. Could a more conclusive chain of evidence be desired?

The mighty river which washed the foot of the Palatine had, at that remote period, no special name; it was called *Rumon*, which means simply " a stream, a river." The inhabitants of the surrounding villages, which were mostly perched on high hills and mountains, Tusculum, Aricia, Alba, Tibur, Præneste, having entered into commercial communications with the new settlement, began to name it from its most prominent topographical feature, from its connection with the Rumon or river: they called it *Roma*, which means the " town of the river," the " Stromstadt," as Professor Corssen has literally translated the word; they called the leader of the settlement *Romulus*, which means " the man from the town of the river."

All that I have said is so simple and matter of fact that it conveys persuasion at once, as plain truth always does. But if another argument is required to prove that the names Roma and Romulus are derived from the aboriginal word Rumon or stream, here it is at hand. The gates of a town are not denominated from the town to which they belong, but from the place to which they lead. Thus some of the gates of Rome were named Tiburtina, Prænestina, and Ostiensis, because the roads issuing from them led respectively to Tibur, to Praeneste, and to Ostia. One of the gates of the early Alban settlement on the Palatine hill was called " Romana." It is evident that the name was given to the gate, not from the settlement itself, but because it led to the Rumon or river. And when the walls of the city were enlarged by Servius Tullius, the new gate leading to the river was likewise named Flumentana.

As to the epoch in which the foundation of Rome, this greatest event in the history of mankind, took place, it was, chronologically speaking, the seven hundred and fifty-fourth year before Christ; prehistorically speaking, it was the age of bronze.

The state of the ancient world in the year 754 B. C. was as follows: Egypt was ruled by the twenty-fourth Saitic dynasty, the last king of which, named Bokenranf by the Egyptians, Bokkoris by Herodotus, was captured and burnt alive by the Ethiopian invader Shabak, sixteen years only after the foundation of Rome. Assyria was ruled by King Assurdanil, of the second dynasty, and was suffering a temporary decadence, which is figured in the legend of a first destruction of Nineveh and in the legend of King Sardanapalus. Oziah was king of Judah, and Zachariah

SITE OF THE PORTA ROMANA.

(the fifth and last sovereign of the house of Jehu, afterwards murdered by Shallum) was king of Israel. The throne of China was occupied by the dynasty of the Cehoo, the third after Yas. Athens was undergoing a change in the form of its constitution, namely, the substitution of an Archon for ten years to an Archon for life. Alcmæon is the last ruler of the old system; Charops begins the new. The year 754 is included in the fifth Olympiad, the champion of which, in the competition of the Stadion, was Polychares from Messene.

Such being the political and ethnographical conditions and divisions of the civilized world when Rome was founded, the inhabitants of Central Italy, Etruria excluded, had only attained that degree of civilization which is called the civilization of bronze. This statement is confirmed by many arguments. First, in the fossil cemetery of Alba Longa, buried by that volcanic conflagration which induced some of the Albans to migrate into the plain below, no trace of iron has been found, only of amber and bronze. Secondly: the same absence of iron has been noticed in the archaic tombs of Rome discovered within the walls of Servius Tullius, and consequently older than the walls themselves. In the third place, early Roman religious rites show such an abhorrence of iron that we may infer from it that iron was regarded as a profane innovation, as a material which could not be substituted for the venerable brass utensils without offence to the gods. I shall enter into more particulars on this subject, because to the attraction of novelty it joins the attraction of a profound interest, especially in a country like America, for which the prehistoric is the only possible kind of national archæology.

Every student is familiar with the verse of Lucretius,—

" Et prius æris erat quam ferri cognitus usus,"

(And the use of bronze was known before that of iron), because it proclaims a scientific law, which, forgotten for nearly twenty centuries, has only lately been revived.   Lucretius must have drawn his information from early Roman rituals, in which the use of iron was anathematized, and forbidden to priests in their religious capacity, and excluded also from places of worship.   Here are some instances of this practice : —

When a village or a town was founded, its limits were determined religiously by a furrow traced with a bronze plough, *œneo vomere ;* and this practice was maintained long after the contrivance of iron ploughs.

The *flamen Dialis,* one of the high priests of Rome, and belonging to an order instituted at a very remote period, could not shave himself or have his hair cut and trained with an iron razor or knife, — *œneis cultris tondebatur ;* it was his duty to make use exclusively of a bronze instrument. I may add that several bronze razors have been discovered in the archaic cemetery on the Esquiline.

The earliest of Roman bridges, built by Ancus Martius across the Tiber, one hundred and fourteen years after the foundation of the city, was called *Sublician,* because it was entirely constructed of wood.   Among the details of its construction which have been transmitted to us, one is very characteristic : no iron had been used in building the bridge ; and, on the strength of religious tradition, no iron was ever used in its subsequent restorations, even in the Christian era, down to the fall of the Empire.   The fact is certified by Dionysius, v. 24 ; Varro, v. 83 ; Ovid, v. 622 ; and Pliny, in the 36th book (c. 23) of his Natural History.   Pliny, ignorant as he was of prehistoric antiquities, gives a wrong explanation of the fact : he says the Romans have always excluded iron from the Sublician bridge because, at the time of its gallant defence by Horatius Cocles, they had such a hard time cutting it down to prevent the enemy from crossing it. The explanation is absurd: iron was proscribed from the structure because iron was not known when the bridge was first thrown across the river, 114 A. U. C.

Remains of the Sublician Bridge.

Macrobius, who wrote in the fifth century of our era, when Christianity had already become the religion of the state, says that, from a very remote period, brass instruments alone could be used for religious purposes. In consequence of this rule, which shows the tenacity and the antiquity of Roman religious practices, every time iron chanced to touch a temple, or a shrine, or any religious building made venerable by age, sacrifices had to be performed to expiate the profanation, except in those cases where the use of iron had been duly authorized and sanctioned by a decree of both the political and the religious authorities.

Many years ago, a bronze tablet was discovered among the ruins of Furfo, near the village of S. Nicandro, in the province of Aquila, which contains a rather remarkable document on this subject, namely, the law passed by the municipal magistrates for the building and dedication of a shrine to Jupiter. The law, dated July 11, of the year 58 B. C., and written in a rude kind of Latin, such as was spoken at that time among the mountains of Abruzzo, declares and provides that although the use of iron in religious buildings was not lawful, still, all circumstances being taken into consideration, its use was authorized in this shrine of Jupiter, and no expiatory sacrifices were required to purify the shrine from the unlawful contact.

More remarkable still is the instance afforded by the laws of the most antique and venerable of Roman religious brotherhoods, the College of the *Fratres Arvales*. The origin of this brotherhood is lost in the darkness of age: it was most likely imported into Rome from Alba together with the institution of the Vestal Virgins; at any rate, it is always mentioned by ancient writers in connection with Romulus, the founder of the city. It was composed of twelve members, selected from the highest patrician families, whose duty was to offer sacrifices on various days and months of the year to a goddess called *Dea Dia*, to implore the blessings of heaven on the produce of the soil, such as crops and harvests of every description, the vintage, and so forth. Their ceremonies correspond, to a certain degree, to the Christian ceremony of the Rogations.

They used to assemble in a little wood at the fifth milestone of the Via Campana, on the slope of the hills which now overlook the farm of La Magliana, the *rendezvous de chasse* of Pope Leo X., where he caught the fever which caused his death. The slope, now occupied by a vineyard belonging to the Ceccarelli family, was excavated from top to bottom in 1868 and 1869, at the expense of the Empress Augusta of Germany, and under the direction of the late Professor W. Henzen. The very temple of the Dea Dia was discovered, a round marble structure raised on a very high platform, on the vertical surface of which the annals, or yearly records, of the fraternity were engraved. To

speak of the importance of these annals, which begin with
the reign of Augustus and stop with that of Gordianus
II., a lapse of two centuries and a half, and which contain
an almost incredible amount of archæological, historical,
and chronological information, would not be consistent with
the spirit of this chapter. I must notice, however, one
particular, which is evidently a recollection of the age of
bronze. The annals of each year were engraved on the
marble basement of the temple during the month of April,
and were engraved, of course, with iron or steel tools. To
expiate this profanation, in the same month of each year
sacrifices were offered, *ob ferri inlationem et elationem*, for
the introduction and removal of iron within the sacred precinct : a sow and a sheep were slain over the altar, and
their flesh was eaten afterwards by attendants and sacristans
of an inferior order.

This horror of iron, however, is not the only recollection of prehistoric ages to be found in the ritual of this
Arvalian brotherhood. There is another one, still more
curious and characteristic. I have already spoken of the
hand-made and sun-dried fossil pottery discovered in the volcanic district of Alba Longa and in the earliest cemeteries of
Rome. The Romans knew that this rough kind of earthenware had been manufactured, as utensils of prime necessity,
by their rough, uncivilized ancestors. Hence Tibullus wrote :
Fictilia antiquus primum sibi fecit agrestis pocula (The
ancient shepherd first contrived clay cups and vessels). In
memory of this primitive state of things, the use of earthenware was obligatory, or at any rate was preferred, in sacrifices
and libations. " It is worth noticing," Pliny remarks, " how,
in the incredible luxury of our age, libations are offered to
gods, not with cups of crystal and *murrha*, but with rough
terra-cotta *pateræ*." The same remark is made by Diony-

sius ; and Valerius Maximus adds that the sacred fire of
Vesta was kept in an earthen jar. Among the most venerable relics preserved in ancient Rome, there was one called
the *simpuvium Numæ*, the drinking-cup of Numa Pompilius. Juvenal (vi. 341) describes it as a simple terra cotta
tazza, of a dark color and evidently made by hand, — a description which fits exactly the whole archaic suppellex discovered at Alba and at Rome. It is easy to understand
that in the reign of Numa Pompilius ceramics were manufactured in Rome with prehistoric roughness, characteristic
of the age of bronze. The worship of this ancient cup of
Numa lasted until the fall of the Empire. In the annals,
also, of the Arvalian brotherhood, the following record is
many times engraved : *Ollas precati sunt* (They have addressed their prayers to earthen jars). Although it was
obvious that a connection could be traced between this practice of the Arvalians and the worship of Numa's cup, still
no evidence of the fact could be produced. But in 1870, a
few weeks before the excavations of the Empress Augusta
were brought to a close, there were found at the foot of the
temple eighteen prehistoric cups, which, although in a more
or less fragmentary condition, could be recognized as absolutely identical with the fossil pottery of Alba Longa.

Other prehistoric souvenirs, besides those already described, are to be found in ancient Rome. First, flint implements, arrow-heads, and *paalstabs* belonging to the age
of polished stone. These were considered by the Romans as
a product of lightning : *inveniuntur in loco fulmine icto.*
Hence they are called *gemmæ cerauniæ*, meteoric gems,
by Pliny ; and *lapides fulminis*, lightning stones, by Sidonius Apollinaris. They were kept as amulets and sacred
relics, on account of their celestial origin. A Latin inscription, published by Montfaucon (Orelli, 2510), speaks of a

diadem ornamented with flint implements offered to Isis. Prudentius describes the helmets of the German tribes as crowned with flint arrow-heads. More important still is the testimonial of Claudianus, who speaks of the same implements discovered in the caverns of the Pyrenees, along the bed of the mountain torrents.

" Pyrenæisque sub antris
Ignea flumineæ legere ceraunia nymphæ."

Who has not heard of the discoveries made by Lartet in the ossiferous caverns of the Pyrenees, of the Perigord, and of old Castile ?

Not every Roman, however, believed this story of the electric origin of arrow-heads. Augustus, the founder of the Empire and a passionate student of palæo-ethnology, made excavations in the prehistoric caverns in the island of Capri ; and the *res vetustate ac raritate notabiles*, " the rare and curious things," which he found there are described by Suetonius (Aug. 72) as bones of giants, that is to say, of fossil gigantic monsters, and as *arma heroum*, weapons of men living in past forgotten ages, which is a tolerably good scientific definition. During my long experience in Roman excavations, twice only have I met with stone implements. An arrow - head, probably kept as an amulet, was discovered in 1874 in a tomb twenty-six centuries old, near the church of S. Martino al Monti, together with other bronze tools. In the same year, a paalstab of jadeite was found buried at a depth of thirty-eight feet under the Monte della Giustizia, near the central railway station ; but it had no scientific value, as it was lying on the mosaic pavement of a Roman house, built in the year 123 of the Christian era. Nevertheless, we possess the evidence of the actual use of stone knives by the Romans. When a treaty of peace or a suspension of hostilities was sworn between Rome and its foes, the negotiator, called *fecialis*, would offer a sacrifice and kill the victims, *saxo silice* or *lapide silice* as Livy describes it (i. 2), a practice imported from the half-savage populations (*Æquicoli*) living in the upper valley of the Anio.

To cut the matter short, I will quote only one more instance, because it gives us an important and unbroken chain from the historic to the prehistoric times, between the age of gold and silver and the archæolithic age.

There was a well-known custom, in ancient times, of throwing votive offerings (*sacræ stipes*) into lakes, rivers, and springs, which were sacred to the gods, or were famous for their mineral hygienic properties. The custom dates from very remote ages, as the following discovery will testify. In 1852, the Jesuit fathers, owners of the celebrated sulphur springs called by us " Sorgenti di Vicarello," by the ancients " Aquæ Apollinares," on the west border of the lake of Bracciano, sent from Rome a gang of masons to clear the mouth of the central spring, and to put the whole into neat order. In draining the well, a few feet only below the ordinary level of the waters they came across a layer of brass and silver coins of the fourth century after Christ. Then they discovered a second layer of gold and silver imperial coins of the best period, together with a certain quantity of votive silver cups. In the third place, they came across a stratum of silver family or consular coins, belonging to the last centuries of the republic, and under this they found bronze coins, sextants, quadrants, trients, and so forth. Seeing that there remained nothing but brass to plunder, after having partaken of the precious booty in equal shares, the masons resolved to announce their discoveries. It is unnecessary to say that when Padre Marchi, the well-known numismatist, ran to the spot, he found only a few hundred pieces of *æs grave signatum,* the earliest kind of Roman coinage. Under these there was a bed of *æs rude,* that is to say, of shapeless fragments of copper, a kind of currency which preceded the use of æs grave signatum. At the bottom of the well, under the shapeless fragments of copper, there was nothing but gravel; at least the workmen and their leaders thought so. It was not gravel, however; it was a stratum of arrow-heads and paalstabs and knives of polished stone, offered to the sacred spring by the half-savage people settled on the shores of the Lago di Bracciano before the foundation of Rome. Thus this admirable chronological series of votive offerings, beginning with the age of stone, and perhaps with the first appearance of mankind in Central Italy, and ending with the fourth century of the Christian era, has been dispersed and made useless, in a certain degree, to science, partly by robbery, partly by ignorance. Still, the few hundred pieces saved by Padre Marchi, and deposited by him in the Kircherian Museum, Rome, are considered the finest numismatic group in existence with reference to the origin of Roman and Italian coinage.

Now that I have come to the end of this chapter, I feel almost sorry that I have confined myself to a strict scientific inquiry in connection with the origin of Rome, and have spoken the language of dry exactness, when I might easily have abandoned myself to the fascination of poetical and legendary traditions. The duty of a modern archæologist is rather hard and unpleasant if he has any spark of enthusiasm and poetry in his soul; compelled as he is to demolish piece by piece theories which have been believed and cherished for centuries, and to refuse credence to legends which have inspired artists and writers in the creation of their masterpieces of art and literature. I recollect the thrill of emotion which I used to feel — and which I feel now in spite of conviction — in reading the speech which Livy attributes to Camillus (v. 54) when he was trying to stop the emigration of his fellow-citizens to Veii : " Not without reason did gods and men select this site for the foundation of Rome : healthy hills ; a convenient river, equally adapted to inland and maritime trade ; the sea not too far off to prevent a brisk international trade, nor so near as to expose Rome to the danger of a sudden attack from foreign vessels ; a site right in the centre of the peninsula, — a site made, as it were, on purpose to allow the city to become the greatest city in the world." We have seen, to our common regret, I trust, that no supernatural influence or inspiration, no deep political thought, presided over the foundation of Rome ; that its origin must be attributed plainly to the *duris urgens in rebus egestas*, the necessity which compelled Alban shepherds to look for surer and better pasture grounds. We have seen that even its name is a matter-of-fact name, derived from the most noticeable landmark of the place. But if we cannot admire the pretended political forethought and wisdom of the founders of Rome, we are compelled, at any rate, to admire their manly vigor, their indefatigable energy, which led them in a short time to exchange their pastoral rod for the sceptre of kings, and which turned them, to use the expression of Homer, from leaders of flocks into leaders of men.

CHAPTER III.

THE SANITARY CONDITIONS OF ANCIENT ROME.

AFTER describing in the last chapter the humble origin of Rome and the simple causes which led to its foundation on the Palatine hill, we must inquire now whether the selection was equally happy as regards the sanitary conditions of the district which surrounded the new town. The question is full of practical interest on account of the mighty struggle into which we modern Romans have actually entered against malaria, a plague which seems to be spreading slowly, but surely, wherever there is a superabundance of moisture, both in the air and in the land; in other words, which is invading one tenth, at least, of the inhabited world.

The history of malaria in connection with Rome must be divided into five periods, — the prehistoric, the republican, the imperial, the mediæval, and the modern; each one marking a distinct stage in the increase or in the decline of the plague, as well as a change in the means adopted by the inhabitants of the fever-stricken district to protect themselves from the evil.

As regards the prehistoric period, we lack, of course, positive evidence, because, when ancient writers speak of the hygienic condition which existed at the time Rome was founded, either they speak at random, or else they describe things as they appeared in their own age. It seems probable that at that time all the lowlands surrounding the Alban volcanoes, as, for instance, the Pontine, the Volscian, and the Latin districts, were comparatively healthy, on account of the purifying action of telluric fires, of sulphuric emanations, and of many kinds of healing mineral springs. In the deadly calm of nature which has succeeded the extinction of the Latin volcanoes, we find it difficult to conceive an idea of the subterranean activity which prevailed at the time. All along the valley of the Roman Forum, which valley corresponds to a fissure or rent of the soil between the Palatine and the Quirinal hills, volcanic phenomena continued to appear even in historic times. The chasm under the northeast spur of the Palatine, into which Marcus Curtius is said to have leaped, seems to have been the crater of a kind of geyser. Near the Janus Quadrifrons there were hot sulphur springs, described by Varro (ll. V. 32). In the fourth century before Christ powerful jets of water sprang up suddenly in a street called Insteia or Insteiana. Julius Obsequens speaks of other jets of reddish water, near the Senate Hall, which he compares to blood (*sanguine fluxit*). A district of the Campus Martius is called *campus ignifer* by Livy, *fumans solum* by Valerius Maximus, τὸ πυρόφερον πεδίον by Zosimus, on account of volcanic smokes and emanations which for centuries had been noticed there.

The Campagna must have been even more strongly purified, especially around the slopes of the Alban hills, where hot mineral springs were particularly abundant. At all events, this is the only way to explain the presence of a thriving, healthy, strong, and very large population in places which, a few centuries later (namely, at the end of traditional and at the beginning of historic times), are described as pestilential. Antemnæ, Collatia, Corioli, Tellene, Politorium, Crustumerium, and many other centres, populous in volcanic ages, seem to have been obliterated more by the deleterious effects of the climate than by the chances of war and the overpowering supremacy of Rome. In the Volscian district, along the marshy Tyrrhenian coast, there were numberless settlements: Ficana, Lavinium, Ardea, Pyrgi, Antium, Alsium, and so forth. As to the Pontine region, Pliny asserts that it was the abode of a dense and thriving population.

It may be a simple coincidence, it may depend upon a mere accident, this fact of the extinction of human life at the precise time in which volcanic life was extinguished in the old Latium, but it is a coincidence worth scientific investigation. There can no longer be any doubt that malaria invaded the volcanic regions the very minute they ceased to be volcanic.

With regard to the site of Rome itself, we can hardly believe the words of Cicero (De Rep., 2, 6), in which he describes it as *in regione pestilenti salubris,* salubrious in a pestilential region, although the same observation is made by Livy, who considers it almost a prodigious fact that the town should prove healthy in spite of the pestilent and desert region by which it was surrounded (5, 54–7, 38). They evidently refer to the state of things prevailing in their own age. How is it possible that a hill like the Palatine, only a few feet high, and surrounded on three sides by poisonous marshes, should be exempt from the effects of malaria? The other hills of Rome were not better favored, from a hygienic point of view: the Cœlian and the Aventine suffered from the effluvia of the swamps near the Porta Metronia;[1] the Quirinal and the Pincian likewise from those of the Caprea Palus;[2] in fact, Livy asserts that, before the

[1] These swamps, called *Decenniæ,* have been drained lately, and filled up with the earth from the excavations of the Forum.

[2] On the subject of the Caprea Palus, see a recent paper of Comm. de Rossi in *Bull. Comm.* Rome, 1885.

construction of the Cloaca Maxima, every valley between the seven hills was nothing but a boggy quagmire. These hot-beds of malaria were fed by numberless springs, running sometimes above, sometimes under ground, impregnating the whole region with dampness, which is one, and perhaps the most active, of the three coefficients of the plague.

The clearest proof of the virulence of malaria in the first century of the history of Rome is afforded by the large number of altars and shrines dedicated by its early inhabitants to the goddess of the Fever and other kindred divinities. At the time of Varro, there were not less than three temples of the Fever left standing : one on the Palatine, one in the square of Marius on the Esquiline, one on the upper end of the *Vicus Longus,* a street which corresponds, within certain limits, to the modern Via Nazionale.

Altar dedicated to Verminus.

The Esquiline quarter seems to have been the worst of all in its sanitary conditions ; in fact, besides the Fever's temple, there was an altar dedicated to the Evil Eye (Mala Fortuna), and an altar and a small wood dedicated to the goddess Mefitis. Near the Prætorian camp, and near the modern railway station, I have found, myself, an altar consecrated to Verminus, the god of microbes ; and lastly, in the very centre of the Roman Forum, there was an altar sacred to Cloacina, a goddess of typhoid, I suppose.

It appears from the particulars just given that the

primitive inhabitants of Rome, acting as men always do act when they find themselves exposed to the ravages of an unknown evil, utterly ignorant of its mysterious nature and of the proper way to fight and to lessen its effect, raised their hands towards their gods, and actually increased the number of their divinities, and contrived new ones, imploring from heaven the help which they failed to secure with their own resources. After the lapse of many, many years, the request of those simple and energetic men was granted, and their town was made comparatively healthy, not in a supernatural or miraculous manner, but as a just and well-earned compensation for the efforts they had made and for the trouble they had taken to establish a better state of things. Strange as it seems, after the fall of the Empire, when Rome, almost annihilated by the inroads of barbarians, found itself in a condition almost worse than that of its early age, powerless to accomplish any work of improvement, and exposed again to the full influence of malaria, the inhabitants raised again their eyes towards God, built a chapel near the Vatican in honor of the Madonna della Febbre — our Lady of the Fever — which became one of the most frequented and honored chapels of mediæval Rome.

The principal works of improvement successfully accomplished in ancient times for the benefit of public health and for checking malaria may be chronologically described as follows: I. The construction of drains. II. The construction of aqueducts. III. The multiplication and the paving of roads. IV. The proper organization of public cemeteries. V. The drainage and cultivation of the Campagna. VI. The organization of medical help.

First, as regards the drains. The plan of the Etruscan engineers employed by Tarquinius Priscus to organize the

drainage of the town seems to have been to give an outlet
to the ponds and swamps and marshes which stretched along
the valley between each couple of hills, more than to carry
off the sewage, in the modern sense of the word. The
Cloaca Maxima, *receptaculum omnium purgamentorum ur-*

The Cloaca Maxima.

bis, the main collector, as Livy describes it, has been praised,
admired, eulogized by Dionysius (3, 67), Pliny (36, 15), Aurelius Victor (V. Ill. 8), Strabo (5, 3), Dion Cassius (49,
43), and in modern times by Niebuhr and Bunsen. There
is no doubt that the work is simply wonderful. An immense sewer, built twenty-five centuries ago, on unstable
ground, under enormous practical difficulties, which still
answers well its purpose, is a work to be classed among the
greatest triumphs of engineering. But the exactness of an
archæologist compels me to say that the Cloaca Maxima, in
spite of its name, can no longer boast of the priority
which it has enjoyed for so many centuries in the department of Roman sewers. In canoeing along the left bank
of the Tiber, I had long noticed the mouth of another cloaca,
a trifle larger than the Maxima, and separated from it by an

interval of some three hundred feet. I had heard it called
the cloaca of the Circus Maximus, but I was ignorant on
whose authority and by what reason such a name had been

Mouth of the Cloaca of the Circus Maximus.

applied. Six years ago, at the bottom of the valley which
separated the Palatine from the Cœlian, between the Arch of
Constantine and the church of S. Gregorio al Monte Celio,
a cloaca even larger and higher than the Maxima was discovered, three quarters of a mile from its opening into the
Tiber, at the depth of forty feet. The enormous size of its

blocks, the beauty and perfection of its masonry, and the wonderful preservation make it compare most advantageously with its rival, the Maxima, to which it is altogethei superior as regards length and extent of district drained.

The sewers of ancient Rome answered their purpose pretty well, especially if we take into consideration the remote age in which they were constructed, and their en-gineers' ignorance of modern sanitary principles and of the theory of microbes. Their greatest defects are, first, that they were used at the same time to carry off the sewage and refuse of the town and the rain-water ; second, that this double employment made it necessary to have large openings along the streets, so that the population was permanently brought in contact with the poisonous effluvia of the sewers. Many of these mouths of drains have come down to us, some exceedingly rough and primitive, some more elaborate and cut in marble. The most celebrated, perhaps, is the so-called Bocca della Verità, a marble disc, five feet in diameter, with the head of the Ocean in alto-relievo in the centre, through the open mouth of which the rain-water would escape. This monument, the scarecrow of children who show an inclination to lie, is preserved in the portico of the church of S. Maria in Cosmedin, near the ancient forum Boarium. The third defect of Roman sewage was that each sewer emptied directly into the Tiber, thus polluting its waters, which were used not only for bathing and swimming, but even for drinking.

The best apology for this state of things is to be found in the fact that not only modern Rome itself, but many other European capitals, not to speak of provincial towns and villages, remained until lately in an absolutely identical condition. The improvement in the department of sewers is one of the last, if not the very last achievement of mod-

THE BOCCA DELLA VERITÀ.

ern science in connection with hygiene, and it is still far from perfection.

The introduction of pure, drinkable water into Rome took place not earlier than the fifth century after its foundation. Sextus Julius Frontinus, a magistrate who presided over the department of aqueducts during the Empire of Trajan, begins his " Commentaries " on the subject with the following remark : " During four hundred and forty-one years the Romans satisfied themselves with the use of such water as they could obtain on the spot, from the Tiber, from wells, or from springs. Some of these springs are still held in great consideration, on account of their supposed healing power. Such are the springs of the Camœnæ, of Apollo, and of Mercury."

The waters of the Tiber, reaching Rome after a run of 249 miles through clay or alluvial soil, are certainly not pure or clear; in fact, they are saturated with mineral and solid matter. It appears from official observations carried on between March, 1871, and February, 1872, that with an average daily efflux of 1,296,000 cubic metres, the river has carried down to the sea 8,582,333 tons of sand, equal to a volume of 4,114,253 cubic metres. In spite of this state of things, what the ancients assert about the potability of its waters is proved by the fact that, after the destruction of imperial aqueducts, the population of mediæval Rome resorted again to this as the only means of quenching its thirst; in fact, the desire and the necessity of being near the river must be considered as the leading cause of the abandonment of the healthy hills, and of the mustering of the population in the Campus Martius. The salubrity of the waters of the Tiber is celebrated by Alessandro Petroni, physician to Gregory XIII., and by Alessandro Bacci, physician to Sixtus V. Clement VII., in the journey to Mar-

seilles, which he undertook in 1553 to celebrate the marriage
of his niece, Catherine de' Medici, with the Duke of Orleans,
afterwards Henry II., acting on the advice of his physician, Corti, brought with him such a quantity of water from
the Tiber as to be sufficient for all the requirements of the
journey. The same precaution was taken by Paul III.,
Farnese, in his wanderings to Loretto, Bologna, and Nice.

Fancy what must have been, in early Roman times, the
sanitary conditions of a town the drains of which, not
washed by any influx of water, communicated from space
to space with the public streets by large unprotected
openings, and emptied into a river, the polluted waters
of which were drunk by the whole population! The first
remedy against the evil was adopted in 442 A.U.C. by the
building of an aqueduct, which was to carry into the city the
water of a spring seven and a half miles distant, called Aqua
Appia, from the name of Appius Claudius Cæcus, the builder
of the aqueduct and of the Appian Way. The first step
in the right direction once taken, it was easy to advance
boldly. I cannot follow stage by stage the history of
Roman aqueducts. I will trace simply a brief and comprehensive sketch of the water-supply of Rome, under the
Empire; that is to say, at the period in which it was brought
to perfection.

Comparing the accounts left by Frontinus and Procopius
on this subject with the remains of aqueducts radiating
from Rome in every direction, and which form such a characteristic landmark of the Campagna, we gather the following information.

Eighteen springs have been collected and canalized by
the Romans from distances varying from a minimum of
seven and a half miles to a maximum of forty-four. The
waters were brought to Rome by means of fourteen aque-

ANIO NOVVS.
CLAVDIA

ARCHES OF THE CLAUDIAN AND ANIO NOVUS AQUEDUCTS.

ducts, the length of which varies from a minimum of eleven miles to a maximum of fifty-nine. The aggregate length of these fourteen aqueducts amounts to three hundred and fifty-nine and one third miles; of which three hundred and four miles are under ground, fifty-five above ground, the channel being carried on the top of really triumphal arcades, at prodigious heights, sometimes exceeding one hundred feet. The quality of the waters varied greatly. The best were considered the Marcia, the Claudia, and the Virgo; worst of all, the Anio Vetus and the Alsietina; these two accordingly were employed only for the irrigation of gardens and for washing away the drains, and were drunk only in cases of absolute necessity. As regards the temperature, the Marcia was the coldest:

"Marsas nives et frigora ducens Marcia,"

as Statius sings. It marks 46° Fahrenheit at the spring of S. Lucia. Tacitus relates among the crazy exploits of Nero his attempt to profane the sacred spring by swimming across it from shore to shore. This pollution of the pure icy waters was avenged by a rheumatic fever, which brought the young emperor to the verge of death.

I have many times been asked the question why the Romans spent such an amount of time, labor, and money in building these prodigious channels across mountains and valleys, tunnelling the former and bridging over the latter, with tunnels and bridges many miles long, when it would have been so easy and so economical to lay down pipes, following at a moderate depth the undulations of the country. In other words, I have been asked whether the Romans knew or did not know the principle of the siphon. To be sure they knew it, in theory and in practice. The siphons of Pataræ and Aspendus in Pamphylia, of Constantina in Mauritania, and

of Lyons in the Gallia Lugdunensis are all well known.
The finest and most daring of all is the siphon of Alatri,
built by a wealthy citizen, Betilienus Varus, a century and
a half before the Christian era, and capable of supporting
a pressure of ten atmospheres. As to the main aqueducts
which supplied Rome with a daily volume of fifty-four million cubic feet of water, it would have been impossible to
substitute metal pipes for channels of masonry, because the
Romans did not know cast-iron, and no pipe except of cast-
iron could have supported such enormous pressure. Let us
rejoice at this state of things, because, had the ancients
known the contrivances of modern industry, we should most
likely have been deprived of the loveliest sight which our
Roman Campagna offers.

Before leaving this interesting subject of the water-supply, I must make two more remarks : the first concerns the
system widely followed in our age, of damming the beds
of rivers in mountainous regions, in order to create artificial
lakes or reservoirs of pure water, from which the supply is
derived. The ancients knew and followed this system on a
magnificent scale. One of our aqueducts, the Anio Novus,
originally drew its supply directly from the river Aniene, at
a place forty miles distant from Rome. It happened that
every time the river was swollen by rains, the aqueduct
carried down troubled and undrinkable water, which would
fill up the main channel with incrustations of carbonate
of lime, and choke the minor pipes. To mend the matter,
and to obtain a constant influx of pure water, the valley
of the Anio was dammed, not once, but three times, across
the picturesque gorge or cañon of the Symbruine mountains, between the modern town of Subiaco and the Benedictine abbey of the Sacro Speco, and three artificial lakes
were thus obtained, in which the water was purified three
times.

The second remark concerns the system employed by the ancients in boring and tunnelling the mountains for hydraulic purposes. Two very curious documents have come down to us on this subject. The first is the official report of the perforation of a tunnel, to bring down to Bougie, Algeria (called then Saldæ or Civitas Salditana), the waters of a spring, fourteen miles distant, now called Aïn-Seur. The report, engraved on a marble altar, discovered in 1866 near Lambæse, begins with a petition addressed in the year 152 A. D. by Varius Clemens, governor of Mauritania, to Valerius Etruscus, governor of Numidia. The petition reads as follows: "Varius Clemens greets Valerius Etruscus, and begs him in his own name and in the name of the township of Saldæ to dispatch at once the hydraulic engineer of the III legion, Nonius Datus, with orders that he finish the work, which he seems to have forgotten." The petition was favorably received by the governor and by the engineer, Nonius Datus, who, when he had fulfilled his mission, wrote to the magistrates of Saldæ the following report: —

"After leaving my quarters I met with the brigands on my way, who robbed me even of my clothes, and wounded me severely. I succeeded, after the encounter, in reaching Saldæ, where I was met by the governor, who, after allowing me some rest, took me to the tunnel. There I found everybody sad and despondent; they had given up all hopes that the two opposite sections of the tunnel would meet, because each section had already been excavated beyond the middle of the mountain, and the junction had not yet been effected. As always happens in these cases, the fault was attributed to the engineer, as though he had not taken all precautions to insure the success of the work. What could I have done better? I began by surveying and taking the levels of the mountain; I marked most carefully the axis of the tunnel across the ridge; I drew plans and sections of the whole work, which plans I handed over to Petronius Celer, then governor of Mauritania; and, to take extra precaution, I summoned the contractor and his workmen, and began the excavation in their presence, with the help of two gangs of experienced veterans, namely, a detachment of marine-infantry (*classicos milites*), and a detachment of Alpine troops (*gaesates*). What more could I have done? Well, during the four years I was absent at Lambæse, expecting every day to hear the good tidings of the arrival of the waters at Saldæ, the contractor and the assistant had committed blunder upon blunder; in each section of the tunnel they had diverged from the straight line, each towards his right, and, had I waited a little longer before coming, Saldæ would have possessed two tunnels instead of one." Nonius Datus, having discovered the mistake, caused the two diverging arms to be united by a transverse channel; the waters of Aïn-Seur could finally cross the mountain; and their arrival at Saldæ was celebrated with extraordinary rejoicings, in the presence of the governor Varius Clemens and of the engineer.

To come back to Rome, however, the longest tunnel constructed in its vicinity for the sake of the water-supply is the one of Monte Affliano, between Tivoli and S. Gericomio, 4,950 metres (about three miles) long. Its boring was intrusted by Domitian to one of the imperial contractors, L. Paquedius Festus. A bold and arduous work it was, especially on account of the difficulty of ventilation in a channel only seven feet high by three wide. The contractor, before commencing the tunnel, made a vow to a local goddess, named the Bona Dea, to restore her decayed temple on the top of the mountain if the enterprise should succeed. The two opposite sections met most successfully on July 3, A.D. 88. The beautiful columns and fragments of

Junction of the Five Great Aqueducts.

statuary discovered on the summit of Monte Affliano prove that the vow of L. Paquedius was not what is called the vow of a sailor.

The influence of this magnificent supply of water on the

health of the inhabitants of Rome and the Campagna can easily be understood. There was no farm, no country-house, no villa, there was no neighborhood, however small and insignificant, of rustic people, which could not be favored with copious fountains of icy-cold, salubrious water. Villages and towns, such as Ostia, Portus, Gabii, Bovillæ, Veii, the ruins of which are scattered to-day in a waterless desert, were in Roman times almost overflowed, and their aqueducts vie in length and magnificence with the main aqueducts of the capital.

The reform and regulation of the public cemeteries — another hot-bed of pestilence — took place even later than the reform in the supply of water. I speak, of course, of *public* cemeteries, for the burial of artisans, of slaves, and of the poorest classes of the people, because persons belonging to higher classes usually provided themselves with private tombs, either within the precincts of their villas and farms, or along the sides of the highways. It is impossible to conceive an idea of the horrors of a common *carnarium* or fosse in the first centuries of Rome. I will give particulars of one only, which occupied a large district on the Esquiline, because these particulars were discovered by myself, and have not yet been fully disclosed to the general public.

The Esquiline cemetery was divided into two sections: one for the artisans who could afford to be buried apart in Columbaria, containing a certain number of cinerary urns; one for the slaves, beggars, prisoners, and others, who were thrown in revolting confusion into common pits or fosses. This latter section covered an area one thousand feet long, and three hundred deep, and contained many hundred *puticuli* or vaults, twelve feet square, thirty deep, of which I have brought to light and examined about seventy-five. In many cases the contents of each vault were reduced to a uniform mass of black, viscid, pestilent, unctuous matter; in a few cases the bones could in a measure be singled out and identified. The reader will hardly believe me when I say that men and beasts, bodies and carcasses, and any kind of unmentionable refuse of the town were heaped up in those dens. Fancy what must have been the condition of this hellish district in times of pestilence, when the mouths of the crypts must have been kept wide open the whole day!

But there is something still worse. Every visitor to Rome knows the great fortification which protected the city on the east side, called the Agger or embankment of Servius Tullius, from the king who raised it. This fortification, more than one mile long, comprised a ditch or moat one hundred feet wide and thirty deep, with ramparts one hundred feet wide and thirty high, supported and strengthened on the outside by a lofty battlemented wall. It seems that under the republican rule, and on the occasion of a stupendous mortality, — to use the words of Livy, — the portion of the huge moat which skirted the cemetery of the Esquiline was filled with corpses, thrown in as if they were carrion, until the level of the embankment was reached. The discovery of these revolting particulars took place in 1876, under the circumstances which I am going to relate. In building the foundations of a house at the corner of Via Carlo-Alberto and Via Mazzini, the architect, deceived by the presence of a solid bed of tufa on the northern half of the building-ground, began to lay his masonry and fill up the trenches to the uniform depth of twelve feet below the level of the street. All of a sudden the southern portion of the ground gave way, and one half of the area fell through into a chasm thirty feet deep. On careful examination of the circumstances of the catastrophe, it was ascertained that, whereas the northern half of the foundations rested on the solid embankment or Agger of Servius Tullius, the southern half had been laid on the site of the ditch, filled up with thousands upon thousands of corpses, which, when brought in contact with the air after twenty centuries, had crumbled into dust or nothing, leaving open a huge chasm. According to measurements which I took at the time, this mass of human remains was, at least, one hundred and sixty feet long, one hundred wide, and thirty deep. Giving to each corpse an average space of twenty cubic feet, which is more than sufficient, there were not less than twenty-four thousand bodies in a comparatively small space.

As if all the evils described were not deemed enough, the town authorities had increased their potency by allowing the daily refuse of a population numbering nearly a million souls to be heaped up within and around the precincts of this Esquiline cemetery. In later times, seven centuries after the foundation of Rome, they endeavored to stop the practice, or at any rate to regulate it. Decree upon decree was issued on the subject, and a line of stone cippi, inscribed with sanitary rules, was set up around the edge of the pestiferous ground. I have found three of these police regulations engraved on square blocks of travertine. Here is the text of one : " C. Sentius, son of Caius, Prætor, by order of the Senate has set up this line of terminal stones, to mark the extent of ground which must be kept absolutely free from dirt and from carcasses and corpses. Here also the burning of corpses is strictly forbidden." Another hand, probably that of a man living in the neighborhood and within reach of the effluvia of the place, had written in huge red letters the following entreaty at the foot of the official decree : " Do carry the dirt a little farther ; otherwise you will be fined." This line of stones, beyond which the refuse of the town could be legally thrown and be allowed to putrefy under the burning sun, was only four hundred feet distant from the walls and embankment of Servius Tullius. On the day of the discovery of the above-mentioned stone, June 25th, 1884, I was obliged to relieve my gang of workmen from time to time, because the smell from that polluted ground (turned up after a putrefaction of twenty centuries) was absolutely unbearable even for men so hardened to every kind of hardship as my excavators.

The reform in this branch of public hygiene, the suppression of the popular cemetery on the Esquiline, took place only under Augustus, at the suggestion of his enlightened prime minister, C. Cilnius Mæcenas, who obtained from his sovereign and friend the concession of the whole district, buried it under an embankment of pure earth, twenty-five feet high and a third of a square mile in area, and on the newly made ground laid down his magnificent gardens, the world-known *Horti Mæcenatiani.* The event proved to be of such unexpected importance for the improvement of the health of Rome that Horace himself thought it worth being sung by his muse:

" Nunc licet Esquiliis habitare salubribus, atque
    Aggere in aprico spatiari, quo modo tristes
    Albis informem spectabant ossibus agrum."

(Sat. i. 8, 14.)

I shall not mention other improvements carried on with the progress of Roman civilization, such as the paving of the streets, the opening of a thick network of roads in the Campagna, the drainage of damp districts, the spreading of suburbs, the careful cultivation of the soil, and the like; because I shall have occasion to speak of these particulars in the chapter on the Campagna. One subject deserves more attention, because little is known about it, — the subject of medical attendance, both public and private, a matter which is one of the most important factors in the sanitary arrangements of a civilized nation.

The hospital, even in its most rudimentary shape, was not known in Rome much before the third century of the Christian era. In fact, Celsus Aurelianus, an eminent physician, who wrote at the beginning of the third century a treatise " On Acute and Chronic Diseases " (*De morbis acutis et chronicis*), reproaches his colleagues for their obstinacy in keeping their patients in absolute confinement, as a practice injurious to the progress of science. It is not difficult to explain this state of things. First, the members of the higher classes of society were not in need of public sanitary institutions; secondly, the slaves, of whom the manufacturing and trading class was chiefly composed, had to be assisted at the expense of their own masters in case of sickness ; and besides, medicine was not known and practised as a science, but only in an empiric fashion. Hence patients were compelled to confide more in gods than in men, and to trust in supernatural help for the relief of their ailments. We must also bear in mind that charity was a virtue altogether unknown in ancient times, and even if it existed, was stifled by the spirit of conquest, by the maintenance of slavery, and by the passion for bloody and revolting gladiatorial shows, which rendered even the most tender Roman hearts and souls insensible to the sufferings of the neighbor.

Livy asserts that the Romans always remained faithful to the precept of Numa : " *Unam opem ægris corporibus relictam si pax veniaque ab diis impetrata esset* " — that the peace and good-will of gods were the only remedies and means to recuperate lost health : a passage which testifies that the famous *faith-cure* is at least twenty-six centuries old. Thus the more common cases of sickness to which mankind is subject were deified and idolized, and temples and shrines were set up in their honor. I have mentioned above the altars of the Fever, the sacred wood of Mephitis, the shrine of Orbona, and so on. Apollo, as a god of hygiene, had a temple near the theatre of Marcellus. This temple, built in the year 321 of Rome, and opened for public worship two years later, on the occasion of a terrific stroke of pestilence, was rediscovered quite by accident nine years ago, in the cellar of a third-class inn, near the Piazza Montanara, called the Albergo della Catena. It will be excavated, we hope, in 1889, in consequence of the destruction of the neighboring Jewish quarter (Ghetto); and considering its remarkable state of preservation, we trust we shall be able to find, at least, fragments of the famous group by Praxiteles or Scopas, representing Apollo annihilating the children of Niobe, described by Pliny (xxxv., 5, 28). Next in importance to the temple of Apollo was the temple of Health, the site of which corresponds nearly to that of the Barberini Palace, on the northern slope of the Quirinal. Women laboring in childbirth could apply to no less than thirteen goddesses, from Juno Lucina down to Deverra, Diana, Alemona, Nona, Decima, Partula, Antevorta, Postvorta, Eugeria, Fluonia, Uterina, Intercidona, etc.

In the year of the city 459, when Rome was in danger of annihilation by another plague, the Sibylline books were consulted, as they always were in cases of supreme danger. The answer was: "*Æsculapium ab Epidauro Romœ arcessendum*" (Livy, x., 32) — Æsculapius must be removed from Epidaurus to Rome — and so he was. The new god was comfortably and neatly installed on an island in the Tiber, now called the island of S. Bartolomeo, and his temple became the greatest sanitary establishment in the metropolis.

The practice followed by the Roman lower classes was this: patients whose life was in danger were brought into the peristyle or atrium of the sanctuary and put to sleep there, evidently by means of narcotic drugs, in order that Æsculapius might manifest in their dreams the proper way of healing their troubles. Once the recipe was obtained, the priests themselves undertook the cure of the patients; and if the cure succeeded, by some unforeseen and wonderful coincidence, then an *ex-voto* was suspended in the sacristy of the sanctuary, together with a tablet describing the happy event. Here is the text of one, given by Thomassinus : " In this last day, said the oracle to Caius the Blind, come to the sacred altar and kneel in front of it, then touch it on the left side, and apply instantly your hand to your eye.   Having obeyed, he recovered at once his eyesight, amidst the applause of the assembled multitudes." [1]   Is it not a striking coincidence, is it not a striking proof of the vitality of tradition in Rome, that the very island of the Tiber, the very spot on the island, always has been since Roman times, and is now, the seat of a hospital, the hospital of S. Giovanni di Calabita ?

Another curious anecdote is this : It seems that at the entrance of the Fabrician bridge (*ponte quattro Capi*), leading from the Campus Martius to the island, there were shops for the sale of *ex-votos* of every description, exactly as similar shops are to be seen now along the approaches to the great sanctuaries of Catholic countries.   One of these shops was discovered in the spring of 1885 in the foundations of the left embankment of the Tiber.   It contained a large number of anatomical specimens in painted terra-cotta, beautifully modelled from nature, and representing heads, ears, eyes, breasts, arms, hands, knees, legs, feet, *ex-votos* to

---

[1] The authenticity of this tablet is rather doubtful.

be offered by happy mothers, etc. The most interesting pieces are three life-size human trunks, cut open across the front, and showing the whole anatomical apparatus of the various organs, such as the lungs, liver, heart, bowels, etc. These pieces have not yet been examined by experts, and consequently I am not able to say whether they are capable of throwing any light on ancient hygienic and anatomical matters.

We must not suppose that men of education would resort to such absurdities as those I have described in connection with the temple of Æsculapius. Cicero has strongly condemned the practice in his book, "De Divinitate," but the populace, in spite of such good advice, adhered to its ignorance and superstition; and this obstinacy had then, and has still, such a firm hold, and such deep roots in the lowest classes of Italy, that only three years ago, in September, 1885, when the cholera broke out in Sicily, physicians trying to exercise their mission of charity were stabbed and killed by dying patients, just as happened in similar circumstances in Hungary and Croatia.

Another strange practice, imported from the East into Rome, was the exposure of the sick in the streets and under open porticoes, in order that passers-by might give them advice from personal experience.

The first physicians in Rome, if such a name can be applied to men knowing only the use of a few herbs and potions, came from the Abruzzi and from the shores of the lake of Fucino. In process of time, patrician families secured, at a high price, the services of slaves, experts in medicine, to whom the office of a modern *valet de chambre* was assigned. These slaves, emancipated after long successful services, used to open shops called sometimes *Medicinæ*, sometimes *Pharmacopolæ*, in which drugs and physic were sold, and surgical operations performed. For these operations the patient was put into an anæsthetic state in a much surer way than is now done with chloroform or laughing-gas. A successful physician was sure to receive high official distinction. Arcagathus, a Peloponnesian who migrated to Rome in 219, not only was rewarded with citizenship, but obtained a residence, with shop and office, bought at public expense. Asclepias from Drusa, Bithynia, was almost deified by the populace, and held in great estimation by Crassus and Cicero. Julius Cæsar was the first statesman to promote the welfare of hygienists, by recognizing them as professors of a liberal art, with rights to citizenship. Augustus, when cured by his freedman, Antonius Musa, of a dangerous illness, by means of fomentations and cold compresses, made him a knight, honored him with a bronze statue in the temple of Æsculapius, and exempted forever his colleagues from any kind of income-tax. Nero organized the service by naming an *archiatrus*, or superintendent of court-physicians. Schools of medicine were opened, and students organized themselves into a corporation, the seat of which was on the Esquiline. When one of the professors was called to visit a patient, he was followed by the whole body of pupils, because, there being no hospitals at the time, this was the only way by which they could learn and gain experience. Martial describes one of these professional visits in the ninth epigram of the fifth book, and relates how Dr. Symmachus, when sent for, came at once to his bed, accompanied by more than one hundred disciples, who, one by one, felt his pulse with hands almost frozen by the northern wind, or tramontana, which happened to be blowing at the time.

The merit of organizing a service of public assistance, in the true modern and philanthropic sense of the word, belongs to Antoninus Pius, who acted, I am sure, under the indirect pressure of Christian influence and charity, for the new faith had made immense progress in Rome under his wise and temperate rule.

The new sanitary codex comprised the institution of head-physicians (*archiatri*) in every inhabited centre, and a set of rules for the medical service in the largest cities of the empire. These medical officers had to be elected by the town council, and to be approved by the *patres-familiæ*. In process of time the election had further to be sanctioned by the College of Physicians practising in the same town, and even by the Emperor himself. Assistance to the poor was compulsory and gratuitous.

CHAPTER IV.

PARKS, gardens, commons, and public squares have been happily compared to the lungs of a city ; and if the health and general welfare of a city depend upon the normal and sound function of its respiratory organs, ancient Rome, in this respect, must be considered as the healthiest city which has ever existed on earth. Comparing the documents we possess on Roman topography, texts of classics, inscriptions, plans, ruins, and so forth, we learn that towards the end of the third century after Christ there were in Rome eight *campi* or commons, green spaces set apart mostly for foot-races and gymnastic exercises ; eighteen *fora* or public squares, and about thirty parks and gardens, which, first laid out by wealthy citizens for their private comfort or for the comfort of their friends, had been absorbed into the imperial domain by right of purchase, by bequest, or by confiscation. These three classes of open spaces, namely, commons, forums, and parks, are far from representing the total amount of free ground which the citizens could enjoy at any hour of the day or night. We must add to the list the cemeteries, those marble cities of the dead, shadowed by stately cypresses and weeping-willows ; the sacred enclosures of temples with their colonnades and fountains ; the porticoes, expressly built for the sake of allowing citizens to move about pleasantly in hot or rainy weather ; and lastly, the great *thermæ*, establishments provided with every possible comfort and accommodation to insure the health of the body and the education of the mind. It is, not possible to describe all these groups of public open places in a single chapter. I shall simply sketch the outline of this important feature of ancient Rome, leaving aside commons, ornamental cemeteries, and sacred enclosures, and confining myself to forums, baths, and public parks.

Beginning with the forums or public squares, I shall speak of them not from a purely artistic or archæological point of view, but with regard to their capacity for giving to the citizens free movement and free air.

The first forum of Rome, the one called afterwards the *Forum Romanum magnum*, was established on newly made land, on ground reclaimed from the marshes of the Velabrum :

> " Hic ubi nunc fora sunt, udæ tenuere paludes :
> nunc solida est tellus, sed lacus ante fuit ! "
>
> (Ovid, *Fasti* vi. 395.)

It answered its purpose very well during the first three or four centuries of Rome, not only on account of its size, but especially on account of its central position, and of the facility of access from the neighboring valleys.

In its first state, the forum was a tract of gently undulating, grassy, damp ground, bordering on a swamp, surrounded on two sides by the lofty perpendicular cliffs of the Palatine and of the Capitol, and used exclusively as a public market. On its sides there were a few conical straw huts, such as the one in which the public fire was kept, transformed in process of time into the beautiful temple of Vesta. On the north side, directly under the Capitoline hill, there were some stone quarries, called *Lautumiæ*, afterwards transformed into the *Carcer Tullianum*, or Mamertine Prison. There were also two fine springs of water, one issuing from these quarries or Lautumiæ, the same which is shown to visitors as a miraculous feature of S. Peter's Prison ; the other issuing from the ivy-clad rocks of the Palatine, and called the spring of Juturna. The first improvement, made at an early date, toward the regular arrangement of the forum was the drainage of the stagnant waters which surrounded it, and the canalization of the two above-mentioned springs.

Other improvements were accomplished under the kings. Numa Pompilius organized the service for the maintenance of a public fire at the disposal of citizens, and built a very convenient and elaborate hut for the young maidens, the Vestals, in charge of the fire, and for the high priest charged with the surveillance of this department. Tullus Hostilius built on the east side of the forum a stone enclosure, called the *Curia*, in which the senators could hold their meetings ; he also fenced in a space in front of the Curia, named the *Comitium*, in which the polling for election took place. Tarquinius Priscus finally gave to the forum the regular shape of a parallelogram, which it preserved down to the fall of the empire,[1] and divided the ground surrounding it into building lots, which were sold to private speculators with the condition that shops should be built there, and porticoes on the fronts of the houses facing the forum.

Such was the character and condition of the public square of Rome during the kingly period. It does not come within the scope of this chapter to follow, stage by stage, even by centuries, its development into a magnificent forum, surrounded by stately edifices. I will satisfy myself by tracing a brief outline of its prominent features as it appeared near the end of the Republic, when, having be-

---

[1] The forum is represented in every existing plan as a trapezium, whereas it is a perfect parallelogram.

come almost ridiculously small for the accommodation of the people, it began to lose its individuality by the addition of other fora, far larger and more luxurious.

Towards the end of the republican period, obscure private edifices, shops, and houses, had totally disappeared from the bordering line of the square, and had made room for more substantial structures of a public character. Beginning at the north side, that is to say, at the side of the Tarpeian rock and of the Capitoline hill, the first conspicuous building was the temple of Saturn, used not only as a place of worship, but also as a public treasury for civil purposes. As a place of worship, it was remarkable on account of its strange ritual : it was the only temple in Rome which the devout could enter with heads uncovered ; it was the first to have inaugurated the use of burning wax tapers ; it was the first temple, the anniversary feast of which — the well-known Saturnalia — has been transformed in progress of time into the Carnival, an institution once famous, now fast dying out in Italy. Other places of interest on the north side were the temple of Concord, used as a military treasury ; the Græcostasis, a space set apart for ambassadors from foreign nations, waiting to be admitted into the Curia, or Senate-house, and the State Prison above referred to.

The east side was occupied by two structures separated by a wide street, — the Senate-house and the Court-house, — called *Basilica Æmilia.* (In the middle of the street separating the Curia from the Basilica, there was the small square temple of *Janus Quadrifrons.*) Of these structures the Senate-house was, politically speaking, the most important building in Rome, in spite of the simplicity of its architecture. It was an oblong hall, eighty-five feet long, seventy-five wide, raised on a platform made accessible by a

flight of steps, the same down which the body of King Servius Tullius had been hurled by Tarquinius.   Inside it con-

The Curia (S. Adriano) in the Sixteenth Century.

tained several rows of wooden benches, the Speaker's desk,
a wooden tribune, and behind the Speaker's chair a small
apartment containing the archives of the House.   So extreme was the frugality and self-denial of those worthy
republican senators, that they had never allowed their hall
to be warmed in the depths of winter, in an age in which
even the houses of the peasantry had been furnished with
heating apparatus.   In a letter addressed by Cicero to his
brother, on January 6, 692 A. U. C., he relates how the
Speaker Appius, having summoned the senators to an important meeting, *tantum fuit frigus, ut populi convicio
coactus sit nos dimittere*, it grew so intensely cold that he
was obliged to dismiss the assembly and expose the senators
to the raillery and derision of the populace.

In the year 700 A. U. C. this venerable edifice, more than
five hundred years old, was burned down by the partisans
of Clodius, the fierce tribune whose name is so familiar
to students of Cicero. The revolutionary instincts of the
mob having been aroused and excited by violent speeches,
a certain Sextus Clodius, a scribe, broke into the adjoining
Senate-hall at the head of a band of roughs, carrying on
their shoulders the corpse of the murdered anarchist ; and
having made a kind of pyre of the benches, tables, books,

The Curia (now the Church of S. Adriano) in its present condition.

and shelves, set everything into a blaze, and burned with
the corpse of Clodius the Curia itself, and the adjoining
Court-house, then called the *Basilica Porcia*.

I have spoken more at length of this building and of its

conflagration in the year 700, because its reconstruction by
Julius Cæsar and Augustus, together with the reconstruction
of the adjoining Court-house, marks the period of the
transformation of the old forum itself, as I shall presently
relate.

To complete our tour along the two remaining sides of
the square, I shall mention on the south side, the *fornix
Fabianus,* a triumphal arch raised in the year 633 of Rome
to Fabius Maximus Allobrogicus, the conqueror of Savoy,
one of the oldest, if not the very oldest, arch in the city,
the remains of which we brought to light in March, 1882;
the temple of Vesta and the convent of the Vestals, the
discovery of which will form the subject of my sixth chapter; and lastly, the *ædes Castorum,* temple of Castor and
Pollux, built on the very spot at which the two Dioscuri
had been miraculously seen watering their horses at the
spring of Juturna, to announce the great victory of Lake
Regillus, gained by the Romans on that same day, in
496 B. C.

The western and last side was still and for the greater
portion occupied by rows of shops. Originally they were
of an inferior order, mostly butcher shops, such as the one
from which Virginius is said to have seized the knife with
which he avenged the honor of his violated daughter. Later
on, the butchers gave up the place to schoolmasters for
elementary teaching. Lastly, towards the end of the Republic, brokers, bankers, and money lenders and changers
took absolute possession of the place, and transformed it
into a real Wall Street. As regards the square itself, the
proper area of the forum, it was full of every kind of obstruction; so much so, that we wonder how in such a small
and encumbered space the actual populace could move
about.

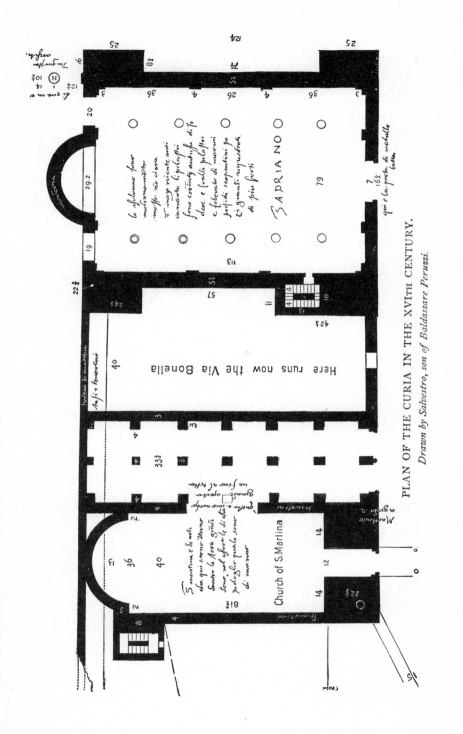

PLAN OF THE CURIA IN THE XVITH CENTURY.

Drawn by Salvestro, son of Baldassare Peruzzi.

In the first place, there was another populace of stone, marble, and bronze : the well known statue of Marsyas, near the Rostra, the daily meeting-place of lawyers and attorneys of an inferior rank, selected also by Julia, daughter of Augustus, for her nocturnal rendezvous : the one of Tatius, marking the spot in which the treaty of peace between the Romans and the Sabines had been sworn ; those of Atta Navius, Pythagoras, and Alcibiades, near the Senate-house ; the bronze statue of Servius Sulpicius, whose descendants had the right of occupying a space of five feet square, free of payment, in front of the statue itself, on the occasion of gladiatorial games, shows, and festivities ; a stone lion, marking the spot in which Faustulus, the tutor of Romulus, had been buried, according to an early tradition ; the statues of Horatius Cocles ; of the ambassadors murdered at Fidenæ ; of Q. Marcius Tremulus, the conqueror of the Hernici, and so forth.   So great was the hindrance created by this army of statues, that in the year 156 B. C. the censor Cornelius Scipio was obliged to clear away the whole crowd, respecting only those which had been put up by a decree of the Senate.   The second obstruction was the trees, of every age and quality : the Ficus Ruminalis, which Tacitus describes as having shown the first signs of decay eight hundred and forty-one years after the twin infants Romulus and Remus had been exposed under its shade ; a lotus-tree growing between the temples of Saturn and Concord, described by Masurius as older than Rome itself ; a fig-tree, which was cut down at the age of two hundred and sixty-one years, because its roots had undermined and nearly overturned an old stone figure of Sylvanus ; a vine and an olive-tree near the spring of Juturna, and others.

I shall not speak of the Rostra or public tribune, of the Columna rostrata raised in honor of C. Duillius, the Roman admiral who defeated the Carthaginian fleet; of the *Puteal Scribonianum,* marking a spot struck by lightning, and made sacred; of the Jani, or four-faced porches, because the description of these prominent features of the forum would lead me far from the special topic of the present lecture. I will conclude my brief sketch by remarking that, besides the obstacles already described, the square and its vicinity were occupied by certain classes of people, not particularly distinguished, who so constantly haunted this or that special corner of the place that they actually were nicknamed from it. Thus we hear of the *Subrostrani,* attorneys and lawyers without employment, who haunted the neighborhood of the Rostra; of the *Canalicolæ,* drunkards keeping themselves near the Canalis, a place the explanation of which is given by Plautus in Curculio, iv. 1; and in a more general manner we hear of the *forenses, habitués* of the forum, who used to spend hours upon hours in laziness and gossip near the *Solarium,* or sun-dial, or near the Tabula Valeria, a kind of panorama of the battle gained by M. Valerius Messalla over King Hieron of Syracuse, painted on the outside wall of the Senate-house in the year 492 A. U. C. Fruit-sellers had taken possession of the ascents leading from the forum to the top of the Velia; jewellers, goldsmiths, makers of musical instruments, of the Sacred Way; perfumers, of the Tuscan Street (*vicus Tuscus*), leading to the Circus Maximus; copyists, sellers of books and literary novelties, of the Argiletum, a street leading toward the ill-famed Subura, which was also the rendezvous of pickpockets, who were in the habit of meeting in the afternoon to partake and otherwise dispose of the morning's booty. Then there was a special place in the forum for usurers, lenders, and changers of money; another, the porticoes of the Basilicæ, for fishmongers, who poisoned the clients of the court-house with the offensive smell of their merchandise.

THE FORUM, LOOKING EAST.

The first important step towards the improvement of this obnoxious state of things was taken in the seventh century of Rome by the construction of a fish-market or *forum piscatorium.* Then followed the construction of the Basilicæ Fulvia, Porcia, Sempronia, which being surrounded by porticoes, and kept constantly open day and night, increased, in a certain measure, the accommodation of the frequenters of the forum. In the year 699, M. Æmilius Paulus bought private property on the east side of the forum for the sum of $2,400,000, and built his superb Basilica Æmilia, called by Cicero *magnificentissima.* The reason for this great undertaking is given by the same writer; *ut forum laxaremus,* to enlarge the area and extent of the forum. The Basilica, the finest ever built in Rome, was dedicated twenty years after the beginning of the work in 719 A. U. C.; eighteen years afterwards, when it had been injured by fire, Augustus and other friends of Æmilius Paulus supplied the funds necessary to restore the edifice, and to decorate it with the famous columns of pavonazetto marble, which were transferred five centuries later to the basilica of S. Paul outside the walls (perhaps on account of the similarity of their names), and almost entirely destroyed by the great fire of 1823.

The work of Æmilius Paulus was continued by Julius Cæsar. So enormous was the sum of money which he spent in the year 702 to purchase the area for his new forum (an extension of the old one) that even the unimpressionable Pliny exclaims, *pyramides regum miramur, cum solum tantum foro exstruendo HS millies Cæsar dictator emerit!* "We wonder at the Egyptian pyramids, when Cæsar, as dictator, spent one hundred millions of sesterces merely for the ground on which to build his forum!" The sum of one hundred millions of sesterces, mentioned by

Pliny and confirmed by Suetonius, corresponds to four million dollars; and as the area purchased by Cæsar does
not exceed ninety thousand square feet, it is evident he
must have paid, on an average, $44.45. per foot.   This
forum of Cæsar took the shape of a sacred enclosure surrounding the temple of Venus Genetrix, so named because
this goddess was considered by Cæsar to be the one from
whom his own family had originated.   The statue of the
divinity was a masterpiece by Arcesilaos, and a masterpiece
also was the equestrian statue of the dictator himself,
placed in front of the temple.   The horse was carefully
modelled from nature.   In the sixty-first chapter of his Life
of Cæsar, Suetonius speaks at length of this famous charger.
It was a charger, he says, whose fore-feet were nearly human, the hoofs being split in imitation of toes.   The animal
was foaled in the family mews; and as the augurs, when
asked to explain the miracle of the hoofs, had declared that
it portended the empire of the world for his master, Cæsar
devoted himself to the education of the colt, and the colt
conceived such an affection for his master that he would
never allow himself to be fed, or taken care of, or ridden
by anybody else.   The temple of Venus Genetrix contained
famous paintings by Greek artists, which Pliny describes;
six collections of engraved gems and cameos; and a breast-
plate for the statue of the goddess, entirely covered with
pearls from Britain.

Augustus followed the example of Cæsar, and in continuation of the two forums built a third one, still more magnificent, named the *forum Augustum*, or else the *forum
Martis* from the temple of Mars the Avenger, which stood
in the middle of it.   The reason given by Augustus himself
for this work was the absolute insufficiency of the two previous forums for the transaction of business and the admin-

REMAINS OF THE FORUM OF AUGUSTUS AND THE TEMPLE OF
MARS ULTOR.

istration of justice. No words could describe the beauty of this architectural *chef-d'œuvre*, the remains of which, known by the modern name of the Arco de' Pantani, rank among the very finest of ancient Rome. The most notable feature of the place was a gallery of statues, representing the generals who by their exploits and victories had increased the power of Rome, and had subjugated to it more than one half of the old world. I can only mention the fourth forum, built by Vespasian, and the fifth, begun by Domitian and completed by Nerva. Although smaller and altogether less remarkable than the three preceding ones, they would have been the pride of any other town than Rome. In Vespasian's forum, dedicated to Peace (*forum Pacis*), the gold vessels and the seven-branched candlestick from the great temple of Zion had been deposited, as a votive offering to the goddess. In Domitian's forum, dedicated to Minerva, there was another gallery of portrait-statues, in imitation, or rather as an extension, of the one exhibited in the forum of Augustus. The statues were of colossal size, and represented the Roman emperors. One only has come down to us, the so-called Pyrrhus, placed at the foot of the staircase of the Capitoline Museum, and noticeable for the really shameful way in which it was restored, altered, and disfigured at the beginning of the last century.

We must now enter the last and most magnificent square belonging to the group I have attempted to describe, the forum of Trajan, the handsomest and costliest monument of ancient Rome. To fully explain its importance as a masterpiece, not only of architecture, but also of engineering, I must lay before the reader's eyes a sketch of the topographical conditions of the centre of the town, in connection with its viability and traffic.

The Capitoline hill, situated in the very centre of the town, originally was not isolated, as it is at present, but was connected with the adjoining Quirinal hill by a high ridge, which sloped sharply down towards the Roman forum on the south side, towards the Campus Martius on the north side. In other words, it was not an isolated hill, which the daily tide of the city traffic could turn on every side, as is the case now; it was a barrier, an obstacle, an obstruction, which cut the town and its traffic right in two, and could only be overcome in one of two ways: either by ascending and then descending the steep ridge which connected it with the Quirinal, along a lane corresponding with the modern Via Marforio,— a lane only ten feet wide, with a gradient of 12 to 100, which crossed the ridge at its lowest point, or by rounding the Capitol on the river-side.. The passage could be accomplished on this side on level ground, it is true, but it was three times as long as a direct line carried across the ridge; and besides, fancy what the condition of the traffic must have been in that narrow strip of land between the Capitol and the left bank of the Tiber, which afforded the only possible line of communication between two halves of a city inhabited by nearly two million souls!

To obviate the evil, to allow citizens freedom of movement, to relieve the streets surrounding the Capitol on the river-side from the pressure of traffic, and, at the same time, to double at once the surface of the five existing forums, Trajan conceived the idea of severing the Capitol from the Quirinal, of cutting away the ridge, and of substituting for it a level passage, nearly six hundred feet wide. His plans were carried into execution by a skilful man, the architect Apollodorus, in about fifteen years' time. To give an approximate idea of the importance of the work, I will men-

tion two things only : first, that private property, built on
each side and on the top of the ridge, must have been purchased and appropriated to the extent of some 275,000
square feet. Supposing the price paid by Trajan to be the
same as that paid by Julius Cæsar for the area of his forum,
namely, $44.45 per square foot, the ground alone must have
cost Trajan the sum of $12,223,000. The second remark
refers to the work of cutting, excavating, and carting away
the mountain. So great was the astonishment created by
the titanic achievement, even in a city accustomed to wonders, that the well-known column, that prototype of monumental pillars, was erected at a public cost *ad declarandum
quantæ altitudinis mons et locus sit egestus,* — " to show
to posterity how high rose the mountain levelled by the
Emperor." Trajan's column is one hundred and forty feet
high, from the pavement of the forum to the top of the
bronze statue. This circumstance helps us to state the total
amount of earth and rock removed to make room for the
forum at 24,000,000 cubic feet. I have made investigations all over the Campagna, within a radius of three or
four miles from the walls, to discover the place where the
24,000,000 cubic feet were carted and dumped, but my
efforts have not, as yet, been crowned with success. This
fact leads me to suppose that the enormous mass might
perhaps have been utilized to fill up some marshy district
in the neighborhood of Rome.

The reader must not imagine this forum of Trajan as a
simple square, surrounded by porticoes, and ornamented
more or less abundantly with works of art. The forum of
Trajan comprised seven different sections, namely : the propylaia, or triumphal arch of the Emperor ; the square itself,
with the equestrian statue in the middle ; the Basilica Ulpia ;
the Bibliotheca Ulpia ; the two hemicycles ; the monumen-

tal column ; and the temple of Trajan.   The *ensemble* of
these various sections was considered not only the masterpiece of Roman architecture of the golden age, but one
of the marvels of the world.   Let me quote the words with

Column and Forum of Trajan.

which Ammianus Marcellinus (xvi. 10) describes the impressions felt by the Emperor Constantius at the first sight of
the group : " Having now entered the forum of Trajan, the
most marvellous creation of human genius, — *singularem
sub omni cœlo structuram*, — he was struck with admiration, and looked around in amazement, without being able
to utter a word, wondering at the gigantic structures, —
giganteos contextus, — which no pen can describe, and which
mankind can create and see only once in the course of centuries.   Having consequently given up any hope of building himself anything which would approach, even at a re-
spectful distance, the work of Trajan, he turned his attention to the equestrian statue placed in the centre of the

forum, and said to his attendants he would have one like it in Constantinople." These words having been heard by Hormisdas, a young Persian prince attached to his court, he turned quietly towards the Emperor, and said, " If your majesty wants to secure and keep such a horse, you must first provide him with a stable like this." So far Ammianus Marcellinus.

Cassiodorius asserts that, no matter how many times one saw this forum, it would always appear a prodigious, a miraculous work, more than the work of man. Such being the estimation in which Trajan's masterpiece was held in ancient times, such being its beauty and perfection, I cannot attempt to enter into details, and describe one by one its various sections and their contents. It is enough to say that by the addition of Trajan's forum to the five which already existed, the whole space put at the disposal of the people of Rome, for meeting in public, for promenading, for the transaction of business or the administration of justice, and so forth, was brought to the grand total of twenty-five and one half acres. This space contained thirteen temples, three basilicas, or court-houses, eight triumphal arches, the house of parliament, thousands of life-size statues in bronze and marble, porticoes more than one mile long, and supported by about twelve hundred columns, public libraries and archives, and the finest and richest shops of the metropolis.

Next to forums I must speak of the baths as places of public resort. At the end of the third century after Christ, Rome numbered 11 large public thermæ, and 926 smaller ones conducted under private enterprise. The baths of Caracalla alone could accommodate, at one time, 1,600 people ; the baths of Diocletian, 3,600. Taking 1,500 as the average accommodation of each of the public *thermæ*, and 50 as that of each of the private baths, we learn that in ancient Rome, at any minute, 62,800 citizens could restore their strength in baths of every nature and description ; and this, without bringing into the calculation the Tiber, the Anio, the Lake of Agrippa, and the bathing accommodations with which every Roman house was abundantly furnished. These dry figures and statistics concern only cleanliness and bodily health. But for those who frequented the great thermæ bathing was the very last thought, — I mean for the fashionable *habitués* of imperial times ; since the earlier generations, those which had made Rome the queen of the world, had always considered the bath as the most important event and the most essential requirement in the every-day life. In course of time, and under the corruption which began to contaminate Roman society after the conquest of the East, bodily health and cleanliness, although the original object, had long ceased to be the only one ; for the thermæ, decorated with prodigal magnificence, and supplied with all the comforts, conveniences, and novelties that a voluptuary could desire, had become places of amusement, whither people repaired for pastime and enjoyment. They were, in a word, gigantic clubs, where the elegant youth passed the whole day, at least the hours in which the establishments were kept open. Of course, the number of hours varied according to the season, or the good-will of the Emperor. The opening was announced by the sound of a bell heard at a great distance. *Sonat æs thermarum !* was the exclamation popular among the anxiously waiting *habitués*. A great deal has been written by Salmasius, Marini, Becker, and other antiquarians about the hours for opening and closing the public baths. The truth is that they varied at different periods, from sunrise until sunset.

THE FRIGIDARIUM, OR SWIMMING BATH, OF THE BATHS OF CARACALLA.

Pliny the younger says that his friend Spurinna bathed in winter at the ninth hour, in summer at the eighth. Vopiscus mentions the ninth as the opening hour. *Thermæ apud veteres non ante nonam aperiebantur.* The Emperor Hadrian made a new regulation. He ordered that nobody should enter the thermæ before the eighth hour of the day except those provided with a certificate from the attendant physician, and absolutely no one after sunset. Severus Alexander not only caused the gates to be opened again at sunrise, but ordered them to be kept open until late at night, defraying the expense of illumination from his own private purse. The Emperor Tacitus again restricted the time to the length of the day, as the concession made by his predecessor had given occasion to great nocturnal disturbances; but probably this did not continue long in force, for we find again in the Codex of Justinian a certain sum allotted to the cost of lighting. Thermæ became by degrees places of the most foolish debauchery. Suetonius relates of Caligula that he imagined unheard-of refinements in bathing and eating, and that he carried the luxury of bathing to such an extent that he took his bath, not in water, but in tepid perfumes. Helagabalus, the mad youth who put vases of murrha (the costliest and most precious material known to the ancients) to the vilest uses of the imperial household, used to swim in basins the water of which had been mixed with the oil of saffron.

With regard to the custom of allowing both sexes to bathe at the same time, the regulations were changed under different emperors. There is no doubt that Roman women, even the noblest of them, visited the public baths; but, as a rule, they were provided with separate rooms. Atia, the mother of Augustus, after the fabulous *rencontre* in the Temple of Apollo, bore on her person the indelible mark of a serpent, to conceal which from indiscreet eyes she was obliged to give up frequenting public baths. Juvenal and Martial allude very often to the gross immorality of the men and women bathing together; but we must not believe that the immorality was general. Hadrian was the first Emperor to put an end to this shameful disorder, though only for a brief period; because the periodical renewal of these interdicts shows that the evil could not be eradicated. In 1870, an inscription was found near some private baths in the Trastevere, containing the following notice: "By order of the mighty god Sylvanus, women are prohibited from stepping into the swimming basin reserved for the men." This inscription shows that police regulations were not enough to keep fast women in order, and that the owners of baths, responsible for the decency of their establishments, were obliged to resort to the intervention of the gods. The last thing we hear on this subject is a general decree promulgated by Helagabalus, by which promiscuous bathing was allowed everywhere and at all hours. Let us follow one of the elegant youths of Rome into one of the great thermæ. He is welcomed at his entrance by the *ostiarius,* or porter, a tall, majestic fellow with a sword at his side, and by the *capsarius,* or wardrobe - keeper, who takes charge of his wraps. Then follows a general salutation and kissing of friends, exchange of the last topics and scandals of the day; reading of the newspapers, or *acta diurna.* The visitor then selects the kind of bath which may suit his particular case, — cold, tepid, warm, shower, or perspiration bath. The bath over, the real business begins, as, for example, taking a constitutional up and down the beautiful grounds, indulging in athletic sports or simple gymnastics to restore circulation, and to prepare himself for the delights of the table.

The luxurious meal finished, the gigantic club-house could supply him with every kind of amusement : libraries, concerts, literary entertainments, reading of the latest poems or novels, popular or Barnum-like shows, conversation with the noblest and most beautiful women. Very often a second bath was taken to prepare for the evening meal. All this could be done by three or four thousand persons at one and the same time, without confusion or delay, because of the great number of servants and slaves attached to the establishment.

The excavations and discoveries which Abel Blouet made in 1824, Guidi in 1878, and ourselves during the last fifteen years in the baths of Caracalla, show clearly how the service was organized. It was carried on entirely underground, by means of crypto-porticoes, which allowed the servants to appear suddenly everywhere, and to meet the requirements of the visitors without crossing the halls and without interfering with the circulation of the noble crowd. In fact, we have discovered a fragment of the " order of the day," or programme of the distribution of service on the nineteenth day of April, A. D. 226.[1]

This unique and most remarkable document, which we were fortunate enough to bring to light in January, 1881, was evidently written by one of the overseers in charge of a special department, say, for instance, the department of the wardrobe ; and for the want of the proper material it was written with a black pencil on a piece of marble, evidently belonging to the incrustation of the walls of the room which was used as an office. It contains, first, the above mentioned date (April 19th) and the name of the Emperor, Severus Alexander. Then follows a list of

[1] The year is not absolutely certain, as of the two consuls only Severus Alexander is mentioned.

names of slaves and servants, such as Zoticus, Gaudentius, Panacius, Januarius, Stephanus, etc., and near each name a number, which varies from a minimum of one half to a maximum of three and a half, — numbers which probably refer to the hours of duty of each individual.

I have spoken of public squares and of baths as places of resort and enjoyment for the people of Rome; I come now to another special characteristic, — that of the porticoes, which occupied the whole plain of the Campus Martius, stretching from the foot of the hills on the left bank of the river to the river itself. They followed one another almost without interval, filling up the spaces between the great buildings, such as the circuses, theatres, *stadia*, temples, etc. Between the Capitol, the Quirinal, and the river, not less than twenty porticoes were erected. Under the republican rule they were almost a rarity; and besides, the few that existed at that time were built, not as mere places of pleasant meeting, but with a definite and more practical aim. Thus the *porticus Minucia* served as a corn exchange; the one surrounding the forum Olitorium as a market for fresh vegetables; that around the theatre of Pompey was a place of rehearsal for choruses, and a refuge for spectators in case of sudden rain. Augustus made porticoes popular; he introduced the fashion and taste for them, either building them with his own money, or else helping and inviting his personal friends and admirers to follow his example. In less than twenty years the whole Campus Martius was covered with colonnades. Augustus himself constructed the Portico of Octavia, the ruins of which are such a prominent landmark in the Ghetto, or Jewish quarter of modern Rome;[1] another near Pompey's theatre,

---

[1] This picturesque corner of the city was levelled to the ground in the spring of 1887.

THE BATHS OF CARACALLA.

called *Ad Nationes,* on account of some colossal statues representing the various nations of the world; and lastly, he rebuilt from the foundations the one named Corinthian, on account of the capitals of the columns being made of gilt Corinthian brass. Cornelius Balbus, an intimate friend of the

Remains of the Portico of Octavia.

emperor, built his famous *Crypta* at the rear of his theatre, the ruins of which we are now engaged in bringing to light. Marcius Philippus built the portico which surrounded the Temple of Hercules; Vipsanius Agrippa, the prime minister and faithful adviser of Augustus, went further, and in the magnificence and grandeur of his constructions cast into the shade both predecessors and contemporaries. To him the Romans were indebted for the *porticus Vipsania,* so named from his sister, Vipsania Polla; for the *Septa,* a portico used for electoral meetings under shelter; the *villa*

Publica, the portico of the Argonauts, and the portico of Europa.   And as if such a superabundance of luxury were not deemed sufficient for the comfort and well-being of

Remains of the Portico of Octavia.

the Romans, the example of Augustus and his courtiers found imitators down to the very fall of the Empire, as shown by the porticoes of Constantine and of the *Bonus Eventus,* and by the *porticus maximæ* of Gratian, Valen·

tinian, and Theodosius. Finally, we have accounts of similar enormous structures, designed but not built, or else begun and not finished. Severus Alexander, for instance, began a portico 1,000 feet long and 100 feet wide, supported by one thousand marble columns, and destined to connect the *Septa* with his baths. Gordianus the younger also began a portico under the Pincian hill, 900 yards in circumference, and enclosing a garden 44,000 square yards in extent. The enterprise was stopped by his premature death. The same fate befell the portico of Gallienus, a prince illustrious for the extravagances of his artistic projects. I shall mention only one of them. He had designed raising on the very top of the Esquiline hill a most unheard-of colossal statue, 219 feet high, — that is to say, twice the height of Trajan's column, — which would have represented him as the sun, holding a rod in his hands. A spiral staircase, to be ingeniously made in the rod, was to allow visitors to reach the very top of the colossus. The same prince began a portico 9,000 feet long, which would have led from the centre of Rome to the Ponte Molle (the Milvian Bridge). We do not know whether the idea was carried out to its full extent.

I doubt whether students of Roman topography have paid due attention to the special nature of these structures, which covered with a network of colonnades the whole space between the hills and the river. Porticoes have been studied individually, and, under this aspect, they appear to us sometimes as simple enclosures of temples, sometimes as picture - galleries and museums of statuary, sometimes as places of rendezvous for elegant, lazy youths and their sweethearts. Their importance, however, increases tenfold if we consider them, not individually, but combined, as successive manifestations of the same original conception or plan, that is, as an institution contrived and developed for the benefit of the public. In Rome, certainly, the need of open, pleasant places of rest and amusement was not felt. I have already spoken of forums and baths; I shall speak presently of that superb crown of parks and gardens which surrounded and adorned the city ; but these public gardens and parks and squares were naturally exposed to the rigor and inconstancy of the seasons, to the sharp tramontana or north wind, to the fierce rays of the sun in the dog-days. To obviate such inconveniences, to allow the inhabitants of the metropolis to take their " constitutional " walk in every season of the year, at every hour of the day, protected from the rain, the sun, and the cold, these porticoes were planned; or, to express my thought better, the idea was conceived of dedicating to this purpose a certain kind of edifice, which up to that time had had an entirely different purpose. It is needless to say that this happened when the contagion of Eastern luxury had begun to contaminate the purity of the true old Roman education. People have thought that the *porticus Vipsania* must have been built to exhibit in public the geographical maps of the provinces of the Empire, surveyed and drawn in the famous census mentioned in the Gospel of S. Luke ; and that the portico of the Argonauts was built to exhibit, likewise, the famous picture representing the history of the Golden Fleece. This was not the design of those buildings, nor the idea the ancients had of them. Whenever classical writers, and especially Martial, speak of the porticoes, they constantly allude to one idea, — to the pleasure of enjoying there the warmth of the sun, when throughout the city people were shivering from the piercing *tramontana*. The place spoken of most frequently by Martial is the portico of Europa, the frequenters of which were protected not only by the colonnades, but also by high walls of boxwood, which intersected in graceful designs the inner space. By looking at a plan of ancient Rome, however defective and antiquated it may be, one sees very easily how it was possible to cross under shelter the whole plain of the Campus Martius, from end to end. The walk, taken either in a direct line from the Forum Boarium to Hadrian's Mausoleum, or by a longer circuit through the forum of Trajan and Agrippa's buildings, would cover a space of from two to three miles; and the sights which would have struck the eye of the foreign visitor at every step were enough to excite an imagination the least susceptible of enthusiasm. I have been tempted to calculate some statistical data concerning this incomparable group. The extent of the twelve larger porticoes of the Campus Martius amounts to 4,600 yards; the surface protected from the sun and rain to 28,000 square yards; the total area of the porticoes, central gardens included, to 100,000 square yards; the number of columns to 2,000, or thereabouts. These columns were cut out of the rarest kinds of breccias and marbles; their capitals were sometimes of Corinthian gilt brass; their pavements were inlaid with jasper and porphyry. Every portico contained, as I said before, a museum of sculpture and a gallery of pictures; and the space enclosed by them was decorated with lovely gardens, and with thickets of box, myrtle, laurel, and plane-trees, bordering lakes, fountains, and waterfalls. Besides, every one of them offered to the stranger some special attraction. In that of Vipsania Polla, the maps of the provinces of the Empire were displayed. The portico of the Septa was transformed into a huge magazine of curiosities, antiquities, and manufactures of the extreme East, China included. Here, also, some wonderful specimens of natural history were exhibited, such as a colossal beam left over from the building of the roof of the Diribitorium (the widest roof in Rome). Lastly, in the portico built by Marcius Philippus, ladies could find the latest and most remarkable specimens of wigs and hair-dressing which the fancy of Roman coiffeurs could contrive.

Having arrived at this point, I must speak finally of the principal subject which I wished to illustrate, namely, the parks and gardens. The city was not only surrounded and enclosed by them, but intersected in every direction. It is necessary to bear in mind that Rome occupies the *thalweg* of the Tiber, a plain less than a mile wide, and about three miles long, flanked east and west by the parallel ranges of hills, the highest of which, now called Monte Mario, rises to a height of about 450 feet. Both ranges were covered with gardens. Let us begin with the east range, overlooking the plain of the Campus Martius. The Pincian hill, the promenade of modern Rome, was occupied by the magnificent gardens of Acilius Glabrio, the existence of which was first made known in 1867 by the accidental discovery of an altar, dedicated to Sylvanus by the overseer or superintendent of Glabrio's gardens. Where the villa Medici, the seat of the French school of fine arts, now stands, were the gardens of the Anician family, as was ascertained in 1789 by the discovery of a pedestal and a statue dedicated to the owner of the place, Anicius Acilius Aginatius. The southwest slope of the same Pincian hill, now crossed by the Via S. Giuseppe a Capo le Case, was occupied by the gardens of Lucullus.

The valley between the Pincian and the Quirinal, from the modern Piazza Barberini to the Porta Salaria and the Porta Pia, a charming and undulating district, with glens and overhanging rocks, rivulets of pure water, and other natural attractions, was the seat of the gardens of Sallust, the finest and most celebrated of ancient Rome. Proceed-

Ruins in the Garden of Sallust.

ing farther south, we should cross the gardens of Lollia Paulina, of Mæcenas, of Ælius Lumia, of Torquatus, of Epaphroditus, of Gallienus, of Pallans, of Helagabalus, of Statilius Taurus, and many smaller gardens, all forming one stretch of verdure, more than two miles long and over half a mile wide. And here I must answer a question which has often been asked of me, namely, How is it possible that there was room for so many and such large pleasure-grounds in a district which we know for a certainty to have been occupied, from a very remote age, by public cemeteries? The careful and almost daily examination I have made of the ground, especially in the new quarters of the Viminal and of the Esquiline, enables me to solve the problem easily. The popular cemeteries having become offensive to public health, and real hot-beds of disease and contagion, Mæcenas, the great statesman, decided to make a bold stroke, and to destroy the evil from the very roots. As I have already stated in the preceding chapter, he obtained from his sovereign and friend a grant of that portion of the Esquiline necropolis in which human bodies and carcasses, slaves and beasts, were thrown in horrible disorder, together with the daily refuse of the town ; then buried the whole space under an enormous mass of pure earth, thirty feet deep, and turned that pestilential den into smiling gardens.

The same thing was done, in process of time, for the rest of the Esquiline cemeteries, even in that portion which was occupied by private family tombs. The way in which I discovered this fact is curious, and worth relating. When the plans for the new quarters were about to be carried into execution, our Archæological Commission obtained from the municipality the permission to explore the ground beforehand, so that, as far as possible, nothing should be left under the new buildings. In carrying on this work of exploration, we left aside, of course, those places which we knew positively to have been searched before. Such, for instance, was the space between the so-called temple of Minerva Medica and the Porta Maggiore, which, according to the accounts left by Ficoroni and Piranesi, had been thoroughly gone over in the second half of the last century. Events have proved that our policy may have found an excuse in the necessity of the moment, but was not a wise one. The first explorers of that rich archæological ground, after crossing the stratum corresponding to the level of the imperial gardens, had stopped their work at the level of the drains, feeling sure that a deeper search would be absolutely fruitless. They labored under a false idea. A deeper search would have brought them, as it has brought us, to the stratum occupied by the republican cemetery, buried in the second century of the Christian era, not only for sanitary purposes, but to provide room for such an extension of public parks as was required by the increase of the population; and as, in the period in which the change took place, the religion of tombs was still deeply rooted even among the commonest workmen, we found those tombs absolutely intact, and full of rich funeral deposits. I will give only one instance. In excavating a space fifty feet long and thirty feet wide, within the gardens of Licinius Gallienus, we discovered between February 7 and May 27, 1871, five *columbaria*, containing 204 inscriptions, 200 lamps, 2 marble and 40 terra-cotta cinerary urns, 195 coins, 150 glass perfume-bottles, 200 *flaçons* of terra-cotta, and a few gold finger and ear rings.

The hills on the west side of the valley were also occupied by an uninterrupted chain of gardens, from those of the Minician family, on the Monte Mario, to those of Julius Cæsar, on the southern ridge of the Janiculum; and the

Ruins in the Garden of Sallust.

banks of the river also had been transformed into a garden by Augustus, Pompey the Great, Domitia, Nero, Caligula, and others.

As I am prevented by want of space from entering into details, I shall mention only the latest discovery made in this department, — the discovery of an altogether unknown park. In building the foundation of Prince Massimo's palace, near the southwest corner of the central railway station, a line of terminal stones was brought to light, inscribed with the following legend : " These stones mark the boundary lines of the gardens of Lollia (*horti Lolliani*), which gardens are now the property of the Emperor Claudius." Many works of art and ornamental marbles were discovered there at the same time, which enable us to form an idea of the former beauty of the place. There is no doubt that the lady mentioned on the stones as the original owner of the grounds was Lollia Paulina, equally famous for her beauty, her wealth, and her misfortunes. She was the granddaughter of M. Lollius, the teacher and tutor of Caligula, who, having been reproached by his imperial pupil for the extortions he had committed on the populations of Asia Minor, had poisoned himself from shame and grief. The untold wealth of which Lollius had robbed that province was inherited by Lollia Paulina, of whom Pliny the elder speaks in the following terms : " I have seen the lady at evening parties, with her hair dressed in emeralds and pearls; in fact, she wore emeralds and pearls as ear-rings, necklaces, breast-plate, bracelets, and also as simple trimming of her robe, to such excess that the value of the whole set was estimated at 40,000,000 sesterces [$1,600,000]." In the year of Rome 790, Caligula fell in love with the lady, and made an empress of her, in spite of the protests of her legal husband, Memmius Regulus. However, he soon grew tired of the alliance, and Paulina was banished from the imperial house, with the injunction that she should live henceforth with no man, not even with her former husband. Eleven years later, the Emperor Claudius, being in search of a wife, after the death of Messalina, hesitated for a while between the two "professional beauties" of the age, Lollia Paulina and Agrippina. Court intrigues made the balance turn, at the end, in favor of Agrippina, and the first act of the new empress was to obtain the banishment of the abhorred rival and the seizure of her personal property. Among the estates thus confiscated and incorporated in the imperial domain were evidently the gardens on the Esquiline, the existence of which has now been accidentally revealed to us for the first time.

CHAPTER V.

THE PALACE OF THE CÆSARS.

THE Palatine hill became the residence of the Roman emperors, and the centre of the Roman Empire, not on account of its historical and traditional associations with the foundation and first growth of the city, nor because of its central and commanding position, but by a mere accident. At daybreak on September 21st of the year 63 B. C., Augustus was born in this region, in a modest house, opening on the lane called *ad Capita bubula,* which led from the valley, where now the Colosseum stands, up the slopes of the hill towards the modern church and convent of S. Bonaventura. This man, sent by God to change the condition of mankind and the state of the world, this founder of an empire which is still practically in existence, never deserted the Palatine hill all through his eventful career. From the lane *ad Capita bubula* he moved to the house of Calvus, the orator, at the northeast corner of the hill overlooking the forum; and in process of time, having become absolute master of the Roman Commonwealth, he settled finally on the top of the hill, having purchased for his residence the house of Hortensius, a simple and modest house, indeed, with columns of the commonest kind of stone, pavements of rubble-work, and simply whitewashed walls.

Whether this selection of a site was made because the Palatine had long before become the Faubourg St. Honoré, the Belgravia of ancient Rome, is difficult to determine.

THE FORUM, LOOKING WEST.

INDEX TO THE PLAN OF THE PALACE OF THE CÆSARS.

1. Entrance to the excavations and ruins, from the Via di S. Teodoro.
2. Lower portion of the *Clivus Victoriæ*, leading from the *Velabrum* up to the *Porta Romana*, or *Romanula*.
3. Site of the *Porta Romana*, restored under Septimius Severus.
4, 4. Upper section of the *Clivus Victoriæ*, leading from the *Porta Romana* to the temple of Victory. This temple was discovered and destroyed by Duke Francis of Parma and Monsignore Bianchini, in 1726.
5. Entrance to a reservoir for rain and spring water, believed to be contemporary with the foundation of Rome.
6. Remains of the earliest fortifications of the Alban settlement on the Palatine, commonly called the walls of Romulus.
7. Altar dedicated to an unknown god (SEI DEO SEI DEIVAE) by Caius Sextius Calvinus.
8. Other remains of the earliest fortifications of the Palatine.
9. Ruins of the *domus Gelotiana*, incorporated by Caligula into the imperial palace.
10. Room in which the caricature of the Crucifix was found. See plate, page 122.
11. *Stadium* for gymnastic and athletic sports, built by Domitian, restored by Septimius Severus, and transformed into a kind of amphitheatre by King Theodoric.
12. Imperial tribune.
13. Bathing-apartments connected with the *Stadium*.
14. A wing of the palace built by Septimius Severus. Its façade on the *Via Triumphalis* was called the *Septizonium*. See plate, page 126.
15. The *Pulvinar*, or balcony from which the emperors could witness the races of the Circus Maximus.
16. Remains of the *domus Augustana*, discovered in 1792 by Rancoureuil.
17. Halls built on an artificial platform over the deepest portion of the gorge which separated the northern from the southern summit of the hill, namely, the *Germalus* from the *Velia*.
18–25. Ruins of the palace built by Domitian for state receptions and banquets.
   (18.) *Triclinium*, or banqueting-hall.
   (19.) Bathing-apartments.
   (20.) *Peristylium*, or colonnade surrounding the great Court.
   (21.) Offices.
   (22.) *Basilica*.
   (23.) State reception hall, or *Tablinum*.
   (24.) *Lararium*, or private chapel.
   (25.) *Atrium*.
26. Remains of the earliest fortifications of the Palatine.
27. Street called *Vicus Apollinis*, leading from the *Sacra Via* to the temple and libraries of Apollo.
28. Probable site of the *Porta Mugonia*, one of the three gates of the Palatine settlement.
29. Foundations of the temple of *Jupiter Stator*.
30. Cellars and storerooms.
31. *Crypto-porticus*, or subterranean passage in which the murder of Caligula took place.
32. Subterranean passage, leading from the palaces of Tiberius and Caligula to the palace of Domitian. It passed under a public square, called *Area Palatina*.
33. Basin or tank, supposed to be a *vivarium* for fish.
34. House of Germanicus, famous for its paintings and for its excellent preservation. See plate, page 109.
35. *Puteal*, or mouth of a well or cistern for rain-water. It dates from the first or second century of Rome.
36. Remains of a building not yet identified.
37. Temple of *Jupiter Propugnator*, or *Victor*.
38. A group of ruins, dating from the kingly period; bordering on a steep ascent, which leads from the *vallis mureia* up the Palatine, and which was called *scalæ Caci*.
39. Temples of Cybele, called *ædes magnæ Deûm Matris*.
40, 40. Southwest front of the *domus Tiberiana*, or palace of Tiberius.
41, 42, 43. Substructions of the palace of Caligula.
44. Baths, opening on the *Sacra Via*, supposed to have been built by Helagabalus.

PLAN OF THE PALACE OF THE CÆSARS

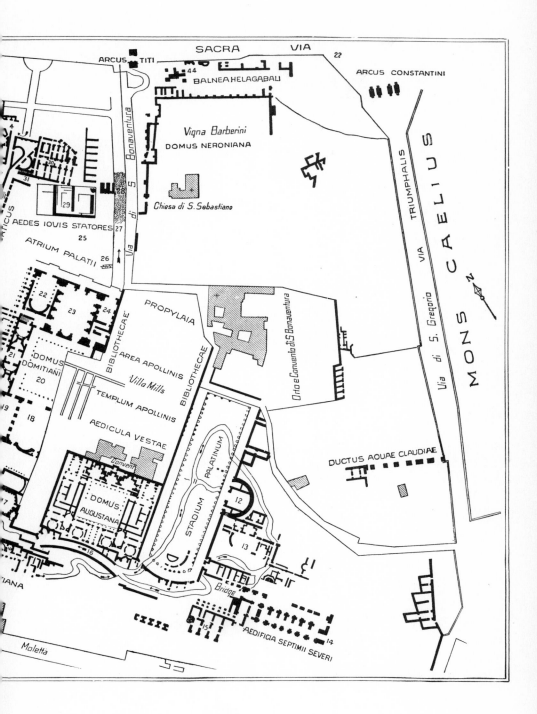

We know that the house of Hortensius, chosen by Augustus, was surrounded by those of Clodius, Scaurus, Crassus, Cæcina, Sisenna, Flaccus, Catilina, and other members of the aristocracy. I am persuaded, however, that the secret of the selection is to be found in the simplicity, I will even say in the poverty, of the dwelling; in fact, such extreme modesty is worthy the good sense and the spirit of moderation shown by Augustus throughout his career. He could very well sacrifice appearances to the reality of an unbounded power. It is just, at any rate, to recognize that even in his remotest resorts for temporary rest and retirement from the cares of government he led the same kind of plain, modest life, spending all his leisure hours in arranging his collections of natural history, more especially the palæo-ethnological or prehistoric, for which the ossiferous caverns of the Island of Capri supplied him with abundant materials.

It was only after the victory of Actium that, finding himself master of the world, he thought it expedient to give up, in a certain measure, his former habits, and live in better style. Having bought through his agents (*per procuratores*) some of the aristocratic palaces adjoining the old house of Hortensius, among them the historical palace of Catilina, he built a new and very handsome residence, but declared at the same time that he considered it as public property, not as his own. The solemn dedication of the palace took place on January 14th, of the year 26 before Christ. Here he lived, sleeping always in the same small *cubiculum*, for twenty-eight years; that is to say, until the third year after Christ, when the palace was almost destroyed by fire. As soon as the news of the disaster spread throughout the Empire, an almost incredible amount of money was subscribed at once, by all orders of citizens, to pro-

vide him with a new residence; and although, with his usual
moderation, he would consent to accept only one denarius
from each individual subscriber, it is easy to imagine how
many millions he must have realized in spite of his modesty.
A new, magnificent palace rose from the ruins of the old
one, but it does not appear that the plan and arrangement were changed; otherwise Augustus could not have
continued to sleep in the same room during the last ten
years of his life, as we are told positively that he did.

The work of Augustus was continued by his successor
and kinsman, Tiberius, who built a new wing (*domus
Tiberiana*) near the northwest corner of the hill, overlooking the Velabrum. Caligula filled with new structures
the whole space between the *domus Tiberiana* and the
Roman forum. Nero, likewise, occupied with a new palace the southeast corner of the hill, overlooking the valley,
where the Coliseum was afterwards built. Domitian rebuilt
the *domus Augustana,* injured by fire, adding to its accommodations a *stadium* for gymnastic sports. The same
emperor raised an altogether new palace in the space between the house of Augustus, on one side, and those of
Caligula and Tiberius on the other. Septimius Severus and
his son restored the whole group of imperial buildings, adding a new wing at the southwest corner, known under the
name of *Septizonium.* The latest additions, of no special
importance, took place under Julia Mamæa (*diætæ Mam-
meianæ*) and Helagabalus (baths on the Sacred Way).

It is impossible for me to give a minute description of
this immense and complicated mass of structures; to render
such a description intelligible I ought to make use of an
indefinite number of plans, diagrams, sections, and photo-
graphs, and even then I am not sure that I could reach
the necessary degree of clearness. One must be on the

RUINS OF THE PALACE OF TIBERIUS.

spot; one must examine *de visu* those endless suites of apartments, halls, terraces, porticoes, crypts, cellars, to appreciate the difficulty of the problem. Every emperor, to a certain extent, enlarged, altered, destroyed, and recon-

Remains of the House of Germanicus.

structed the work of his predecessors; cutting new openings, walling up old ones, subdividing large rooms into smaller apartments, and changing their destination.

Coming now to some particulars concerning a few of the leading portions of this immense group of buildings, I must remark that one section alone of the imperial Palatine buildings remained unaltered, and kept the former simplicity of its plan down to the fall of the Empire, — the section built by Augustus across the centre of the hill, which comprised the main entrance, or *propylaia*, the portico surrounding the temple of Apollo, the temple itself, the Greek and Latin libraries, the shrine of Vesta, and the imperial residence.   A brief description of this group, so simple and yet so magnificent, will be easily understood, and will convey to the mind of the reader the true idea of the aspect which the palace of the Cæsars, taken as a whole, presented in the golden age of the Roman Empire to the astonished eyes of a foreign visitor.

The state entrance was approached from the Sacra Via by a wide street, named *vicus Apollinis*, the street of Apollo, from the sanctuary to which it led.   On the top of the central arch of this state entrance Augustus had placed one of Lysias's masterpieces, a chariot drawn by four horses, driven by Apollo and Diana, the whole group being cut out of a single block of marble.   This archway seems to have been rediscovered about 1575.   Flaminius Vacca, a sculptor and an antiquarian of the time of Sixtus V., who has left a diary or register of discoveries which took place in his lifetime, says : " I remember to have seen in the palace of the Cæsars, near the Farnese grounds, the remains of a colossal gate, with posts of Greek marble twenty-nine feet high, and with a niche of African marble which must have been formerly on the top of it."

Passing across the threshold of the *propylaia*, the visitor found himself at once before the most marvellous sight which human eyes have ever witnessed.   There is certainly no exaggeration in the words of contemporary writers, when they give to this group the epithet of golden, of perfect, and of the *chef d'œuvre* of Augustan magnificence.

The peristyle, surrounding the sacred area paved with white marble, contained fifty-two fluted columns of *giallo antico*, many of which, more or less broken, were discovered on the spot by Pope Alexander VII., by Vespignani in 1869, and by ourselves in 1877.   As regards the number of the shafts, there is no doubt that there were at least fifty-two, because fifty intercolumniations were occupied by the statues of the Danaids, and one by the statue of their prolific father. In the open space, in front of the figures of the Danaids, stood equestrian statues of their miserable husbands, the sons of Egypt. Many torsos and fragments belonging to this army of statues, the work of the best Greek chisels of Augustus's age, were recovered on the spot, just three centuries ago. The account of their discovery is given by the same Flaminius Vacca whom I mentioned above : " I remember to have witnessed the discovery of eighteen or twenty torsos, or statues, representing Amazons, a trifle larger than life-size. They were lying under the Ronconi garden, in the centre of the palace of the Cæsars. I recollect, also, that in mending the wine-press, the said Ronconi discovered a beautiful marble statue imbedded in the wall. It represents Hercules, and bears on the plinth the signature ΛΥΣΙΠΠΟΥ ΕΡΓΟΝ, the work of Lysippus. Duke Cosimo de' Medici bought the figure from Ronconi for 800 scudi, and removed it to Florence, where it is still to be seen." It is evident that Flaminius Vacca, a faithful but simple and unlearned diarist, mistakes Danaids for Amazons. As to the fate of the twenty statues, I am afraid they must have come to their end in a limekiln or in a foundation wall.

On the west side of the portico, behind the temple of Apollo, was the library of the same name, in two sections, the Greek and the Latin, with a reading-hall between them large enough to accommodate the whole Senate on state occasions, and to hold a colossus fifty feet high. This library did not contain books upon every branch of human learning. It is certain that historical works were not included in the catalogue. Vopiscus, the imperial biographer, declares that he collected the materials for the life of Probus from books preserved in the library of the palace of Tiberius and in that of Trajan's forum. This means, we believe, that no such documents were to be found in the library of Apollo. Its formal destination has been made known to us by an anonymous scholiast of Juvenal, who, commenting on the 128th verse of the first satire, says: *bibliothecam iuris civilis et liberalium studiorum in templo Apollinis palatini dedicavit Augustus.* "The Augustan library by the temple of Apollo is devoted to books on civil law and on the liberal arts." The Romans, after all, knew perfectly well how much more advantageous to science is the institution of special libraries for one single branch of human learning than the institution of miscellaneous, universal, encyclopædic arsenals of books, which can scarcely keep up with the times, and reach the necessary degree of completeness in every department. Another peculiarity of literary Roman establishments and reading-rooms was the absolute exclusion of trash; the honor of appearing on the *scrinia*, or shelves, was reserved to standard works only, even when the productions of contemporary writers.

The Greek and the Latin sections of the library of Apollo were placed under the supervision of a carefully selected staff of officials, under the high directorship of a *procurator bibliothecarum Augusti,* superintendent of imperial libraries.

The principal ornament of the hall was a colossal bronze statue, fifty feet high, representing Augustus with the attributes of Apollo. It was the work of an Italian artist, and was cast successfully in Rome, in spite of its enormous size. Nardini attributes to this colossus the bronze head, six feet high, which is preserved in the Palazzo dei Conservatori on the Capitol, because its size is exactly proportionate to that assigned by Pliny to the whole figure, — whereas it would be too small for the colossus of Nero, the height of which was exactly double that of the Palatine statue. The walls of the reading-room were covered with medallions of the most celebrated authors and orators, some in *repoussé* work of gold and silver, some cast in bronze. Tacitus relates how the son of M. Hortalus, having been called to defend himself before the Senate assembled in this reading-hall, would sometimes turn towards the medallion of Hortensius the orator, sometimes towards the image of Augustus. The medallions were disposed in groups of poets, historians, lawyers, orators, and so forth. In the same library, rare specimens of palæography were exhibited. Pliny, in the seventh book of his "Natural History," after declaring how closely old Greek handwriting resembled the Latin, adds: "I can bring the evidence of an archaic bronze inscription from Delphi, which Augustus has placed in his library as a specimen of palæography." It is probable that in this reading-room were held the sittings of the literary academies and societies, described by Pliny the younger in his letter to Sosius Senecio (I. 13), which were the delight of the Emperor Claudius, the abhorrence and the horror of literary men, who were obliged by their connection with the imperial court to lose hours upon hours in listening to silly and narcotic lecturers. Nothing could be more graphic than the description by Pliny of one of these compulsory sittings. "We approach the hall," he says, "as if we were compelled by main force; many of us sit outside of the door, and try to overcome the *ennui* by discussing the gossip of the town. Messengers are surreptitiously sent in to inquire whether the lecturer has really made his appearance, whether he has finished his prologue, or how many sheets are still left to be read. Then, when we hear that the moment of deliverance is not very far off, we come in slowly, sit on the edge of our chairs, and do not even wait for the end of the discourse to slip or steal quietly away."

The temple of Apollo, which stood in the centre of the square portico, between the *propylaia* and the libraries, was built entirely of Carrara marble.   The front of the temple was covered with bas-reliefs in Parian marble, the work of Bupalos and Anthermos of Chios, the favorite artists of Augustus.   On the top of the pediment, the chariot of

Section of a Frieze from the Temple of Apollo.

Apollo, of gilt bronze, shone under the rays of the sun. The two sides of the door were incrusted with ivory bas-reliefs, representing on one side the extermination of Niobe's family, on the other the flight of the Gauls from Delphi.   Inside of the temple, the attention of the visitor was particularly attracted by the group of Apollo playing on the lyre, between his mother and sister, the work of three famous sculptors.   Scopas had made the Apollo ; Cephisodotos, son of Praxiteles, Latona ; and Timotheos had modelled the figure of Diana.   The central group was surrounded by the nine Muses.   Other works of art are described by Pliny.   " Great predilection," he says, " is shown by artists and amateurs for hanging chandeliers, or for candelabras cast in the shape of trees, which bear lamps instead of fruit.   The finest specimen of this kind of work is preserved in the temple of Apollo on the Palatine, a work remarkable also for its historical association, having been seized by Alexander the Great in the storming of Thebes, and afterwards dedicated in the Temple of Cyme." There was also a collection of gold plate, and especially of tripods. Augustus had ordered these to be made out of the money raised by the melting of all the silver statues which provincial servility had set up in his honor and against his will. Finally, we have the record of a collection of engraved gems and cameos, a present offered to the god by Marcellus, son of Octavia and nephew of Augustus.

Inside of the pedestal that supported the statue of Apollo two golden chests were concealed, in which Augustus had deposited, as in a safe, the Sibylline books. The last account I have been able to find of these Sibylline books, so intimately connected with the history of Rome and of the world, belongs to the year 363 of the Christian era. In the winter of that year, more precisely in the night between the 18th and 19th of March, the Temple of Apollo caught fire, and was destroyed to the very foundations. The only things which the firemen, led by Apronianus, prefect of police, could save from the conflagration were the Sibylline books. Their subsequent fate is utterly unknown. Of the shrine of Vesta, which occupied the space between the libraries and the palace of Augustus, there is but little to say, except that it was round in shape and built in imitation of its prototype on the Sacred Way.

Summing up the brief description I have given of the architectural group raised by Augustus on the Palatine, and which formed, as it were, the vestibule to his own imperial residence, we know with absolute certainty that it contained at least one hundred and twenty columns of the rarest kinds of marbles and breccias, fifty-two of which were of Numi-

dian marble, with capitals of gilt bronze; a group by
Lysias, comprising one chariot, four horses, and two drivers, all cut in a single block of marble ; the Hercules of
Lysippus ; the Apollo of Scopas ; the Latona of Cephisodotos ; the Diana of Timotheos ; the bas-reliefs of the pediment by Bupalos and Anthermos ; the quadriga of the
sun in gilt bronze ; exquisite ivory carvings ; a bronze
colossus fifty feet high ; hundreds of medallions in gold,
silver, and bronze ; gold and silver plate ; a collection of
gems and cameos ; and, lastly, candelabras which had been
the property of Alexander the Great, and the admiration of
the East.

Has the world ever seen a collection of greater artistic
and material value exhibited in a single building ?   And
we must recollect that the group built by Augustus comprises only a very modest section of the Palatine ; that to
his palace we must join the palaces of Tiberius, Caligula,
Nero, Vespasian, Domitian, Septimius Severus, Julia Mamæa, and Helagabalus ; that each one of these imperial residences equalled the residence of Augustus, if not in pure
taste, certainly in wealth, in luxury, in magnificence, in the
number and value of works of art collected and stolen from
Greece and the East, from Egypt and Persia.   By multiplying eight or ten times the list I have given above, the
reader will get an approximate idea of the "home" of the
Roman emperors in its full pride and glory.

I have deliberately excluded from my description the residence or private house of Augustus, because he himself
had deliberately excluded from it any trace of that grandeur
he had so lavishly bestowed on the buildings which consti-
tuted the approach to it.

As regards Caligula's buildings, which extended from
Tiberius's palace to the northeast corner of the hill, over

SUBSTRUCTIONS OF THE PALACE OF CALIGULA.

looking the forum, the best preserved portion of them is
a long cryptoporticus, or subterranean passage, represented
in the illustration below.

On January 24th, A. D. 41, a scene of horror took place

Corridor in which Caligula was murdered.

in this dark corridor, — the murder of the Emperor Caligula. Whoever will endeavor to picture in his mind all
the revolting circumstances of that death, as described by
Flavius Josephus, will hear echoing again in the long
vaulted crypt the last cries of the frantic young prince,
fallen on his knees, and trying to avert with his feeble
hands the last implacable blows of his assassins.

Caligula had spent the morning of that eventful day in attending to the *ludi palatini,* or scenic plays, which Livia had instituted permanently in honor of Augustus, and which were usually performed on a wooden stage, built for the occasion, in front of the palace itself. Having left the performance towards noon, Caligula walked with his attendants towards the palace, entering by the main gateway. But once inside, instead of proceeding by the usual way, that is, by the state court-yard and staircase, where the body-guard was in attendance, and whither he had been preceded by Claudius, he suddenly turned to the right, and entered, as the historian says, a solitary and obscure corridor, which led to the bathing apartments. He was tempted to pass this unusual way by the desire of meeting some young noblemen from Asia, whom he had invited to the imperial court to be trained in singing hymns and in performing the sacred pyrrhic dance.

Having halted a few minutes to speak to them, and to ascertain the state of their training, he was met by Cassius Cherea, the captain on duty and leader of the conspiracy, who asked the young prince the password for the day. Receiving an exceedingly profane answer, Cassius Cherea with his poniard struck the first blow. Caligula tried to escape towards the group of terrified youths from Asia, but Cornelius Sabinus, who had joined the conspiracy, knocked him down, and held him firm until the deed was accomplished.

The conspirators, now that they had succeeded in their murderous attempt, fearing for their own safety, tried to escape unobserved. Not daring, however, to go back the same way they had entered the crypt, for the dread of the sentinels who kept watch at the main gateway, they ran through the other end of the corridor, and concealed themselves in the house of Germanicus, which had been incorporated in Caligula's palace. A strange occurrence, indeed, that the murderers of the son of Germanicus should seek refuge in the house of his own father !

The historical corridor just described, and the apartments which adjoin it on the north side, are not the only additions

The Domus Gelotiana.

made by Caligula to the imperial palace. He appears to have purchased and embodied in the crown property another large house, belonging to a certain Gelotius and hence called *domus Gelotiana ;* and this acquisition was made, not for any want of additional space and accommodation, but to satisfy the mania of the prince for the games of the circus, for horses and grooms. Caligula was a passionate supporter of the squadron of the greens,[1] so much so that he used to spend days and nights in their stables, sharing their dinners and suppers, and indulging with them in all

[1] For details about the various squadrons or *factiones*, see chapter on Police.

sorts of excesses. This house of Gelotius was bought because it lay nearer to the circus than any other building
on the Palatine, and because, by simply crossing it, the
prince could reach, undisturbed and unseen, his favorite
place among the "greens." From an inscription discovered
in Rome in the seventeenth century, which mentions a *Sym-
phorus tesserarius,* or ticket collector, *de domo Gelotiana,*
we gather that this house on solemn occasions could contain a large number of guests. Its importance to us, however, is not derived from its connection with the circus, but
from the considerable number of *graffiti,* or scribblings,
which cover its walls.

The mania for writing on the plaster in public or private
buildings, with a nail or a sharp point of any kind, was perhaps stronger in ancient times than it is now. It must have
been tolerated by municipal regulations. In that portion of
Pompeii which has been unearthed up to the present time,
not less than six thousand *graffiti* have been copied and
published ; and we have gained more knowledge of the
life and habits, the love and business transactions, and the
political feelings, of the Pompeians from this source than
from any other written or engraved documents. In Rome,
not a single edifice escaped the nail and the pocket-knife of
idlers or schoolboys. Wherever there was a flat surface of
marble or plaster, no matter whether horizontal or vertical,
there you are sure to find some more or less interesting record : checked gambling-tables, caricatures, alphabets, profane words, sentences, emblems, and the like. The dread
which neat people felt for scratchers on walls was such
that we have actually found a marble inscription outside
the Porta Portuensis, which had been put up by a gentleman, in front of his property, and in which he begs
passers-by not to *scariphare* or scratch the walls of his

buildings. When *graffiti* are found in large numbers in one and the same place, they gain the importance of an historical document. Such are, for instance, those discovered in the barracks of the seventh battalion of police,[1] which have revealed to us the most minute details regarding the organization and duties of that body; and such are, also, the *graffiti*, discovered in the year 1857, in the *domus Gelotiana*, which introduce us into the intimacy of the life of court servants of a higher class. It appears from them, and from the records they contain, that after the murder of Caligula the house became a residence and a training-school for court pages, who had received their first education in the imperial elementary school, called *pædagogium ad caput Africæ*, from the name of a street which led from the Coliseum to the aristocratic quarter of the Cœlian. The boys must have been delighted at their deliverance from the rod of the master, and their admittance into the palace; and accordingly they chronicle the happy event on the walls of their new residence with inscriptions modelled on the same pattern: *Corinthus exit de pædagogio; Marianus afer exit de pædagogio,* and so forth. There is another very spirited and bright allusion to the hardships of school life, composed of a vignette and its explanation. The drawing represents a donkey turning the mill; and the legend says, LABORA ASELLE QVOMODO EGO LABORAVI ET PRODERIT TIBI: "Work, work, little donkey, as I have worked myself, and thou shalt be rewarded for it." But by far the most interesting and most widely celebrated *graffito* of the whole set is the one discovered at the beginning of the year 1857 in the fourth room on the left of the entrance, re-

---

[1] These barracks were discovered twenty years ago, near the church of S. Crisogono, in Trastevere. See chapter on the Police.

moved soon after to the Kircherian Museum at the Collegio Romano, where it is still to be seen. This *graffito*, illustrated by Garrucci, Visconti, Becker, De Rossi, and Kraus, contains a blasphemous caricature of our Lord Jesus Christ, — a caricature designed only a few years after the first preaching of the gospel in Rome by the Apostles. Here is a photographic reproduction of the precious sketch. Our Lord is represented with the head of a donkey, tied to the cross, with the feet resting on a horizontal piece of board. To the left of the cross there is the figure of the Christian youth Alexamenos, with arms raised in adoration of his crucified God, and the whole composition is illustrated and explained by the legend, ΑΛΕΞΑΜΕΝΟΣ ΣΕΒΕΤΕ ΘΕΟΝ : " Alexamenos worships (his) God."

During the rule of Claudius, the successor of Caligula, little or nothing was done towards the enlargement or the embellishment of the palace of the Cæsars. Nero, however, the successor of Claudius, conceived the gigantic plan of renewing and of rebuilding from the very foundations, not only the imperial residence, but the whole metropolis ; and as the metropolis was crowded at every corner with shrines and altars and small temples which religious superstition made absolutely inviolable, and as the slightest work of improvement was fiercely opposed by private owners of property, and gave occasion to an endless amount of lawsuits, and appraisals, and fights among the experts, he rid himself of all these difficulties in the simplest and cleverest way: He ordered his favorite architects, Severus and Celer, to draw a new plan of the city, and to draw it according to the best principles of hygiene and comfort ; then he caused an enormous quantity of wooden booths and tents to be secretly prepared, and ordered fleets of grain-

CARICATURE OF THE CRUCIFIXION.

In the Kircherian Museum, Rome.

laden vessels to be kept in readiness to sail from the various harbors of the Mediterranean at a moment's notice.

Having taken all these precautions, and insured the success of his stratagem as far as human foresight could, Nero set the whole city into a blaze of fire, and did it so neatly that although, of the fourteen regions, or wards, into which Rome had been divided by Augustus, three were annihilated completely and seven for the greater part, yet not a single human life seems to have been lost in the gigantic conflagration.

The homeless crowds found a ready and comfortable shelter under the booths and tents, raised by thousands in public parks and squares; at the same time, a large number of vessels laden with grain from Sardinia, Sicily, Numidia, and Egypt appeared at the mouth of the Tiber, and relieved the emperor from any anxiety as far as famine was concerned. These vessels, as soon as they had discharged their cargoes, were filled up again with the *débris* of the conflagration, which was thrown into the marshes surrounding the delta of the Tiber.

Even in our age of progress, and material improvement, and comfort, we cannot help admiring the profound wisdom shown by the two imperial architects, Severus and Celer, in designing and rebuilding the city. The straight line and the right angle were followed, as far as could be done in a hilly region, in tracing the new streets and avenues through the still smoking ruins. Hasty and irregular constructions were forbidden; the line of frontage of each new building had to be sanctioned and approved by one of the official surveyors. Large squares were opened in place of filthy, thickly inhabited quarters. The height of private houses was not allowed to exceed double the width of the street, and porticoes were to be built in front of each one, to provide the citizens with cool, sheltered walks in case of rain or of excessive heat. Lastly, wooden ceilings were excluded from the lower story of private dwellings, and absolute isolation on every side made compulsory.

In the rebuilding of the city the emperor secured for himself the lion's share; and his Golden House, *domus aurea,* of which we possess such beautiful remains, occupied the whole extent from the Palatine to the Viminal, where now the central railway station has been erected. Its area amounted to nearly a square mile: and this enormous district was appropriated, or rather usurped, by the emperor, right in the centre of a city numbering about two million inhabitants.

Of the wonders of the Golden House it is enough to say that there were comprised within the precincts of the enchanting residence waterfalls supplied by an aqueduct fifty miles long; lakes and rivers shaded by dense masses of foliage, with harbors and docks for the imperial galleys; a vestibule containing a bronze colossus one hundred and twenty feet high; porticoes three thousand feet long; farms and vineyards, pasture-grounds and woods teeming with the rarest and costliest kind of game; zoölogical and botanical gardens; sulphur baths supplied from the springs of the *aquæ Albulæ,* twelve miles distant; sea baths supplied from the waters of the Mediterranean, sixteen miles distant at the nearest point; thousands of columns crowned with capitals of Corinthian gilt metal; thousands of statues stolen from Greece and Asia Minor; walls encrusted with gems and mother-of-pearl; banqueting-halls with ivory ceilings, from which rare flowers and precious perfumes could fall gently on the recumbent guests. More marvellous still was the ceiling of the state dining-room. It was spherical in shape, and cut in ivory, to represent the con-

RUINS OF THE FLAVIAN PALACE.

stellated skies, and kept in constant motion by machinery in imitation of the movements of the stars and planets. All these details sound like fairy-tales, like the dream of a fertile imagination ; still they are described minutely by contemporary and serious writers, by Suetonius, by Martial, and by Tacitus. Suetonius adds that the day Nero took possession of his Golden House, he was heard to exclaim, " At last I am lodged like a man."

The wonders created by him, however, did not last very long. Otho, his successor, on the very day of his election to the throne, signed an order of fifty millions of sesterces (two million dollars) *ad peragendam auream domum,* — to bring the Golden House to perfection ; but after his murder Vespasian and Titus gave back to the people the greater portion of the ground usurped by Nero. They built the Colosseum on the very spot of Nero's artificial lake, and the *thermæ* of Titus on the foundation of his private palace ; they respected only that portion of Nero's insane constructions which was comprised within the boundaries of the Palatine hill. This section of the imperial palace, facing the Colosseum and the great fountain named the *Meta sudans,* has been charmingly described by Cardinal Wiseman as the scene of St. Sebastian's martyrdom. It is the only portion of the Palatine that has never been excavated, — at least, as far as we can judge ; and, accordingly, I have little or nothing to say about it. Vespasian and his sons, in their turn, could not resist the temptation of doing something to the imperial residence ; and as the houses of Tiberius and Caligula (on the northern summit of the hill) were separated from the house of Augustus (on the southern summit) by a deep gorge, they filled up the gap by means of huge vaulted substructures, and on the artificial platform thus obtained they raised a new building, the Flavian palace, the handsomest and noblest of the whole Palatine group, and used exclusively for state receptions and state banquets.

The chronology of the group, as far as important or interesting additions are concerned, ends with Septimius Severus, who built a magnificent palace at the south corner of the hill, facing the Appian Way and the road to Ostia, in order, as his sharp-tongued biographer says, that his African countrymen, arriving in Rome by the way of Pozzuoli and Ostia, might be struck at once with a specimen of his grandeur. And magnificent indeed was the wing of the palace built by Septimius Severus, and called *Septizonium*, because it was seven stories high. The terrace on the top of the building towered to the height of 210 feet above the level of the surrounding streets, commanding one of the finest views over the metropolis.

After Severus, we have records of more or less important restorations to the palace, not of additions; unless this name may be given to some baths constructed by Helagabalus, between Nero's house and the Via Sacra, the remains of which were brought to light in 1874. The mention I have made of that infamous youth leads me to speak of a very curious and scarcely known incident in which he plays a prominent part.

In the year 549 of Rome, the high-priests, after consulting the Sibylline books on the issue of the second Punic war, found that, to insure the safety and the prosperity of the Roman Commonwealth, it was necessary to send an embassy to Pessinus in Phrygia, to get possession of a meteoric stone, fallen from heaven, which was worshipped there under the name of the " Great Mother of the Gods," or Cybele. The embassy succeeded in securing the stone, and I need not repeat the beautiful description which Livy has left

THE SEPTIZONIUM IN THE XVItH CENTURY.

From a drawing by an unknown artist in the Uffizi, Florence.

(xxiv. 14) of its arrival and solemn reception in Rome. On April 4th of the following year, 550, the precious relic was deposited temporarily in the temple of Victory, on the Palatine; and twelve years later it was finally located in a temple built for the purpose by the censors M. Livius and C. Claudius, known to topographers and historians as the temple of the great mother of the gods: *ædes magnæ Deum Matris.* We possess a very accurate description of this meteoric stone: it was conical in shape, of a deep brown color; it looked like a piece of lava, and ended in a point so sharp that Servius calls it *acus Matris Deum*, the "needle" of Cybele. The stone was set in a silver statue of the goddess, in place of the head.

Among the wild manias of Helagabalus, Herodianus describes the attempt to collect in his private chapel, attached to the palace of the Cæsars, the most sacred relics of the Roman Empire, such as the Palladium, the ancilia, and, of course, the meteoric stone of Pessinus. So far as this last is concerned he succeeded in his attempt: he stole the relic from the temple, and placed it in his chapel, under the name of *Sol Helagabalus*, the Sun Helagabalus. The description left by Herodianus of the stone is absolutely identical with the description of the needle of Cybele. "The stone," he says, "is very large, shaped as a cone, and black in color. People think it a stone fallen from heaven, and believe also that some accidental irregularities in the surface represent the image of the sun, modelled by supernatural hands."

When the excavations of the palace of the Cæsars began, about twenty years ago, I felt sanguine of the recovery of this relic, since it was an object too common to have attracted the attention either of the barbarians, when they pillaged the palace, or of former excavators, unacquainted with its value. My hopes were disappointed, however; and it is only lately that I have learned of its discovery, and probable destruction, in 1730. In reading the book written by Monsignor Francesco Bianchini on the excavations carried on in the Palatine by Duke Francis of Parma, at the beginning of last century (a book which is little known in spite of its enormous size and the useful information it contains), I have found the following passage. After describing the discovery of the private chapel of the emperors, Monsignor Bianchini says: "I am sorry that no fragment of a statue, or bas-relief, or inscription has been found in the chapel, because this absence of any positive indication prevents us from ascertaining the name of the divinity to whom the place was principally dedicated. The only object which I discovered in it was a *stone nearly three feet high, conical in shape, of a deep brown color, looking very much like a piece of lava, and ending in a sharp point.* No attention was paid to it, and I know not what became of it."

I shall bring this chapter to a close with a few remarks on the inhabitants of the enormous mass of dwellings which the palace of the Cæsars formed.

The organization of the imperial household, the number of the servants and attendants, the title and the nature of their duties, are details perfectly well known and full of interest, especially if compared with the organization of modern "*maisons royales ;*" and the way we have gained our information on the subject is this. Servants attached to the person or to the house of an emperor or an empress, as well as servants attached to the person or to the house of a patrician, usually bound themselves into a corporation, a *collegium* as it was called, for the purpose of providing themselves with a common and decent resting-place, with a proper funeral, and with the view of securing a suitable commemoration on the anniversary day of their death. Sometimes the *columbaria* were bought by subscription, raised among the servants of one family or of one person; sometimes servants of two or more persons or families joined in the purchase; sometimes their lords and masters would present them with the much-wished-for resting-place. Columbaria of ordinary size contain from thirty to fifty incinerated bodies, and each cinerary urn is labelled with a marble slab, giving the name, the age, and the official title of the deceased. I need not explain what an amount of useful and genuine information can be gathered from the discovery of well-preserved columbaria belonging to one household. We are able to make a personal review of its various members; we can investigate their life and condition; we can picture in our minds the organization of a rich house, no matter whether patrician or imperial.

Hundreds of these columbaria have been discovered since the Renaissance. Two, however, deserve special attention, as capable of throwing ample light on the matter which I have undertaken to illustrate: the columbaria of the servants of the Statilii and the columbaria of the servants of the Empress Livia: one describing the household of a patrician family, noblest among the noble, and connected with the imperial family by the marriage of one of its members, Statilia Messalina, to Claudius; the other describing the household of an empress. I bring the two instances into comparison to show what little difference in luxury and comfort there was between the house of the sovereign and that of a wealthy subject; and to show also how poor the millionaires of to-day must feel in presence of such a display of grandeur and of such legions of attendants.

The columbaria of the servants of the Statilian family came to light in 1875, in that portion of the Esquiline cemetery which stretches from the so-called temple of Minerva Medica to the Porta Maggiore. The excavations lasted only a few weeks; but in this short time not less than five hundred and sixty-six inscriptions were discovered, together with many hundred objects in terra-cotta, glass, bone, ivory, bronze, gold, silver, marble, belonging to the funeral *supellex* of the deceased. Later excavations, carried on in the same place in 1880 by the municipality of Rome, have brought the total number of inscribed tombstones, discovered within an area of a few thousand square feet, to more than eight hundred.

The columbaria of the servants and freedmen of the house of Augustus, and especially of Livia, his empress, were discovered between November, 1725, and January, 1726, in a vineyard then belonging to Giuseppe Benci, on the left side of the Appian Way, at the exact distance of 5,800 feet outside Porta S. Sebastiano. The discovery was beautifully illustrated by an eye-witness, Monsignore Francesco Bianchini, from whose book, dated 1727, I quote the following particulars. He begins by remarking that between the first and the second milestone of the Appian Way many tombs had been discovered already, all built by Augustus for his household ; that one of them, found by Fabretti near the bridge spanning the river Almo, contained in its three rooms more than three thousand cinerary urns. The ashes of an equal number of persons had been deposited in the tombs which he describes. The consequence is, that in two sepulchres only, comprising six rooms, not less than *six thousand* servants and officials of one emperor and of his relatives were buried, — a number which would seem altogether incredible if we did not possess the evidence of many eye-witnesses and that of the tombs themselves, which still exist, although in a state of great dilapidation. It is true that Augustus reigned for nearly half a century, and that, for a reason which I fail to comprehend, many of his servants died very young, and consequently were replaced by others many times during his lifetime. It is true that, besides the servants strictly so called, their children and brothers or sisters were sometimes buried with them. Still, the number of six thousand, as a minimum, is simply astonishing. Out of this powerful army not less than six hundred were attached to the person of Livia.

One circumstance which helps us to explain such an extraordinary state of things is this: the offices and duties which in modern times, and even in the richest houses, are intrusted to one or two individuals, in ancient times were divided and subdivided to an almost ridiculous extent. Take, for instance, the department of the wardrobes. There were, in Livia's household, a Parmenius, *a purpura*, keeper of purple robes; an Arion, *a veste matutina*, keeper of the morning-dresses; a Rhodanus, *a veste regia*, keeper of the imperial robe; a Bira Canaciana, *a veste magna*, keeper of state robes; a Eutactus, *capsarius*, keeper of overcoats; a Blastus, *lanipendius*, keeper of the manufactured woollen goods; and then many *vestiplici* or *vestiplicæ*, folders of clothes. Take also the department of the personal toilet. We have a general officer *ab ornamentis*, whose duties, however, are not well defined; an Aponia, *a tutulo ornatrix*, a specialist in dressing the hair in the fashion of a high *toupet;* a Helico, *ad unguenta*, keeper of perfumery; eight *aurifices*, or goldsmiths, an indefinite number of *margaritarii*, or jewellers; a Secundus, *aquarius*, or regulator of hot and cold water for the bath; a M. Livius,

calciator, keeper and maker of imperial shoes; a **Verania,**
a sandalio, keeper of that special kind of shoes which were
called sandals; a Julia Hilara, *ornatrix;* another Julia,
auriculæ ornatrix; a Calene, *untrix,* and so forth.   The
same subdivisions of duties occur in the department of
silver and gold plate.   Then there was a Lydus, *a sede
Augustæ,* keeper of Livia's chair; an Aurelia, *a cura
catellæ,* governess of the favorite pet dog; a Syneros, *ad
imagines,* keeper of family portraits, and so on.   It is no
wonder, with the particulars which I have given, that the
servants of the various members of the imperial family
reached such large numbers; indeed, their number was so
large that, to provide for their assistance in case of sickness, not one, but many physicians of both sexes were permanently engaged, and placed under the direction of a
head physician, *supra medicos,* named M. Livius Orestes.
The servants attached to the person of Statilius Taurus,
consul in the year 764, and to his children, numbered at
least three hundred and seventy.   I say at least, because the
columbaria discovered in 1875 on the Esquiline could not
have contained the whole body of servants; there were
other tombs of the Statilian household, as proved by inscriptions discovered much nearer the Porta Maggiore in
1880, in which the mention of Statilian freedmen occurs
many times.   I shall give the titles of such of them as
seem curious and full of interest.

First of all comes an *Asturconarius,* keeper of the
Spanish horse which Statilius Taurus had bought in the
province of Asturia, a province famous for its breed of easy
riding-horses.   Then comes a *puer capsarius,* a boy who
carried the overcoat for his master; two wet-nurses, *nu-
trices;* a midwife, *obstetrix;* a collector of legacies and
bequests; a locator of town and country property; a keeper

of the family tomb ; a keeper of the clothes of the grand-
father ; a keeper of bathing implements, such as sponges,
scraping-knives, ointments, and so on. Amidst this variety of duties intrusted to male servants, from the washer-
man, *fullo*, to *medicus ocularius*, or oculist, we find females
employed in a very restricted number of occupations, almost
exclusively in carding wool. The carding of wool at home
was one of the oldest traditional occupations of a Roman
lady, held in great estimation as late as the beginning of
the Empire. The highest praise which could be bestowed
on the mother of the family was contained in the words,
Domum servavit, lanam fecit, "She stayed at home to card
the wool." The family of Statilius Taurus seems to have
kept faithful to the simplicity of good old times, in spite
of the high rank and the honors and riches acquired at
the beginning of the Empire. On the tombstones discovered in the columbaria at the Porta Maggiore, we find
the mention of a female director of the wool manufactory
(*lanipenda*), a weaver and carder of wools (*tonstrix*), and a
large number of dressmakers and spinners (*sarcinatrices*
and *quasillariæ*). The wool manufactory was probably
established in a separate wing of the mansion, apart from
the men's quarters, and its entrance was watched by a
doorkeeper, *ostiaria*.

CHAPTER VI.

THE discovery of the House of the Vestals, at the foot of the Palatine hill, has supplied the friends and admirers of old Rome with a new and fascinating subject of inquiry. After toiling so long over ground searched and pillaged many a time before, with no prospect or hope of surprising discoveries, our perseverance in excavating the Roman forum and its vicinity has at last been splendidly rewarded. The discovery of the Atrium Vestæ (the official denomination of the convent) settles at once all controversy concerning the topography of this famous district of ancient Rome; and this scientific achievement has been accompanied by no less important material results. Between the middle of December, 1883, and the end of the following January, we brought to light fifteen marble pedestals, with eulogistic inscriptions describing the life of the *Vestales Maximæ* (the official title of the elder Vestals, or high-priestesses of Vesta); five inscriptions relating to historical subjects; eleven life-size statues; nine important fragments of statues; twenty-seven busts and portrait heads; eight hundred and thirty-four silver coins; one gold coin; two pieces of jewelry; several columns of *breccia coralina* and of *breccia di Egitto*, which rank among the finest specimens of antique marbles; besides many other fragments, which, in a less promising land, would be regarded as a treasure by themselves.

In my long experience and practice of archæological re-

THE ATRIUM VESTÆ, LOOKING EAST.

search and literature, never have I met with a subject more delightful and interesting. Historical accounts of this lovely sisterhood have a charm of their own, which we fail to recognize in other Roman religious corporations. In speaking of the Vestal Virgins, in describing their house, — the secrets of which, from the foundation of Rome to the fall of the Empire, were never revealed to mankind, — it is impossible not to give the reins to imagination and sentiment. Let us recall to life the silent ruins; let us vivify these halls, these porticoes, with the presence of maidens clad in snow-white garments, which reflected, as it were, the purity of their minds and souls; in the very prime of beauty, youth, and strength; daughters of the noblest families; depositaries of state secrets, confidants of the imperial household, and faithful keepers of the sacred tokens of the Roman Commonwealth. The very faults committed by a few Vestals in the lapse of eleven centuries, and the penalties they underwent to expiate their shame, quivering under the bloody rod of the high-priest, or breathing their last breath in the solitude of the tomb, in which they had been buried alive, — these sins and these expiations, I say, deeply affect the minds of visitors to the house, and still more, the minds of those who have selected it as a special subject of investigation.

The origin of the worship of Vesta is very simple. In prehistoric times, when fire could be obtained only from the friction of two sticks of dry wood, or from sparks of flint, every village kept a public fire burning day and night, in a central hut, at the disposition of each family. The care of watching the precious element was intrusted to young girls, because girls, as a rule, did not follow their parents and brothers to the far-away pasture-grounds, and did not share with them the fatigues of hunting or fishing expeditions. In course of time, however, this simple practice became a kind of sacred institution, especially at Alba Longa, the mother country of Rome ; and when a large party of Alban shepherds fled from the volcanic eruptions of the Alban craters into the plain below, and settled on the marshy banks of the Tiber, they followed, naturally, the institutions of the mother country, and the worship of Vesta — represented by the public fire and the girls attending to it — was duly organized at the foot of the Palatine hill, on the borders of the market-place (forum).

We possess many models of prehistoric huts and temples, made by the very people who inhabited or built them. I speak of the terra-cotta hand-made and sun-dried cinerary urns (called by Lubbock *hut-urns*), discovered for the first time in 1817, in the cemetery of Alba Longa. On page 29 is the drawing of one, from the Vatican collections, which may be taken as representing exactly the shape and appearance of the original temple of Vesta.

No girl under six, no girl above ten, years of age could be chosen as a priestess of the sacred fire. It was necessary, besides, that both her parents should be living, both of free condition, both irreproachable in public and in private life. In the election described by Tacitus (Ann. ii. 86), which took place A. D. 19, and in which the noble daughters of Domitius Pollio and Fonteius Agrippa stood as candidates, the Senate gave the preference to the former, because there had been some kind of misunderstanding between Fonteius Agrippa and his wife, and this misunderstanding of the parents was thought by the Senators to make the little girl less acceptable to the goddess.

Even the body of the candidate had to be perfect ; girls with defective eyesight, or a lisp, or marked by the slightest physical imperfection were absolutely excluded from the sisterhood.

The number of the Vestals was limited to six; no new election could take place, unless a vacancy was caused by the death of one of the sisters. Among the many documents which certify this particular, I cite one only, the well-known medallion of Julia Domna, showing the six Vestals sacrificing before the shrine of their goddess, which had just been rebuilt at the private expense of the empress.

As soon as the election was duly sanctioned, the virgin was shown into the Atrium Vestæ, where the ceremony of inauguration took place. It began by cutting her hair, which was

Medallion showing the Six Vestals.

appended, as a votive offering, to the *Lotus capillata*, a tree which, when Pliny wrote his "Natural History," was more than five hundred years old. Next, the girl was clothed in white garments, and duly sworn to her sacred duties. And as everything was sweet and gentle in this worship of Vesta, the novice exchanged, for the time being, her own name for that of *Amata*, the beloved. The legal term of service was thirty years; after which, the Vestal, being between thirty-six and forty years of age, was free to return home, and even to marry. The trentennial service was divided into three periods of ten years each: in the first decade the novice was initiated into the mysteries of the place, and instructed by the senior sisters; in the second decade she practised her duties; in the third she taught the novices. The eldest among them was called

Maxima, and presided over the institution. On page 141
is the portrait-bust of an abbess, discovered in the Atrium
on December 12, 1883, which gives a perfect idea of the
monastic dress of that age.

Very few Vestals, however, took advantage of the permission given by law to leave the Atrium and reënter the
wicked world, because the honors, the privileges, and the
riches they enjoyed as Vestals far exceeded any conceivable
advantage of worldly or married life.

In the first place, they were exceedingly wealthy : wealthy
from the revenues of the order, which possessed a large
amount of landed property ; and also from special allow-
ances made to each one of them by their families, or by the
head of the state. When Cornelia was elected in Scantia's
place, A. D. 24, Tiberius presented her with a sum corresponding to $87,705 (438,525 francs of our money). The
same emperor gave 2,192,625 francs ($438,525) to the
daughter of Fonteius Agrippa, as a consolation for the
preference shown by the Senate for her successful rival,
the daughter of Domitius Pollio.

The Vestals did not come under the dominion of the
common law ; they were not even subject to the authority
of the censor. By the simple fact of their adoption into
the order, they were at once delivered from the *patria po-
testas*, the paternal authority, and obtained the right of
making their will (*jus testamenti*). The only annoyance
they could encounter was that of being summoned as witnesses in state trials. Their presence made the wrong
right, of course within certain limits. We are told by Suetonius of a curious instance of this wonderful power of a
Vestal. One of Tiberius's ancestors, Appius Claudius, was
possessed by the most violent desire of celebrating a triumph. His application having been negatived by the

PORTRAIT OF A VESTALIS MAXIMA.

Discovered in the house of the Vestals.

majority of voters, instead of yielding to the popular decree, he induced his daughter, a member of the sisterhood,
to take a seat in the triumphal chariot, and, under her
protection, he succeeded in driving, undisturbed, up to the
Capitol.

The seats of honor were reserved for the Vestals in the
theatres, in the amphitheatre, and in the circus. The empress
herself was obliged, by a decree of the Senate, dated A. D.
24, to sit among the Vestals, whenever she wished to appear
in these public places of resort.

The right of driving in the streets of Rome must also be
ranked among their most extraordinary privileges. Ladies
generally used the *lectica,* or sedan-chair. The Vestals, on
the contrary, had two kinds of carriages : the state carriage,
called *plostrum,* or *currus arcuatus,* a heavy old-fashioned
sort of vehicle, and the daily carriage, called by Prudentius
molle pilentum. They drove out preceded by a lictor, and
every one, even the consuls, was obliged to make room for
them in their passage.

They owned a stable of their own, and therefore were
not obliged to hire horses or carriages. This particular
was revealed by a curious discovery. Every citizen, according to the Roman law, was subject to the *collatio equo-*
rum, or compulsory seizure of horses, whenever the state was
in need of them. Exceptions were made in favor of the imperial family, of high officers, of high priests, of diplomatic
" couriers," and of the Vestals. In 1735, a bronze tablet
was discovered in the farm of Prata-porcia, near Frascati,
with the inscription : " [This horse belongs to] Calpurnia
Prætextata, Abbess of the Vestals. [This horse is] exempt
from compulsory drafting." Two more such tablets, from
the stables of Flavia Publicia and Sossia, both *Vestales*
Maximæ, have been seen and described. The one found at

" Prata-porcia " proves that the farm belonged to the order, unless it was a private property of Calpurnia.

In state ceremonies, in the most solemn civil or religious meetings, they performed important duties. On June 21, A. D. 71, when the first stone of the temple of Jupiter was laid by Vespasian on the Capitoline hill, the Vestals headed the procession, surrounded by the sons and daughters of the aristocracy, and sprinkled with pure water the foundations of the new building.

Wills of emperors, secrets and documents of state, were intrusted to their care. Augustus, a few months before his death, placed in the hands of the abbess four documents, namely : his will, the directions for his funeral, the account of his life, and a description of the newly organized Empire.

In troubled times, in civil wars, in supreme emergencies of the Commonwealth, they were selected as ambassadresses, and even as umpires, to restore peace and tranquillity between the contending parties. During the terror of Sulla's proscriptions the life of Cæsar was spared, thanks to the powerful request of the Vestals. When Messalina's infamies were discovered by Claudius, Vibidia, the venerable abbess, was asked to intercede in favor of the profligate culprit. On the approach of Vespasian's armies, Vitellius begged for a suspension of hostilities ; the Vestal messengers did not succeed in stopping bloodshed, but were treated by the generals assembled in a council of war with special marks of consideration. The same mission was accomplished by them under Didius Julianus.

Any offence against their person was punished with death. Again, if a Vestal met by chance a criminal led to the scaffold, he was reprieved at once. Their influence in every branch of state administration is made evident by the legends engraved on the pedestals discovered in the Atrium, which are shown on page 134. They are described in these marbles as women to whom no request could be denied. Æmilius Pardalus offered a statue to Campia Severina, an abbess of the third century, as a token of gratitude for having been knighted. Q. Veturius Callistratus was made superintendent of the imperial libraries, on the recommendation of the same lady. Ulpius Verus and Aurelius Titus were made captains of the army, thanks to Flavia Publicia, abbess A. D. 247. It appears from these and other instances, which it would be superfluous to quote, that all state departments, including that of war, were to a certain extent subject to these virgins.

STATUE OF FLAVIA PUBLICIA.
Discovered in the Atrium of the Vestals.

The highest distinction conferred upon the Vestals was the right of interment within the walls of the city. The site of their burial-place is unknown; it will remain unknown, I presume, forever. This supposition is founded on the following fact. Among the thirty thousand inscriptions discovered in Rome since the Renaissance, only *one* tombstone with the name of a Vestal (Clodia, the niece of C. Claudius, prætor A. U. C. 698) has been found; and it was not found *in situ*. This dearth is at least singular, as the order is known to have flourished for more than eleven centuries. The Vestals, perhaps, like the nuns and the monks of the present day, had a common place of rest, a crypt, a *columbaria*, furnished with hundreds of *loculi*. What a magnificent event would be the discovery of such a place!

I have hitherto described the privileges of the Vestals, to prove how their moral, social, and material condition was far superior to that of married ladies, of matrons, or of maidens, even of the highest aristocracy. And what were the duties and obligations imposed upon them in exchange for so many advantages? Two only: to remain pure for thirty years, and to fulfil the rules of the order with the utmost care. The least deviation from the rules was punished with the rod; a breach of the vows was punished with death by starvation and strangulation.

Many and careful precautions were taken to prevent the virgins from falling into temptation. No man was allowed to approach the temple of Vesta at night; no man was allowed to step over the threshold of the Atrium upon any pretence. Even physicians were excluded, however urgent and needful their presence might be. In fact, no case of sickness was permitted to develop itself within this strongly protected citadel of chastity. As soon as the first symptom of a serious case of sickness made its appearance, the patient was removed from the Atrium, and put under the care of her parents, or else of a distinguished matron. The behavior of the attendant doctors was in each case closely watched.

Although a place of honor was reserved for them in dramatic, gladiatorial, or racing performances, they were not admitted to the athletic fights, lest perchance the sight of those admirable plastic forms should cast a shade over the serene purity of their minds. Nero, according to Suetonius, broke this rule, and the Vestals were officially invited by him, in his double capacity of emperor and high-priest, to come and look at the athletes. The excuse he gave for this freak was that the Grecian priestesses of Ceres could freely taste of this forbidden fruit in the Olympian games. We know not whether Nero's invitation was accepted or refused by the Vestals; but we do know, as an actual fact, that from the time of Nero to the time of Domitian their conduct did not escape blame and suspicion. But this must be considered as an exception, as a passing shadow over the brilliant, pure fame of the sisterhood.

The *pontifex maximus,* to whose paternal care the sisterhood was subject, kept a vigilant eye over it, watching the slightest suspicious sign. Every detail of their life was reported to him by secret informers, chosen evidently among the female servants of the house. The Vestal Minucia was denounced to the pontiff (329 B. C.) by one of these spies, because she had been noticed to have a special regard for her personal appearance, *propter mundiorem justo cultum.*

One door only seems to have been left open to attack, — the door which afforded direct communication between the house of the Vestals and the house of the high-priests themselves. Through this opening the enemy appears, at very rare intervals, to have entered and stormed the place.

The fall of a Vestal was regarded as incest. The expiation was terrible. The unfortunate girl, as soon as the trial was over and the condemnation pronounced, was divested of the distinctive garments of the order, and

flogged by the judges themselves.   Then the funeral procession was organized.   The culprit, covered by a pall and
lying in the hearse, was brought through the Forum, the
Long Street (*Vicus longus*), and the High Street (*Alta
Semita*), to the Porta Collina,[1] amidst the mourning and
dejected crowd of her friends and relatives.   Let us quote
the thrilling account of an execution given by Plutarch :
" The Vestal convicted of incest is buried alive in the
neighborhood of the Porta Collina, under the Agger of
Servius Tullius.   Here is a crypt, small in size, with an
opening in the vault, through which the ladder is lowered ;
it is furnished with a bed, an oil lamp, and a few scanty
provisions, such as bread, water, milk, and oil.   These provisions (in fact, a refinement of cruelty) are prepared because
it would appear a sacrilege to condemn to starvation women
formerly consecrated to the gods.   The unfortunate culprit is
brought here in a covered hearse, to which she is tied with
leather straps, so that it is impossible that her sighs and
lamentations should be heard by the attendant mourners.
The crowd opens silently for the passage of the hearse ; not
a word is pronounced, not a murmur is heard.   Tears stream
from the eyes of every spectator.   It is impossible to imagine a more horrible sight ; the whole city is shaken with
terror and sorrow.   The hearse being brought to the edge
of the opening, the executioner cuts the bands, and the
high-priest mutters an inaudible prayer, and lifts up his
arms towards the gods, before bidding the culprit good-
bye.   He follows and assists her to the top of the ladder,
and turns back at the fatal instant of her disappearance.
As soon as she reaches the bottom, the ladder is removed,

[1] This gate was discovered in 1872, under the northeast corner of the Palazzo del Ministero delle Finanze, not far from the Porta Pia and the English Embassy.

the opening is sealed, and a large mass of earth is heaped
upon the stone that seals it, until the top of the embankment is reached, and every trace of the execution made to
disappear."

The exact spot of the crypt is described by Livy, near

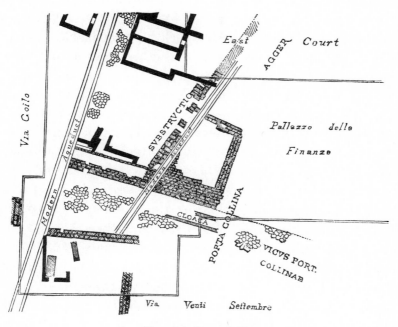

Plan of the Porta Collina.

the gate (*ad portam Collinam*) on the paved road on the
right (*dextra via strata*), and the place was called *Campus Sceleratus*. Comparing these precise indications with
the present state of that quarter, the crypt must lie under
the street named *Via Goito*, within a radius of some fifty
yards from the east door of the Palazzo delle Finanze.

How many touching inspirations this sad end of the
fallen Vestal has suggested to the poet, to the artist! I
believe, however, that no creation of the pencil or of the

lyric pen can be compared with the splendid letter addressed by Pliny to Minucianus (IV. 11), in which he
describes the last moments of one of Domitian's victims.
This tyrant was determined to make his reign illustrious
by the sacrifice of a Vestal. He found an accomplice
named Celer, who impudently confessed a pretended crime
with Cornelia, the very abbess of the Atrium. Whether
there was any foundation for such an abominable accusa-
tion, one thing is certain : the trial directed and presided over by Domitian was just as great a crime as that
imputed to Cornelia. The judges were not summoned to
the *Regia,* the official seat of the ecclesiastical court of
law, but to Domitian's private grounds at Albanum ; and
here the unfortunate abbess, without being heard, without
being allowed to exculpate herself, was sentenced to death.
" The priests and the executioner were despatched in great
haste to drag their victim to the *Campus Sceleratus.*
Raising her hands to Vesta and the immortal gods, she
protested her innocence, and kept exclaiming, ' The emperor declares me guilty of incest, knowing that my
prayers alone have given him victory, triumph, and an
immortal name ! ' I do not know whether this was said
sincerely or ironically; to mitigate the fury of the tyrant
or to ridicule and abuse him. At any rate, she was heard
repeating these words until she reached the fatal spot. In
descending the ladder, the folds of her veil being caught
somewhere, she stepped back to adjust it ; and as the executioner offered her the help of his hand, and attempted
to escort her down, she was horrified, and shrank from his
impure contact. She met her fate, certainly, as the purest
and noblest of women." The fate of the accomplice was
not less cruel. According to the ancient custom, he was
flogged to death in the *Comitium,* a small square between
the Forum and the Senate-Hall.

We come now to a rather difficult and mysterious point of inquiry: we must discover the secret of the order; we must find out what were the sacred tokens of the Roman Commonwealth intrusted to the care of the Vestals. Within the sacred enclosure there was an innermost sanctuary, in which some wonderful relics were concealed. According to the general belief, the safety, the prosperity of the Empire, depended upon the preservation of these relics; but nobody knows what they were. One of the most learned men of the present age, Francesco Cancellieri, has published a volume on the subject, entitled " Le Sette Cose Fatali di Roma Antica," but in spite of his prodigious erudition Cancellieri has not solved the mystery. He depends entirely upon the well-known words of Servius (Æn., vii. 188): " There were seven pledges of the prosperity of the Roman Empire, namely: the meteoric stone from Pessinus;[1] the terra-cotta quadriga from Veii; the ashes of Orestes; the sceptre of Priam; the veil of Iliona; the Palladium; the shields named *Ancilia*." Surely all this trash was not kept by the Vestals. Ancient writers use the general and indefinite expression *sacra quædam*, or *sacra fatalia*, " some sacred things," " some fatal things," and when they specify they only mention the Palladium. Cicero distinctly affirms that " in Vesta's penetralia is kept the statue fallen from heaven," and nothing else.

When the Atrium was burned down, in the great conflagration of 191, described by Herodianus, the Vestals fled to the Palatine across the Sacra Via, carrying with them, of course, the mysterious relics. " On this occasion," the historian says, " the Palladium was seen for the first time by profane eyes." Of one particular we are sure:

---

[1] Worshipped by the Romans under the name of " Great Mother of the Gods." See page 126

these things were of small size, and could be concealed inside a terra-cotta jar. When the Gauls stormed
Rome, in 364 B. C., the Vestals, before escaping to Veii,
buried between the Cloaca Maxima and the house of the
Flamen Quirinalis, a jug containing the relics. Hence
the name of the spot, *Doliola;* and hence the superstition
which forbade any one spitting upon it. The same feeling
of curiosity which impels us to inquire into this subject
scientifically was the cause of one of the most daring attempts against the privileges of the Vestals. The author
of it was Helagabalus, and it is described by his biographer, Lampridius.

Let us follow the mad prince into the Atrium ; let us
share with him the sacrilege ; violence may help us more
than science, perhaps, to solve the problem.

" Helagabalus " (I quote the words of the historian) " was
determined to substitute by main force the worship of his
own god, Helagabalus, for that of Roman gods. Vesta
was not spared in the persecution, and he tried repeatedly
to extinguish the perpetual fire. Disappointed in his attempts, he resorted to violence. Contaminated as he was
with every excess of immorality, he broke into the innermost sanctuary of the convent *penetralia,* the approach to
which is permitted only to the Vestals and to the high-
priests, and actually stole the jar containing (as he was led
to believe) the pledges of the Empire. Finding it empty,
he smashed it to pieces. Religion, however, lost nothing
from the sacrilege, because many such jars are kept in the
sanctuary, and nobody knows which is the right one. After
renewed attempts, he finally succeeded in obtaining the
Palladium, and placed it in his own temple, fastened with
chains of gold."

The account of Lampridius is rather obscure. At any

rate, if the real Palladium (the only relic mentioned by him) was actually stolen, there is no doubt that the successor of the crazy prince must have restored it to its legitimate keepers.

When the Atrium was discovered, in December, 1883, we had a faint hope of tracing the exact place of the *penetralia ;* but the hope was to a certain extent frustrated. In the very centre of the cloisters we came upon the foundations of an octagonal shrine, purposely and deliberately destroyed to the level of the ground.

Foundation of the Shrine in which the Palladium was kept.

As the house itself stands in a tolerably good state of preservation, and still contains many valuable works of art, who could have taken such a special interest in the disappearance of this central shrine ? Not the men of the Middle Ages, certainly : they knew little about the Vestals, nothing about the *penetralia* and its relics ; there was no reason, besides, why they should destroy the shrine, built of bricks as it was, more than other, richer portions of the house, which were left undisturbed. We believe that the destruction of this innermost sanctuary was accomplished by the Vestals themselves in the last days preceding their banishment from the cloisters and the suppression of their order (A. D. 394); we believe the secret to have been buried with the last Vestal.

The house of the Vestals is a rectangular building, 345 feet long and 171 feet wide, bounded by public streets on every side. The street skirting the house on the east, along the *Porticus Margaritaria,* is the famous *Sacra Via;* the one on the west side is the not less famous *Nova Via;* the name of that on the south is unknown; the name of that on the north has been quite recently discovered under the following curious circumstances. The architects of the basilica of S. Paul-outside-the-walls, in digging the foundations of the portico in front of the basilica itself, found at a considerable depth many Christian tombs of the sixth century, made up of every kind of material, and particularly of slabs and blocks of marble removed from older buildings.

One of these slabs, discovered in 1878, contained the following inscription : —

" Under the consulship of L. Marius Maximus and of L. Roscius Ælianus " (A. D. 223), " the shrine or chapel which stood at the corner of the street of-Vesta, and which had been allowed to fall almost into ruin, has been rebuilt by the magistrates of the (ward or) district, and dedicated to the domestic gods of the imperial family, and to the Genius of our emperor, Severus Alexander, the Pious, the Fortunate," etc., etc.

Six years later, in the spring of 1882, not only did we succeed in laying bare the pavement of the lane running between the temple of the Dioscuri and the north side of the house of the Vestals, which evidently must be the one mentioned in the inscription, but we brought to light the very shrine or chapel to which the marble slab above described was originally affixed. This shrine is a *bijou* of Greco-Roman architecture ; and although its various members and marble decorations lay scattered far and wide, all over the valley of the Forum, we have picked them out one by one, and expect to restore them soon to their proper places, and to reconstruct the whole shrine.

Many of my readers may have been struck by the remarkable instance, which I have quoted, of a marble slab of great dimensions, removed from the Roman Forum in the sixth century after Christ, — that is to say, at a period in which old imperial Rome had still a certain amount of vitality left, — and employed by an obscure Christian as a cover to a humble tomb, fully three miles distant from the Forum. This instance is by no means remarkable or extraordinary ; the amount of dispersion which the inscribed marbles and stones of Rome have undergone is simply wonderful. This is the reason which impels us to be always exceedingly careful in drawing conclusions from the discovery of an inscription. Unless found in its original place, or unless we can prove beyond doubt, by other means of comparison, that although somehow out of place, it belongs to the building among the ruins of which it happens to be brought to light, an inscription has no topographical value. I shall explain better this important rule in the study of Roman topography by instancing one or two cases, which prove how easily one can be misled in this branch of archæological research by trusting too confidently to appearances.

Not many years ago, the old marble pavement of the church of S. Maria in Trastevere was demolished, in order that a mosaic one might be substituted in its place. It was ascertained, in the progress of the work, that nearly one fifth of the marble slabs with which the old floor was paved were nothing but ancient inscriptions laid upside down; that is to say, with the letters embedded in cement, and the plain back exposed to view. One of these epigraphic fragments of a monumental character spoke of a forum built, or rather reconstructed, by the emperors Valens and Gratianus, for the benefit of the citizens of Rome. The discovery led some to believe that in ancient times there must have been a forum or square in the neighborhood of the church of S. Maria in Trastevere, within the limits of the fourteenth ward or region, and that this forum must have been restored in the fifth century by the emperors above named. The deduction was utterly groundless : the monumental inscription set in the pavement of the church had travelled all the way down from the Esquiline hill, a distance of about two miles ; it had been seen and copied in its original place, near the church of S. Vito, by the so-called " Anonymus " of Einsiedlen, eleven centuries before. This copy enables us to fill up the lacunæ in the fragments dug up at S. Maria in Trastevere, and shows that the forum in question was officially called Forum Esquilinum, the square of the Esquiline, and at the same time Macellum Liviæ, the market of Livia.

Not less extraordinary in this respect is the discovery of the fragments of the *acta fratrum Arvalium* (annals of the Fratres Arvales), a brotherhood which closely resembled, in organization and in religious character, the sisterhood of the Vestals. From fragments of the annals discovered, we know not where, in the Middle Ages, it was evident that the Arvales held their meetings in a wood five miles distant from Rome, and worshipped in a temple dedicated to the *dea Dia ;* but where the temple stood, and how far and in what direction the adjoining woods extended, it was impossible to ascertain. Many more fragments of the annals, that is to say, of the marble slabs on which they are engraved, have come to light during the last three centuries, but from such widely separated, out-of-the-way, incongruous places that the problem was considered, until late years, as utterly insoluble. Some have been found in the foundation of the sacristy of S. Peter's, some in the catacombs of S. Agnes on the Via Nomentana, some on the Esquiline, some under the foundations of a house near the Jewish quarter, some on the road to Fiumicino, five miles and a quarter outside the Porta Portese. This last place, the fifth ·mile - stone of the ancient Via Campana, has been finally ascertained to be the true one. The magnificent work of exploration carried on in this spot for two consecutive years by the late Dr. Wilhelm Henzen, under the auspices and with the help of Empress Augusta of Germany, brought to light not only the remains of the temple of the *dea Dia*, the place of worship of the Arvales, but also their banqueting-hall, called the *tetrastylum*, and about one thousand lines of the annals, or yearly records of the brotherhood. After the instances I have related, which I could multiply *ad libitum*, we shall not wonder any more at the curious fate of the Farnese Hercules, that colossal masterpiece of Greco-Roman sculpture, now in the Museo Nazionale in Naples, the torso of which was discovered in the baths of Caracalla, the head at the bottom of a well in Trastevere, the legs in the farm of " le Frattocchie," ten miles from Rome. At all events, these instances of dispersions of ancient marbles in Rome and its suburbs will not surprise any one acquainted with the history of the decline and fall of the city, and of its subsequent vicissitudes in the Middle Ages, and even in modern times. As Thomas

Dyer remarks in the seventeenth chapter of his History:
" To the use and abuse of building and ornamental materials the destruction of the Roman monuments must principally be referred. . . . The process of spoliation, conversion, and destruction was pursued by the emperors, by
the popes, by noblemen and prelates, and by private individuals. . . . The Romans were thus the principal demol-
ishers of their own city."

If it were in our power to snatch the secret of the origin
and former purpose and use of the marbles, stones, and
bricks with which our palaces, our cloisters, and our villas
have been built and embellished, or to recall to life the
masterpieces of Greek and Roman statuary, hammered and
ground into dust or burnt into lime, our knowledge of the
city of the Cæsars would be almost perfect. The rebuilding of S. Peter's alone, from the pontificate of Martin V.
to that of Pius VII., caused more destruction, did more injury to ancient classic remains, than ten centuries of so-
called barbarism. Of the huge and almost incredible mass
of marbles, of every nature, color, value, and description,
used in building S. Peter's, until the beginning of the present century, not an inch, not an atom, comes from modern quarries;[1] they were all removed from classic buildings, many of which were levelled to the ground for the
sake of one or two pieces only.

In order not to wander too far from the main subject, I
will cite one item only of these annals of destruction : I
will mention what happened in the valley of the Forum
between 1540 and 1549. In less than ten years' time, the
men employed by the contractors of S. Peter's to search for
building materials crossed the valley of the Forum from end

---

[1] Exception must be made in the
case of the few columns of *cottanello*
marble, which were quarried near
Moricone, Sabina.

to end, like an appalling meteor, destroying, dismantling, splitting into fragments, burning into lime, the temples, the arches, the basilicas most famous in Roman history, in the history of the Old World, together with the inscriptions which indicated their former use or design, and the statues and bas-reliefs which ornamented them. In 1540 the podium, steps, and pediment of the temple of Antoninus and Faustina were removed to S. Peter's or otherwise made use of. Between 1541 and 1545 the same fate befell the triumphal arch raised in honor of Fabius Maximus, the conqueror of Savoy; the triumphal arch raised in honor of Augustus. after the battle of Actium; the temple of Romulus, son of Maxentius; and a portion of the Cloaca Maxima. In 1546 the temple of Julius Cæsar was levelled to the ground, together with the Fasti Consulares and Triumphales engraved on its marble basement; in 1547 the temple of Castor and Pollux was dismantled; in 1549 the temple of Vesta, the temple of Augustus, and the shrine of Vortumnus.

I have not mentioned this sad page of the history of Roman monuments to vituperate or condemn to excess the memory of the authors of so great a destruction, — popes, princes, artists, who, after all, in lieu of the ruins destroyed by them, raised and left to us monuments and edifices which, in beauty and perfection, will bear comparison with the old ones. I have mentioned the subject because it strikes me as one of the most curious and inexplicable problems in the history of art, — the fact that the great masters of the Renaissance and the cinquecento, ardent admirers as they were of ancient architectural and plastic works, should have taken willingly their share in that abominable crusade. One must examine carefully, sheet by sheet, the note-books and studies left by such men as Michael Angelo, Baldassarre Peruzzi, Salvestro Peruzzi, Antonio di Sangallo, Sangallo il Gobbo, Bramante Lazzari, Antonio Dosio, Piero Santo Bartoli, Giovanni da Udine, as I have done myself, to get the true idea, to fathom with the right line their immense love and admiration for ancient art. Even the most obscure and uninteresting bits and fragments of mouldings were taken up by them as subjects of study and investigation. However, all this love, all this admiration, was purely platonic and material : they all considered ancient remains and architectural masterpieces not as things of beauty in themselves, worth being respected and cared for, as we do now ; they looked upon them as a simple means of learning art, and of perfecting themselves in the practice of their profession. When they had got from the original all the advantage which they thought it capable of affording, they abandoned it to its fate, as an altogether useless thing.

I am sure that if I were to make up my mind to publish the documents which I have collected by thousands, on the share which every one of the great cinquecento masters took in the destruction of ancient Rome, my book would be read and regarded as a startling revelation. They all shared in the sacrilege. Let me quote a few instances. The pedestal of the equestrian statue of M. Aurelius on the Capitol was cut by Michael Angelo out of one of the columns belonging to the temple of Castor and Pollux ; another fragment of the same columns was transformed by Raphael and Lorenzetto into the admirable statue of Jonah in the Chigi chapel in the church of S. Maria del Popolo. The coat of arms of Pius IV., on the top of the Porta Pia, was cut by the same Michael Angelo out of a marble capital of colossal size, discovered under the palace of Piero della Valle. The temple of the Sun, on the

Quirinal, furnished the materials for the Cesi chapel in S. Maria Maggiore, for the fountain of the Piazza del Popolo,[1] for the fountain in the Piazza Giudea, for the Pope's palace on the Quirinal, and so forth. The materials for the church of S. Maria dell' Anima and for some portions of the Villa Medici were quarried from the ruins of the temple of Jupiter Capitolinus ; those for the Sixtine chapel, in the Vatican, from Hadrian's mausoleum. The columns of *verde antico* which adorn the Farnese palace and the villa of Julius III., on the Via Flaminia, come from Zenobia's bath-house, at the sulphur springs near Tivoli. The house of Lorenzo Bernini, near S. Andrea delle Fratte, is built with the materials of the baths of Licinius Sura, on the Aventine.

Strange to say, even the work of restoration and preservation of ancient monuments was accompanied with destruction : one monument paid the ransom for another. Thus, for instance, the obelisk raised by Augustus as a sun-dial, in the Campus Martius, was restored by Innocent XII. with the granite of the monumental column of Antoninus Pius, discovered in the garden of the " Casa della Missione." Thus, also, the arch of Constantine was restored by Clement XII. with the large blocks of marble belonging to the temple of Neptune, near the Pantheon. The Pantheon itself, or rather its portico, was restored by Alexander VII. with columns from the baths of Severus Alexander, and with marbles from a triumphal arch called in the Middle Ages the " arch of Piety."

There is no longer any doubt that the Romans have done more harm to their own city than all invading hosts put together. The action of centuries and of natural phenomena, such as hurricanes, earthquakes, fires, and inundations,

---

[1] Now in the public gardens on the Janiculum.

could not have accomplished what men have, willingly and deliberately. As regards the barbarians, the damage inflicted by them to our monuments is comparatively small, because they had at their disposal less powerful means of destruction. We know that the gardens and palace of Sallust were destroyed by Alaric; that the bronze roof of the temple of Jupiter Capitolinus was dismantled by Genseric; that the aqueducts were cut down by Vitiges. These deeds, however, are nothing in comparison with the robberies and spoliations committed by the Emperor Constans during his short visit to the Eternal City in the spring of the year 663. For many centuries private individuals had an unrestricted right over the ruins existing in their own lands; and when, finally, state or municipal authorities determined to take or to show an interest in this matter, their actions were inspired, not by love of art, but by material and pecuniary considerations. The apostolic chamber, or treasury, would sell this or that ruin as a quarry (*petraia*), reserving to itself thirty-three per cent. of the product of the work of destruction. An official document, discovered by Eugène Müntz in the state archives of Rome, certifies that in the year 1452 one of the treasury contractors, named Giovanni Foglia, from Como, removed from the Colosseum alone two thousand five hundred and twenty-two cart-loads of travertine!

But it is time that I should come back to the house of the Vestals, and to the description of its different apartments. In order to obtain the necessary degree of clearness, I will lay before the eyes of the reader a map of the house, and lead him, as it were, by the hand during the interesting excursion.

The extensive building, covering an area of 58,995 square feet, has but one entrance, that marked with the letter A.

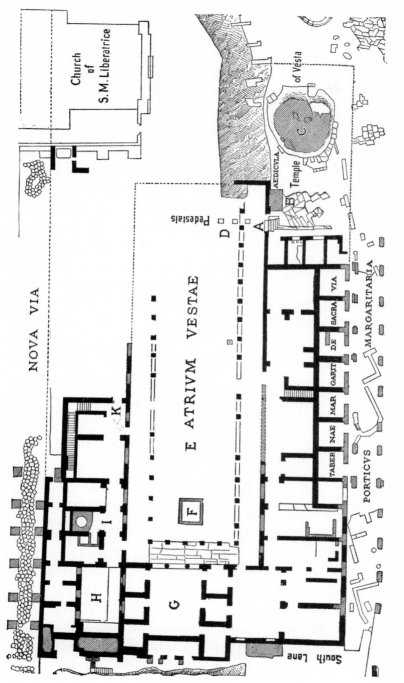

PLAN OF THE HOUSE OF THE VESTALS.

Here began, in ancient times, the monastic *clausura*. Next to it, on the right, are to be seen (B) the remains of the shrine restored under Severus Alexander, a description of which has been given above.

The foundations of the round temple of Vesta are marked C. This lovely structure, rebuilt for the last time by Julia Domna, after the great fire of Commodus, was discovered first in 1489, in an excellent state of preservation. Rediscovered in 1549, it was completely demolished, and levelled to the ground. Only thirty-six marble fragments belonging to its architecture by a great chance escaped destruction. These were found by us in 1883 scattered far and wide. With their help we have been able to reconstruct most carefully the architecture of the temple, as shown in the following cuts.

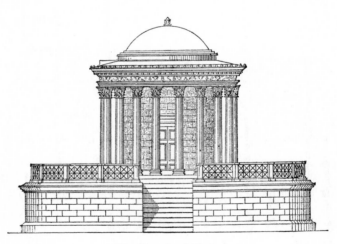

The Temple of Vesta.

D. Three marble pedestals, dedicated one, A. D. 364, to an abbess whose memory was afterwards condemned (see page 170); the second, A. D. 286, to Cœlia Claudiana; the

third, A. D. 247, to Flavia Publicia.   These three pedestals are not in their original places; they were put here during the Middle Ages, and built into the foundations of a small

Capital from the Temple of Vesta.

house belonging to an officer of Pope Marinus II., whose name is not known. We have been able to ascertain this fact from the discovery of a small terracotta jar buried under the pavement of the house, containing, first, the insignia of the officer, in *niello* work, with the legend DOMNO MARINO P A P A; secondly, a collection of 835 coins, one of gold, the others of silver. The gold coin is of Theophilus, emperor between 829 and 842. All but four of the silver coins are Anglo-Saxon. Following is the catalogue of them: —

Alfred the Great	3
Edward the First	217
Athelstan	393
Edmund the First	195
Sitric, King of Northumbria	1
Anlaf, King of Northumbria	6
Plegmund, Archbishop of Canterbury . .	4
Mint of Pavia	2
Mint of Limoges	1
Mint of Ratisbon	1
Uncertain	11

THE ATRIUM VESTÆ, LOOKING WEST.

The remains of the mediæval house were unwisely destroyed in the course of the recent excavations.

We have now entered the cloisters, the Atrium itself, the size of which is so extraordinary in comparison to that of the house that it is no wonder the whole building was named from it. We find in the plan of the building itself the prototype of all the convents and nunneries of the world, the characteristics of which are a large court-yard surrounded with porticoes, both necessary to give air, light, and the possibility of a little exercise to women condemned for life to almost solitary confinement. The portico surrounding this Atrium Vestæ was ornamented with columns of *cipollino* on the ground floor, with columns of *breccia corallina* on the floor above. Near the southern extremity of the court there is a basin, or tank, for the supply of water, which the Vestals drew from one of the neighboring sacred springs, as the use of water running through pipes was against the rules of the order. The basin is marked with the letter F.

G. *Tablinum*, state, or reception hall of the Vestals, with traces of marble pavement and marble incrustations. Six small rooms open on this apartment, three on each side, the pavements of which are raised in a peculiar way to avoid dampness, namely, by laying the new floor on half amphoræ, through the interstices of which the dry air could circulate.

H. A small court-yard containing the furnaces for the heating of the whole house.

I. A mill used by the Vestals to grind meal, with which the *mola salsa* (the most primitive kind of a cake) was prepared on February 15th of each year, during the celebration of the Lupercalia.

K. Small staircase leading to bedrooms on upper floor. Remains of these bedrooms have been found only on the west side; that is to say, on the side facing the Nova Via. These cells are exceedingly small and simple, and are separated from the bath-room which belongs to them by a small corridor.

Apartments not marked on the plan have not been identified.

LAST DAYS OF THE VESTAL VIRGINS.

The second half of the fourth century of our era was one of the most exciting periods in Roman history, on account of the stupendous fight between the Christian majority and the minority of those who still clung to polytheism in its decrepitude. Both parties were determined to put an end to a state of things which had become intolerable to each; both were determined to strike the final blow; and although the emperors themselves were disposed personally to gain the victory with time and persuasion, the impatience of the pagan leaders in Rome caused the catastrophe to be violent and marked by bloodshed.

It is rather difficult to describe the character, the feelings, the behavior, of those who distinguished themselves during the fight, because contemporary writers are not impartial; they judge of men and things from their own point of view, from the interest of their party. This discrepancy of appreciation is noticeable even in points of supreme importance, in events which had been seen and shared by thousands and thousands of witnesses. Christian writers, as a rule, attribute to their antagonists any amount of depravity, even in private life and affections; pagan writers reproach their opponents with conspiring to destroy the Empire, with being determined to open the gates of the Eternal City to the barbarians, provided the triumph of their new faith could be secured. The author of the libel against Virius

Nicomachus Flavianus,[1] the leader of the pagan aristocracy in the Senate, describes him as being polluted by unmentionable vices; whereas Theodosius II. and Valentinian III., in their official messages to the Senate, A. D. 431, proclaim him *nominis illustris, et sanctissimæ apud omnes recordationis,* an illustrious name, a man whose character was as pure as gold. Another instance of this more or less sincere discrepancy of opinions is supplied by the well-known quarrel about the statue of Victory in the Curia or Senate-hall, which statue for centuries had been considered as the personification of the power and destinies of imperial Rome. This statue, formerly worshipped at Tarentum, had been placed by Augustus himself on the tribune of the Curia, and ornamented with the rarest kind of jewelry, which he had collected in Egypt. An altar stood before it, to receive the votive offerings of the *patres conscripti.* From the day of Constantine's conversion to Christianity to the year 382, the statue and the altar had been left undisturbed. In 382, however, they gave rise to the memorable duel fought between S. Ambrose on the Christian and Symmachus on the pagan side before Valentinian II. and Theodosius. Symmachus accused his rivals of enmity, not toward the statue of Victory, but toward the symbol of the fortune of the Roman armies, just then engaged in trying to check the invasion of the barbarians. S. Ambrose, on the other hand, never mentions the statue, venerated by every one because of its glorious origin, won-

---

[1] This libel was discovered by Delille in 1867, at the end of the famous manuscript of Prudentius, which manuscript contains marginal notes in the handwriting of Vettius Mavortius Basilius Agorius, consul A. D. 427. This statesman was a clever classical student for his age. Herr Horkel has shown that Horace's Satires have come down to us through one copy only, from the library of Mavortius Basilius, somewhat altered by his marginal notes and corrections. The libel against Flavianus, discovered by Delille, was published by Morel in the *Revue Archéologique,* June, 1868.

derful beauty, and great age; he contends simply that the altar and the official worship of the goddess should no longer be imposed on the Christian senators, or offend their feelings and trouble their consciences. The want of trustworthy contemporary documents is compensated to a certain extent by the admirable series of inscriptions collected in class five of the sixth volume of the *Corpus Inscriptionum Latinarum,* which refers to Roman patrician magistrates of the fourth century, from the time of Diocletian to the fall of the Empire. These inscriptions derive their importance from the fact that, in describing the political, religious, and military career of each statesman and senator, they reveal at the same time absolutely authentic particulars otherwise unknown and events and names concerning which contemporary writers have not spoken, or have spoken with passion and prejudice. These marbles tell us the names and the exploits of the last champions of polytheism in the Senate. They describe how, during the last outburst of fanaticism, the most absurd superstitions, the most mysterious and contemptible ceremonies, were revived, — those especially which bore a certain analogy with the ceremonies of Christian worship. They throw a new light also on the catastrophe which brought to an end the worship of Vesta, and the life, eleven centuries old, of the sisterhood of the Vestal Virgins.

The leaders of the pagan faction in the Curia were Clodius Hermogenianus, Cælius Hilarianus, Clodius Flavianus, Petronius Apollodorus, Sextilius Agesilaus, the two Rufii Ceionii, Nonius Victor, Aurelius Victor, and other representatives of the old aristocracy. But, alas! how miserably they represented the former conquerors of the world! The whole party was initiated into the mysteries of secret Eastern sects,[1] and their religious fanaticism stood in contrast to the original purity and simplicity of Roman re-

ligion as did their civil and military virtues to the wisdom and valor of the statesmen and generals of the Republic, and also of the Empire, in its first three centuries of glorious life.

They had selected as the scene of their grand exploits, as a place for confidential meetings, two sanctuaries, both of recent construction, — the shrine of

Mosaic discovered at Pompeii.

Cybele and Atys on the Vatican hill, and the grotto of Mithras in the Campus Martius. The shrine of Cybele is mentioned by ancient writers among the buildings of the fourteenth region, *Transtiberim,* under the name *Phrygianum.* Although there was no doubt that such a name belonged to a place of worship of the Phrygian goddess, and that such a place was in the neighborhood of the Vatican, still no positive notice of its history and exact situation was obtained until the reign of Pope Paul V., Borghese. In laying the foundations of the southeast corner of the new façade of S. Peter's, between 1608 and 1609, at a depth of thirty feet below the level of the ground, several altars and pedestals were discovered, on which the history of the shrine was engraved. These marbles apparently had been hammered and split into fragments at some unknown period; perhaps after the great religious catastrophe of 394,

[1] To the mysterious symbolism of one of these sects must belong the curious mosaic discovered at Pompeii, and represented above.

of which I shall presently speak.   The sacred grotto of
Mithras, in the Campus Martius, was within the limits of
the seventh region, on the east side of the Via Lata, between the modern
Corso and the gen-
eral post-office in
the Piazza of S. Sil-
vestro in Capite,
and, more precisely,
in the plot of
ground which is
now occupied by the
Marignoli palace. It
was discovered at
the end of the fif-
teenth century, but
no satisfactory ac-
count of the dis-
covery has come
down to us.   Fra
Giovanni Giocondo
and Pietro Sabino,
who seem to have
witnessed the event,

The Symbolic Grotto of Mithras.   Relief recently
discovered on the Esquiline.

only copied the inscriptions of the sanctuary, without describing any details of its architecture and disposition.
Both places, the Vatican *Metroon* and the *Mithræum
Campense*, as they were officially named, had been filled
with numberless altars and pedestals, as was said above,
to commemorate the initiation of eminent men, mostly
senators of the Empire, into those horrid mysteries and
into the various degrees of the sect.   And do the records
engraved upon these marbles enumerate according to the

ancient custom, the civil, military, and diplomatic offices honorably discharged in the interest of their sovereigns and country? Not in the least. These men pride themselves upon titles and names which would have made their noble and gallant ancestors blush with shame and burst with indignation. They call themselves *pater sacrorum*, father of mysteries; *hierocorax invicti Mithræ*, sacred crow of Mithras the omnipotent; *archibucolus dei Liberi*, great shepherd of Bacchus; *hierofantes Hecatarum*, high-priest of Hecate, and so forth. And they make use of a peculiar

Mithras Cautes.

kind of phraseology, unknown in classic times, and evidently copied in a ridiculous manner from Christian models. One speaks of the gods *animæ suæ mentisque custodes;* another proclaims himself *delibutus sacratissimis mysteriis*, or else *in æternum renatus*, after the baptism of blood; all of them, likewise, testify with unbounded pride to having received this bloody baptism, under the form of *criobolium* or *taurobolium*,[1] or to having renewed the ceremony after a lapse of twenty years, because it appears that the abominable sacrament was thought to lose its redeeming power after a certain time, like some of our cutaneous injections.

Two senators, Nonius Victor Olympius and Aurelius Victor Augentius, presided over the Mithræum Campense, and were the grand-masters of this kind of Free-masonry. In

---

[1] The *criobolium* was administered with the blood of a ram; the *taurobolium* with the blood of a bull.

the tablets discovered there nearly four centuries ago, we can follow step by step the career of many illustrious adepts. Between A. D. 357 and 377 Nonius and Aurelius administered right and left the degrees of *corax* (crow), *cryphius* (griffin), *leo, Perses, Heliodromos,* and *pater.*[1] In 377, however, the practice was stopped, probably, by the prefect

Mithras — Sun.

of the town, Gracchus, who attempted to destroy all the Mythraic grottoes in Rome.

The worship of Vesta was not forgotten in this last outbreak, in this last revival of pagan superstitions. We are glad to acknowledge, however, that our virgins did not contaminate the last days of their life by altering the ancient purity and simplicity of the institution; they fell nobly and gallantly, faithful to the rules of the order eleven centuries old, free from any suspicion, and respected even by their enemies, in whose diatribes we are happy to find a certain sense of kindness and respect every time the Vestals are mentioned. We are also glad to testify that their name is not profaned in the records of the Phrygian and Mythraic sects; the senators, who caused those records to be engraved on marble, only occasionally call themselves *pontifices Vestæ* and *pontifices Vestales.*

The infidel majority in the Senate fought the last battles under two able and determined leaders: Virius Nicomachus Flavianus, the senior (with his relatives the Sym-

---

[1] The 'numbers' or degrees of the society were six : the Venerable of the lodge was called *pater patrum.*

machi), and Vettius Agorius Prætextatus. Flavianus took
little or no interest in the Vestals, perhaps because the simplicity of their worship did not sufficiently excite a soul
vitiated by the violent mysteries of the Phrygian and
Persian rites. The author of the libel discovered by
Delille, and mentioned above, ridicules Flavianus for his
performances of the *Amburbalia,* of the *Isia,* of the *Megalesia,* of the *Floralia ;* but he never speaks of the *Ves-
talia,* of the perennial fire, or of the *Palladium.* Vettius
Agorius Prætextatus, on the contrary, was intensely devoted
to the Virgins, as was also his wife, Fabia Aconia Paullina. Their palace stood at the corner of the Via Meru-
lana and the Via delle sette Sale, on the site of the new
palazzo Brancaccio. It was surrounded by a garden, which
extended as far as the present railway station. Many
monuments concerning the history of their family have
been discovered within these limits. I shall mention,
however, one only, on account of its connection with the
events which I am relating. When the house of Prætextatus was excavated for the first time in 1591, there were
found a pedestal and a statue erected in honor of Cælia
Concordia, the last (or next to the last) abbess of the
Atrium Vestæ. The pedestal bore the following dedication :
" Fabia Aconia Paullina sets up (in her own palace) this
portrait-statue of Cælia Concordia, the Abbess of the Vestals,
not only as a testimonial to her virtues, her chastity and
her devotion to the gods, but also as a token of gratitude
for the honor conferred by the Vestals upon her husband
Prætextatus, to whom they have dedicated a statue in their
own convent." By a remarkable chance, this last-named
statue has been discovered in our excavations. Its head, at
first missing, was found by accident two years later. It is
represented in the accompanying illustration. There seems

to be no doubt of its being the very one alluded to by Fabia Aconia Paullina. It represents a senator in the official robe of the fourth century, and it is the only male statue found in the Atrium Vestæ ; its presence there would have remained almost inexplicable, had we not heard of it before, from the above-quoted inscription.

STATUE OF PRÆTEXTATUS.

Discovered in the Atrium of the Vestals.

I must now mention a pedestal discovered near the northeast corner of the Atrium on November 5, 1883, dedicated to one of the abbesses, A. D. 364, from which the name of the lady appears to have been erased purposely. Here is the text of the remarkable inscription : —

OB MERITVM CASTITATIS
PVDICITIAE ADQ· IN SACRIS.
RELIGIONIBVSQVE
DOCTRINAE MIRABILIS
C · · · · · ·   E· V· V· MAX·
PONTIFICES· V· V· C· C·
PROMAG· MACRINIO ·
SOSSIANO· V · C · P · M·

"[This statue and this pedestal have been raised] in honor of C—— [name erased], abbess of the Vestals, by the college of the high-priests, under the vice-presidency of Macrinius Sossianus, as a testimonial to her chastity and to her profound knowledge in religious matters."

It would be very interesting in connection with the history of the last years of the priesthood to ascertain why the name of the abbess was hammered out, to know why the memory of the lady was condemned by the pagan faction, after it had bestowed so many praises upon her. The *memoriæ damnatio* must have taken place between 364, which is the date written on the right side of the marble, and 394, the date of the abolition of the order. Three causes only can be suggested: first, the conversion of the priestess to Christianity; secondly, an offence against the rules; and lastly, a secession from the order. It is quite probable that she became a Christian. Prudentius, in the hymn to S. Lawrence, says, *Ædemque Laurenti tuam Vestalis intrat Claudia,* — "Claudia, the Vestal Virgin, enters thy shrine"; and these words have been interpreted by some, not as a general and impersonal indication of the conquests made by the gospel in the most famous strongholds of polytheism, but as positive evidence of a special conquest made in the Atrium itself. We must observe, however, that the conversion of an abbess would have been considered such an enormous victory for the faithful that it is remarkable that it is not mentioned and extolled by other, more serious writers than a poet.

No less extraordinary an event would have been the incest of a Vestal; above all, the incest of an abbess. Here, again, we can produce the testimony of a man above suspicion, that such a crime was actually committed by a Vestal Virgin towards the end of the fourth century. Symmachus, the great pagan orator, describes the fall of a Vestal named Primigenia, and insists that she be punished according to the ancient rules. The culprit, however, did not belong to the Roman house of the order; she belonged to the house at Albanum. This explains why the crime of the

priestess did not create more sensation in Rome.   A secession from the order is mentioned by the same authority,
Symmachus.   One of his letters has come down to us, addressed to a Vestal, whose name is not given, in which he
inquires anxiously whether he must believe the rumor, spread
far and wide, of her intended secession from the order.   Of
course, such an act was perfectly legal after thirty years of
service, and the lady whose name was erased from the pedestal being a Vestalis Maxima, had surely gone far beyond
the legal term.   But the anxiety of Symmachus is very natural.   A leader of the infidel party could not help feeling
the wrong done to its interests by the desertion from the
battle-field of a woman of such high standing and consideration as a Vestalis Maxima.   And as her behavior was not
punishable in any way, Symmachus and his colleagues, the
Pontifices majores, resorted to the only possible revenge,
— erasure of her name from the pedestal which they had
dedicated some time before in the Atrium, and covered with
her praises.

The signs of an approaching catastrophe were first noticed in 383, with joy on one side, with ill-concealed rage
on the other.   By an imperial decree of that year, signed
by Gratianus, the privileges and patrimonies of all pagan
places of worship were abolished and confiscated, on the
ground that it was not becoming a Christian government
and a Christian state to supply unbelievers and infidels
with the means of persevering in their errors and of op-
posing the conquests of the gospel; that it was unjust and
intolerable that profane and offensive sacrifices should be
offered, as it were, in the name and with the money of a
Christian government.   At the same time the pagans were
left entirely free to keep their temples and shrines in good

order, and to perform their ceremonies even in public, provided this was done at their own cost.

The pagan senators, who still commanded a majority in that body, not, perhaps, because there were so many pagans among the populace, but owing rather to the glorious traditions which clustered around many of the pagan family names, did the best they could to obtain a revocation of the decree ; but Valentinian II. was inexorable in demanding the accomplishment of the edict of his brother Gratianus. He went even a step further. By a second decree, dated 391, superstitious sacrifices were prohibited in Rome and throughout Italy, even if offered under a private name. Then, as happens generally in such momentous circumstances, when a disaffected party has the good or bad fortune to find an energetic, unscrupulous, daring leader, well known to the populace for his social position, for riches, or for nobility of descent, — then the infidels resorted to their last chance, that of open rebellion. Their flag was hoisted by Nicomachus Flavianus himself.

In 392, Valentinian II., upon whom the hatred of the rebels was concentrated, was brutally murdered by Arbogastes, the Gallic commander-in-chief of the Western armies, and Eugenius was elected in his place. Eugenius, although brought up as a Christian, was a feeble, superstitious, vacillating man ; and placed, as he found himself, at the head of a revolution, political and religious at the same time, did not at once repudiate his former persuasion. Twice the Senate sent him embassies to obtain the revocation of the decrees of 383 and 391 ; twice he refused to restore to the pagan faction the property of its temples, the privileges of its priests. The third embassy was more successful. Eugenius made a kind of compromise between his conscience and his duty: he made a personal gift to Flavianus and his colleagues of the property seized in 383.

Furnished with such powerful means, the victorious faction indulged at once in an outburst of fanaticism. Every long-forgotten exhibition of pagan ceremonies was conducted, as it were, in the name of the Empire, with gorgeous and triumphal *mise en scène*. They began by the *lustrum* or *sacrificium amburbale* of Rome, a ceremony which had never been celebrated since the time of Aurelian, when the fear of the invasion of the Marcomanni caused him to fortify the capital, materially with the walls which are still in existence, morally and religiously with the *amburbium*.

Next came the *Isia*. During four days Rome enjoyed the ridiculous sight of Flavianus and his partisans mourning over the death of Osiris, and marching in procession, with the hair shaved, in long white woollen clothes, carrying cynocephali in their hands. Next, they resorted to the *Megalesia*, the mysterious worship of Cybele. After being baptized in blood, they carried through the principal thoroughfares the chariot of the goddess, with lions of solid silver. The last celebration mentioned by contemporary writers is that of the *Floralia*, which in ancient times was considered the most profligate and indecent of all festivals.

Against the army of the avenger, Theodosius I., provisions were made worthy of the faction. Images of Hercules Invictus were substituted for the glorious *Labarum* of Constantine, and hundreds of statues of Jupiter, with golden thunderbolts in his hand, were set up on the Alpine passes and military roads through which the army of Theodosius was expected to advance.

The exact spot at which the decisive battle took place in upper Italy is not known; we are ignorant also of its date. Socrates, the historian, mentions the 6th of September, 394; perhaps it was fought two or three days later. One thing is certain : the people of Rome, on the 17th of that month, were still ignorant of the result of the battle. In 1864, while the central crypts of Priscilla's catacombs were being excavated, a tombstone was found, erected in memory of Urania Aurelia by her servant Leontius, and dated *xv kalendas Octobres Nicomacho Flabiano consule* (the 17th of September under the consulship of Flavianus). Now Flavianus had lost his life in battle, and if the event had been known in Rome, when the city was trembling from fear of reaction and revenge, no one would have dared to engrave on marble the name of the leader of polytheism, who had just paid with his life, and with the life of his emperor and supporter, Eugenius, the folly of the rebellion.

Who could properly describe the hopes, the anxieties, the despair, of our Vestals during these terrible days of uncertainty ? See them kneeling before the statue of the goddess, which from hour to hour they expected would be mutilated by the populace ; see them trying to screen and protect behind the rampart of their chaste bodies the fire which, after burning with no interruption for eleven centuries, was in peril of being extinguished forever ! And when the fatal tidings of the defeat of Eugenius came to their knowledge, when the order for their banishment from Vesta's Atrium was issued, did they find time to conceal the sacred tokens of the Roman Empire (as they had done on the occasion of the Gallic war), to save the Palladium from profanation, to destroy every trace, every sign, which could reveal to the outer world the mysteries of their house, the secrets of their institution ? We believe they did ; we believe, as we have said, that the secret was buried with the corpse of the last Vestal. We have no doubt that the destruction of the penetralia, or innermost sanctuary in which the relics were kept, was accomplished by the Vestals

themselves, during the few days that elapsed between the
defeat of Eugenius and the suppression of their order.

The reaction of the victorious party was not violent.
Theodosius named as *commissaire extraordinaire* for Rome
and the Peninsula (*agens vicem præfectorum prætorio et
urbi*) a gentleman of moderate ideas, Fabius Passifilus
Paolinus. He enforced, no doubt, absolute obedience to
imperial decrees concerning paganism, but did not resort to
violence or persecution. One thing is absolutely certain:
when the gates of the Atrium were thrown open to public
curiosity, and the crowd entered the cloisters (confiscated
as the property of the state) and stepped over the threshold
which no man had crossed before without danger of death,
no damage whatever was committed, no injury done either
to the building or to its artistic treasures. In spite of
mediæval lime-burners, in spite of natural decay, in spite of
the excavations of 1497, 1549, and 1785, we have discovered statues and busts, pedestals and inscriptions, bronzes,
glass, and jewelry, of which some were still in their ancient
places.

We are informed by Zosimus, the historian, that some
time after the secularization of the building the young
Princess Serena took possession of a precious necklace
which still ornamented the statue of the goddess; a daring attempt, indeed, which the lady expiated soon after in
a horrible manner. The circumstance is thus described by
the historian: "Rome being surrounded and besieged by
Alaric, the senators began to suspect Serena of secret con-
nivance with the barbarians. The whole assembly, and
even Claudia, the sister of the emperor, were determined
to put her to death, hoping that her execution would induce
the besieger to withdraw. The suspicion, nevertheless, was
unjust and groundless, Serena having never dreamed of

opening the gates to the enemy; but she was doomed to expiate her sacrilege against the gods, as I shall relate presently. When Theodosius II. entered Rome, after the defeat of Eugenius, and priests and priestesses were expelled from temples, and the temples were closed, Serena manifested a desire to enter and examine one of the temples, the shrine of Rhea [Vesta]. Here she was so captivated by the beauty of a necklace that she took it with her own hands from the shoulders of the goddess, and fixed it on her own neck. An old woman, the last surviving Vestal, having witnessed by chance the profanation, cursed the princess, and predicted that sooner or later she would sadly expiate her crime. Serena, at first, took no notice of the awful malediction; but the old Vestal had told the truth, — Serena died by strangulation!"

CHAPTER VII.

THE history of the public libraries in ancient and mediæval Rome has not yet been written, and is only to be gathered in a fragmentary and imperfect way from isolated passages of the classics and from inscriptions. There is no doubt that, in ancient times, special books concerning these libraries were written and published. It appears that one of the eighty volumes which Varro is said to have written was entitled "De Bibliothecis." According to Suidas, Telephus, a school-teacher of Pergamon, issued a volume, a *notitia librorum* in three sections, one of which described minutely the leading libraries of his age. These special works, however, have not come down to us; and the subject which I have selected for this chapter has in a certain sense the attraction of novelty, in spite of the more or less successful attempts made up to the present time to illustrate it, as it were, piecemeal.

The essays on ancient libraries, published between 1606 and 1876 by Lipsius, Saint-Charles, Lomeier, Struve, Lürsen, Petit-Radel, Michaud, and others, are not only incomplete, but almost worthless, because we have gained more knowledge on this subject within the last few years, by the results of the excavations at Pergamon, Pompeii, and Rome, than the authors above named could gather in the space of two centuries and a half. An exception to the rule must be made in favor of a few absolutely recent publications, which, although relating to some special chapters in the history of ancient libraries, have still brought many new important facts and particulars under our knowledge. Such is the essay by Professor Alexander Conze, " Die pergamenische Bibliothek," read at a session of the Royal Prussian Academy of Sciences on December 18, 1884 ; such also is the pamphlet by Carlo Castellani, " Delle Biblioteche nell' Antichità, dai tempi più remoti, alla fine dell' Impero Romano," published at Bologna in 1884. I have myself been a contributor to the history of public libraries, by describing in 1883 the one annexed to the palace of Augustus on the Palatine hill. All these publications, however, have been superseded by the latest work of Commendatore de Rossi, the title of which is " Commentaries on the Origin, History, and Catalogues of the Archives and Libraries of the Holy See."

The first important library in ancient Rome was that which L. Æmilius Paulus, the conqueror of Macedonia, brought over from the palace of King Perseus. Sulla, the dictator, when in Athens, laid his hands on a far richer collection, — on the library, namely, of Apellikon, which had belonged previously to Aristotle himself. The vicissitudes of this library were remarkably strange. Aristotle bequeathed it to his disciple Theophrastus, who largely increased its value and importance by the addition of his own works and of works of contemporaries, secured at a great sacrifice from various lands. Neleus, a disciple and heir to Theophrastus, removed the library to Scepsis in Troas, where it fell to the lot of some ignorant relatives of his. Strabo, the geographer, relates how these relatives, having heard that the king of Pergamon was collecting books for his new library, and fearing for the safety of their own, ·actually buried it underground in a damp place, in which it remained for some time, until Apellikon, of Teos, a Peripatetic philosopher, bought it, and carried the precious collection back to Athens. Strabo adds that Apellikon, when he found many manuscripts of the great master damaged by mildew and dampness, patched them up according to his own fancy, and published them, in course of time, as genuine works of Aristotle. Sulla, however, the purchaser or the usurper of Apellikon's library, seems to have guarded his books so jealously that when Tyrannio, Cicero's librarian, was asked by Andronikos, from Rhodes, to compare some passages in Aristotle's books, he could obtain admission into the sanctum only by bribing Sulla's librarian. Lucullus seems to have been more liberal in placing at the disposal of learned men the literary treasures he had brought home from the kingdom of Pontus. His munificence and kindness to scholars and students is highly praised by Plutarch, who says that Lucullus's house was more a temple of the Muses than a private mansion.

T. Pomponius Atticus, the faithful and intimate friend of Cicero, seems to have put together his library more from love of speculation than of literature. Cicero, in one of his letters (i. 7), reminds him not to forget his request for literary novelties ; in another he asks Atticus to send over two bookbinders, with a supply of parchment, upon which the titles of the books could be written, or rather illuminated, in bright colors. Atticus dispatched two of his cleverest assistants, named Dionysius and Menophilus, and they put the whole of Cicero's library in order so skilfully and neatly that the illustrious orator actually wrote a letter of thanks and praise to his friend Atticus, the bookseller. Strange to say, even at this early stage of bibliophily there were stealers of books. In another letter, addressed by Cicero to P. Sulpicius (*Ad fam.* xiii. 77), he relates

how one of his more trustworthy servants, named Dionysius, had run away with a certain number of valuable
volumes, and begs his correspondent to try to discover the
runaway in Dalmatia, to which province he was thought to
have made his escape. *Res ipsa parva*, Cicero writes in
despair, *sed animi mei dolor magnus est.* I will not describe other private libraries of imperial Rome: the one of
Epaphroditus of Chæronæa, the secretary of Nero; the
one of the poet Persius numbering 700 volumes; the one
of both Plinys, and so forth. I will relate a few anecdotes
only which enable us to enter into the secrets of these private temples of learning.

According to Vitruvius, the apartment of the house used
as a library should be exposed towards the east, not
only because such an exposure is the most convenient
for reading in the early
hours of the morning, but
also because a southern or
a western exposure would
favor the development of
moths and mildew and the
deterioration of books.
These apartments were, as
a rule, of small size.

In 1753, a private library
was discovered at Herculaneum, with bookcases around
the walls, and one bookcase
in the middle of the floor.
Although containing at

Scrolls, Writing Utensils, and Bookcase. Relief from a Roman Sarcophagus. After Mazois, Le Palais de
Scaurus, pl. 8.

least 1,700 volumes or rolls of papyrus, the size of the room did not exceed fifteen feet by twenty. This was due to the fact that libraries were never warmed, even in the depths of winter, either by steam, hot air, or open fires; not only so that the dangers of conflagration might be avoided, but also because heat is injurious to books and bindings, and favors the development of moths. This is the reason why students in our own Vatican library have always been condemned to freeze for four months of the year. The ancients avoided both extremes, freezing and burning, by keeping their literary treasures in small rooms, such as the one discovered at Herculaneum.

With regard to the number of volumes collected in private libraries, it varied, of course, according to the taste and pecuniary resources of the owner. Persius, as I have just remarked, satisfied himself with 700 volumes; Q. Serenus Sammonicus, a physician of the third century, collected not less than 62,000, which afterwards became, by bequest, the property of the crown. As a rule, private collectors were exceedingly fond of rare and costly *éditions de luxe*, of dainty little volumes in which a skilful hand had concentrated the contents of an ordinary folio. Such were the three pocket volumes described by Martial, one of which contained the Iliad and the Odyssey of Homer, one the Metamorphoses of Ovid, one the *opera omnia* of Virgil: —

"Quam brevis immensum cepit membrana Maronem!
Ipsius vultus prima tabella gerit."

We learn from this epigram that the front or title page of these fashionable editions contained, as a rule, the portrait of the author. No wonder that rare or elegant editions would sometimes cost a small fortune. According to Gellius, Aristotle gave a sum corresponding to $3,300 for a copy of Speusippos; Plato, likewise, paid $1,833 for three volumes of Philolaos.

King Ptolemæus Euergetes II., in his efforts to improve the stock of the two royal Alexandrian libraries of the Bruchion and of the Serapaion, sent messengers to Athens to collect new books, and to try to obtain, above all, copies of the tragedies of Æschylos, Sophokles, and Euripides. He promised that as soon as copies of the tragedies could be finished by the Alexandrian amanuenses he would send back to Athens the original, and deposited fifteen Attic talents (or $16,500) as a guarantee for the restitution. It is needless to say that the $16,500 were willingly lost and forfeited; King Ptolemæus kept for himself the originals, and sent back to Athens only the copies.

The great book market, the " Paternoster-row " of ancient Rome, was the Argiletum, a quarter situated between the Roman Forum and the Subura. Here the *librarii* and the *antiquarii*, booksellers and copyists of old works, kept their richly furnished shops, so often mentioned and described by Martial and Horace. On either side of the entrance door there were hung elaborate advertisements, giving the title and the price of literary novelties. Each of the leading booksellers secured the privilege of the works of a leading author. Thus the brothers Sosii were the agents for Horace, and Atrectus and Secundus were the publishers of Martial, Tryphon of Quintilianus, and Dorus of Seneca. Editions of one thousand copies were generally issued, as certified by Pliny the younger, and appeared in various literary markets at the same time : in Athens, where the great meeting-place of bibliophiles was in the orchestra of the theatre of Bacchus; in Alexandria near the Serapaion; in Lyons, and so on. So great was the demand for rare books that spurious ones were freely put in circulation, a practice strongly denounced by Galenus, who complains that he found in book-stalls volumes bearing the name of Hippocrates which had never been written by the great master.

The first public library in Rome was built and opened, about A. U. C. 717, by Asinius Pollio, the brilliant and spirited writer, so much admired by Horace and Catullus. The library was organized in the Atrium Libertatis on the Aventine, one wing being set apart for Greek, one for Latin, literature. Four years later, Augustus determined to carry into execution the project of Julius Cæsar and of his literary counsel, Terentius Varro, to make of public libraries a state institution. He named Pompeius Macer director of the department, and put at his disposal large sums of money collected during the Dalmatian war. The first state public library, opened according to the new programme, was the *Bibliotheca Octaviæ*, so called in honor of Augustus's sister, Octavia; and the first librarian was C. Melissus, of Spoletum. Then followed the *Bibliotheca Palatina Apollinis*, organized by the librarian C. Julius Hyginus, of which library I have already spoken in the chapter on the palace of the Cæsars. Tiberius gave up a wing of his own palace for a third institution of the kind, which, although called by Gellius and Vopiscus *Bibliotheca Tiberiana*, seems to have contained state papers and documents, rather than books.

The fifth imperial library was established by Vespasian in his *Forum Pacis;* the sixth by Trajan in his own forum. This last, the richest and most magnificent in the metropolis, and famous for its collection of *libri elephantini* (books with leaves of ivory), was removed, at the end of the third century, by Diocletian, from Trajan's forum to his own *thermæ* on the Quirinal.

I cannot enter into particulars of the material and scientific organization of these libraries, because I must confine myself to a sketch of their main features. The number of volumes which they contained must have been immense.

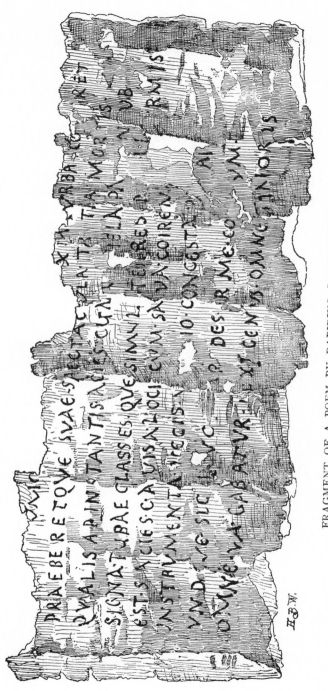

FRAGMENT OF A POEM BY RABIRIUS, 1ST CENTURY, B. C.

Specimen of papyrus MS. from Herculaneum.   In the Museum at Naples.

The two Alexandrian libraries of the Bruchion and of the Serapaion contained 132,800 different works : making a total of more than 400,000 volumes, according to Kallimachos ; 500,000 according to Flavius Josephus ; 700,000 according to Gellius. This difference between the number of works and the number of volumes is easily explained by the fact that it was customary, in ancient times, to subdivide each work into as many volumes as there were chapters or cantos. Thus the Iliad and the Odyssey could form a set of twenty-four volumes each, and the *œuvres complètes* of Aristotle a set of many hundred. In 1821, a papyrus was discovered in the island of Philæ, containing 677 verses from the twenty-fourth canto of the Iliad. The papyrus was eight feet long and ten inches wide. It is easy to understand that this copy of the poem was distributed over forty-one rolls or volumes ; and when we hear authors issuing a prodigious number of volumes, — of Kallimachos, for instance, to whom 800 volumes are attributed ; of Didymos, who is asserted to have written 3,500, — we must never attribute to the phrase the modern meaning, but regard it simply as denoting chapters and paragraphs. From the library of Pergamon, M. Antonius, the triumvir, alone was able to steal 200,000 volumes.

Doubt has been expressed as to whether books could be borrowed from these libraries by private individuals ; that is, for a definite length of time. Beyond doubt, I think, they could, and the librarians could lend books to trustworthy applicants. Aulus Gellius relates that, one day, being the guest of a distinguished friend in a villa near Tibur (Tivoli) a discussion rose amongst the company as to whether the use of iced water, as an ordinary drink in warm weather, was injurious to health. One of the personages present, in condemning the practice most decidedly, quoted the authority of celebrated physicians, and of the great Aristotle himself. As the audience expressed some doubt in regard to Aristotle's opinion, the gentleman ran to the public library of Tibur, borrowed a volume of Aristotle, and read the passage in which the use of iced water was strongly denounced as pernicious. Gellius adds that such was the impression created on the assembly by the words of Aristotle that they all decided at once to give up forever the habit of using water with ice or snow.

To come back to Roman libraries, we are tolerably well acquainted with the circumstances and date of their final destruction. The library of Octavia was destroyed by fire in the year 80, under the rule of Titus. The one in the palace of Tiberius appears to have met with the same fate in the great fire of 191, under the reign of Commodus. The one connected with the temple of Jupiter Capitolinus seems to have been annihilated at the same time from the effects of a thunder-bolt. The famous library of Apollo, on the Palatine, was likewise completely destroyed by fire in the night between the 18th and 19th of March of the year 363. As I have stated already in the fifth chapter, on the authority of Ammianus Marcellinus, such was the violence of the flames that only the Sibylline books could be saved out of many hundred thousand volumes.

We must not believe that these catastrophes could carry with them the complete destruction of ancient Latin literature. Not only hundreds and hundreds of private libraries were left intact, but, before these catastrophes took place, Christian libraries had already been established, and were flourishing in many places. That Christian communities, soon after the propagation of the gospel, provided themselves with libraries pertaining to sacred literature is proved by many passages in the *Acta sincera Martyrum* ("Annals of the Persecution of the Church ") from the time of Nero to that of Julian the Apostate. In the "Acts" of Minucius Felix, from Cirta, now Constantine, it is related how the magistrates went to the house in which the Christians met, and opened the library to seize the books; but *inventa sunt ibi armaria inania.* Alfius Cæciliánus, magistrate of Autun, is said to have found in the local Christian library *epistolas salutatorias,* namely, correspondence between the bishops. Mensurius, Bishop of Carthage, as soon as he heard of the imminent confiscation of the books belonging to the central library of his diocese, concealed *codices pretiosos vel pretiosissimos,* and put in their place *scripta hæreticorum,* which he was only too happy to have seized.

The finest libraries of the first three centuries of Christendom were of course in Rome. They contained not only books and documents of local interest, such as the *gesta martyrum,* the *matriculæ pauperum,* and so forth, but also copies of the official correspondence between the see of Rome and the dioceses of the Christian world. Such was the importance attributed to books in those early days of our faith that, in Christian basilicas, or places of worship, they were kept in the place of honor, next to the episcopal chair. Many of the basilicas which we discover from time to time, especially in the Campagna, have the apse *trichora ;* that is, subdivided into three smaller hemicycles. The reason and the meaning of this peculiar form of an apse was long sought in vain ; but a recent discovery made at Hispalis proves that, of the three hemicycles in those apses, the central one contained the tribunal or episcopal chair, the one on the right the sacred implements, the one on the left the sacred books.

The first building erected in Rome, under the Christian rule, for the study and preservation of books and documents was the *Archivum* (Archives) of Pope Damasus, who occupied the chair of S. Peter between 366 and 384. This just and enterprising Pope, the last representative of good old Roman traditions as regards the magnificence and usefulness of his public structures, selected for the site of his establishment the barracks or stables of the *factio prasina,* the green squadron of charioteers and riders of the Circus Maximus, and modelled it on the pattern of the typical library at Pergamon, of which the Palatine library of Apollo in Rome had been the·worthy rival. He began by raising a basilica, or hall of basilical type, in the centre of the area, which he dedicated to S. Lawrence, and which corresponds to the temple of Minerva Polias in the library of Pergamon, and to the temple of Apollo in that of the Palatine. The hall of S. Lawrence, called still in our days S. Lorenzo in Damaso, or in Prasina, was surrounded by a square portico, into which opened the rooms or cells containing the various departments of the archives and of the library.

A commemorative inscription, composed by Damasus himself, in hexameters, seven in number, and engraved on marble by the skilful hand of Furius Dionysius Philocalus, the Pope's calligraphus, was set in the front of the building, above the main entrance. The text has been discovered in a MS. formerly at Heidelberg, now in the Vatican (n. 833). The first four hexameters do not bring out in a good light the poetical faculties of the worthy pontiff, — in fact, their real meaning has not yet been ascertained; but the last three verses are more intelligible : —

> "Archibis, fateor, volui nova condere tecta;
> Addere præterea dextra lævaque columnas,
> Quæ Damasi teneant proprium per sæcula nomen."

("I have erected this structure for the archives of the Roman church; I have surrounded it with porticoes on

either side ; and I have given to it my name, which I hope
will be remembered for centuries.") These hopes have been
splendidly realized, because, as I have already remarked,
the church of S. Lawrence is still called " in Damaso." I
may add that around the apse of the inner hall there was
another distich of about the same poetical value, the text of
which has been discovered by Commendatore de Rossi in a
manuscript at Verdun : —

> " Hæc Damasus tibi, Christe deus, nova tecta levavi
> Laurenti sæptus martyris auxilio."

(" With the help of S. Lawrence the martyr I have raised,
Lord Christ, this ' hall in Thine honor.") Mention of
Damasus's archives is frequently made in documents of the
fourth and fifth centuries. The official *comptes-rendus* of
the council held in Rome in 369, together with the auto-
graph signatures of the 146 bishops who attended the
sittings, were certainly deposited in them. S. Jerome calls
them *chartarium ecclesiæ Romanæ,* and asserts that the
epistles, circulars, decrees, and constitutions of the popes,
the *regesta Pontificum,* as they were called in later ages,
were shown to everybody, and could be copied on application to the keeper-in-chief. Among those who have consulted the copious documents of the place, we can mention,
on contemporary evidence, Pope Boniface I. in 419 ; Pope
Innocent I. in 412 ; and the members of the Roman synod
of 531.

I need not say that the library of Damasus has long since
disappeared. The first blow aimed at the noble institution
came from the centralization at the Lateran of all the documents connected with the Church, which took place in the
seventh century. Finally the building itself, repaired and
probably disfigured from time to time, was levelled to
the ground, four hundred years ago (1486) by Cardinal

Raphael Riario, nephew of Sixtus IV. A new church was then built, two hundred feet east of the Basilica Damasiana, and incorporated by Riario in his magnificent Palazzo della Cancelleria.

Those who have visited Rome, or are otherwise acquainted with its prominent buildings, will recollect, I am sure, the wonderful court-yard of this Palazzo della Cancelleria, the *chef d'œuvre* of Bramante, resting, as by a miracle of art, on a double tier of light columns of red Egyptian granite. These are the very columns which Pope Damasus carried from Pompey's theatre to his library, and which Cardinal Riario, in 1486, removed from the library to his palace.

During the fifth century we hear no more of literary institutions in Rome. In 535, however, Cassiodorius (commonly miscalled Cassiodorus), then prefect of the Prætorium, induced Pope Agapetus to institute a kind of university or higher school for Christian teaching, and to connect with it a select library. Pope Agapetus yielded to the suggestion, and gave up for the new institution his own paternal house, which stood on the Cœlian, on the Clivus Scauri, the modern picturesque Salita dei SS. Giovanni e Paolo. The library was placed in the principal hall of the house, and above its entrance a commemorative inscription was set up, the text of which has been transmitted to us by the author of the well-known "Codex of Einsiedlen," and which begins as follows: "Here you see assembled, together with Agapetus, the founder of the library, the venerable array of the Fathers of the Church, ready to explain to you the mystic words of the Scriptures."

To understand the meaning of this sentence we must examine, although as briefly as possible, the material and practical organization of Christian libraries, from the fall of the Empire to the Renaissance of classical studies.

There is no doubt that the words of the inscription just quoted refer to the medallions or images of the Fathers of the Church, painted on the frieze of the cases which contained their works. This praiseworthy custom is of very ancient origin. In the chapter on the Palace of the Cæsars, I have mentioned the medallions in *repoussé* work of brass or silver which ornamented the walls of the famous library of Apollo. But without resorting to the testimony of ancient authors, who very often allude to these iconographic galleries connected with public or private libraries, I can draw upon my own experience, and describe an ancient private library which I have seen with my own eyes. I think I am the only living man of letters who can boast of

Lararium, or private chapel discovered in the Via dello Statuto, 1883.

having been favored by chance with such rare good fortune. The discovery took place in December, 1883. A new road, the Via dello Statuto, was then in course of construction between the Piazza Vittorio Emmanuele, on the Esquiline, and the Via Cavour, in the Subura.   Not far

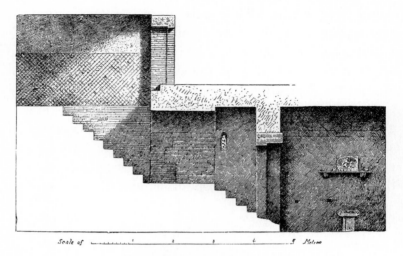

Crypt of Mithras discovered in the Via dello Statuto.

from the northeast corner of the church of S. Martino ai Monti, the remains of a private house began to appear in the trench, of which house some apartments were in the most wonderful state of preservation; others had been robbed even of their marble and mosaic pavements.   To the intact portion of the building belongs — to cite only one instance — the *lararium*, or domestic chapel, and the *Mithræum* (an underground cell, in which the secret mysteries of Mithras were performed), represented in the accompanying plates.   In the chapel, besides the statue of Fortune, occupying the *place d'honneur*, there were some seventeen statuettes and busts of domestic divinities still standing upright on the side shelves.   In the *Mithræum* there were — there are still, because we have saved the place from destruction, and added it to the curiosities of Rome —

the remnant of the seven torches, that is to say of sticks of fir-wood coated with tar, which were kept burning before the image of Mithras Tauroktonos. The ruined apartments, from which no more discoveries were expected, and the excavation of which we did not watch with the same anxiety as we did that of the others, occupied the northern portion of the atrium, and consisted mostly of bath-rooms. I was struck, one afternoon, with the appearance of a rather

MITHRAS TAUROKTONOS.
Marble group recently discovered on the Esquiline.

spacious hall, the walls of which were plain and unornamented up to a certain height, but beautifully decorated above in stucco work. The decoration consisted of fluted pilasters, five feet apart from centre to centre, enclosing a plain square surface, in the middle of which there were medallions, also in stucco work, two feet in diameter. As always happens in these cases, the frame was the only well-preserved portion of the medallions. Of the images surrounded by the frames, of the medallions themselves, absolutely nothing was left *in situ* except a few fragments piled up at the foot of the wall, which, however, could be identified as having been representations of human faces. My hope that at last, after fifteen years of excavations, I had succeeded in discovering a library, was confirmed beyond any doubt by a legend written, or rather painted, in bright red color on one of the frames. There was but one name,

APOLLONIVS THYAN...

but this name told more plainly the purpose of the apart ment than if I had discovered there the actual book-shelves and their contents.

The form, disposition, and ornamentation of book-shelves and book-cases, which the ancients called *armaria,* are well known from the authentic description we possess of the library of S. Isidorus at Hispalis. This library was divided into classes or departments of geography, natural philosophy, theology, and so forth. The books of each class were neatly arranged in separate *armaria,* on the frieze of which the portraits of the most famous authors were painted, together with an epigram explaining what the contents of the *armaria* were. On the book-case containing works on law there were the portraits of the famous jurisconsults Gaius and Paul, and of the Emperor Theodosius, the author of the Codex Theodosianus. The legend read as follows : —

> " Conditur hic juris series amplissima legum
> Veridico latium quæ regit ore forum."

On the book-case containing historical works were the portrait of Eusebius and Orosius, with the legend : —

> " Historias rerum et transacti tempora sæcli
> Condita membranis hæc simul arca gerit."

Likewise, on the *armarium* set apart for works on medicine there were four pictures or medallions, representing Hippocrates, Galenus (misnamed Gallienus), and the brother saints Cosmas and Damianus, with the epigram : —

> " Quos claros orbe celebrat medicina magistros,
> Hos præsens pictos signat imago viros."

The text of the other inscriptions of this well-organized library can be found in the manuscript formerly at Lauresheim, now in the Vatican (No. 1877). It appears from what I have said that the founders of Christian libraries in Rome and elsewhere followed faithfully the clas-

The Vatican Library, showing style and arrangement of book-cases in ancient Rome.

sic prototypes, not only in the general architecture of their buildings, but also in the minute details of interior arrangement; and the illustration above shows the force of tradition in such matters, the arrangement of the Vatican library to-day being precisely that of the ancients.

The portraits of learned men were not always painted on the wood of the cases or on the plaster of the walls; there was an endless variety of arrangement. In a letter addressed to Eucherius, Bishop of Lyons, by Rusticus, Bishop of Narbonne, at the beginning of the fifth century, mention is made of a library in which Rusticus himself had studied classic literature in his younger years.   In this library, exclusively devoted *sæcularibus litteris*, there were many portraits of orators and poets in mosaic (*expressa lapillis*), or in terra-cotta (*formata*), or in a kind of pastel (*ceris discoloribus*), and each image was accompanied by a biographical inscription.

But the ancients by no means confined themselves to simple medallions, in their desire to honor the memory of learned men ; they actually set up life-size statues in the vestibules and porticoes of their libraries, and *hermæ* or busts in the inner halls.   The taste for this display of literary luxury was introduced into Rome in the Augustan era, by Asinius Pollio.   *Asinius Pollio primus Romæ bibliothecas publicavit* (græcam atque latinam) *additis auctorum imaginibus in atrio*.   In a fragmentary inscription discovered by Stevenson at Bolsena four years ago, the will of a gentleman is praised, who had bequeathed to his Volsinian fellow-citizens *bibliothecam cum libris et statuis*, with the books and statues.   Statues and busts that have belonged to libraries can easily be recognized, at least in some cases, because the list of the *œuvres complètes* of the authors they represent is generally engraved on the base of the bust, or on the plinth of the statue.   Monuments of this kind, such as the famous Euripides of the villa Albani, have been illustrated by Ennio Quirino Visconti in the "Iconografia Greca," by Winckelmann in the " Monumenti Inediti," and quite recently by Comparetti and Di Petra in their volume on the " Villa dei Pisoni " and its library.

In spite of the decadence of art and refinement, in spite of the poverty of the age, the Christians followed classic traditions even in this particular, as we see from the famous life-size sitting statue of S. Hippolytus, doctor of the Church and martyr, on the plinth of which the catalogue of his works is engraved in minute Greek letters. The importance of this document has always been considered so great that when in 1756 the two learned brothers, Stephen Evodius and Joseph Simon Assemani, by order of Benedict XIV., published the first volume of the catalogue of the Vatican library, they began the preface with the list of S. Hippolytus, considering it as the oldest specimen of an index of sacred literature.

Books were not placed upright on the shelves, as with us, but horizontally. The first illumination of the volume offered by the Abbot Ceolfridus to the Holy See in 716, now in the Biblioteca Laurenziana at Florence, of which book I shall speak again presently, represents an *armarium* with open shutters, and with the books lying horizontally on the shelves. The same particular is represented in one of the mosaics of S. Apollinare in Classe at Ravenna.

Church and house of S. Gregory.

I have mentioned above the name of Cassiodorius as the one who suggested to Pope Agapetus the establishment of a Christian university on the Cœlian, an institution which was enlarged and improved by S. Gregory the Great, and which has in a certain measure come down to our age, as the library of the convent of S. Gregorio at Monte Celio. Tired of his political career, Cassiodorius left the wicked world in 536, and retired to one of the most secluded spots in Calabria, to devote himself to monastic life; I ought to say, rather, to devote himself to his passion for rare books and well-organized libraries. The one he founded in his Calabrian monastery of Vivarium is spoken of so frequently and so passionately in his book, " De Institutione Divinarum Litterarum," that we know every particular connected with it. I shall mention one or two.

In the first place, great care and taste were displayed in binding the volumes; a body of *docti artifices*, clever bookbinders, was attached to the establishment, and a collection of models and specimens was placed at their disposition for instruction.

In the second place, some wonderful lamps were contrived for the assistance of students and copyists in their nocturnal work. Cassiodorius describes them as *mechanicas lucernas quæ, humano ministerio cessante, prolixe custodirent uberrimi luminis claritatem* (mechanical lamps, which, even when left entirely to themselves, would continue to shine brilliantly for many hours), — lamps, I suppose, built on the *modérateur* or " Carcel " principle.

In the third place, the library was furnished with sundials and clepsydræ, *horologium solare* and *aquatile*, to regulate the hours of study and work by day or night, in clear or cloudy weather.

Lastly, a large staff of amanuenses and copyists, called

antiquarii in classical times, was kept at work without interruption, like the printing departments of our libraries. A. Reiffersheid shows, in a pamphlet published at Breslau in 1882, what an incredible number of books was put in circulation by Cassiodorius at Vivarium, and by his friend Eugippius at the *cœnobium Lucullianum*, near Naples. Their joint literary productions and copies of first-rate books inundated not only lower and central Italy, but even the African bishoprics, as proved by the epistles of S. Fulgentius to Eugippius.

As to catalogues, in the strict modern sense of the word, we know they must have existed, but we have no positive evidence about them, except, perhaps, the unique passage in the ninth chapter of Seneca " De Tranquillitate," in which he mentions *voluminum frontes*, frontispieces ; *titulos*, titles ; and *bibliothecarum indices*, real catalogues. The titles, as Cicero describes them, were beautifully illuminated on a small piece of parchment, and pasted on the back of the volume. The oldest catalogue of a Christian library is that inserted by Eusebius in the third book of the life of Pamphilus. Others, anterior to the thirteenth century, have been quite recently collected and edited at Bonn by Professor Gustav Becker, beginning with the catalogue of the Fontanelles library, written in 745. The series of Professor Becker, although numbering 136 catalogues, is far from complete, and many important documents have escaped his attention. Such are, for instance, the index of books offered to the church of S. Clement in Rome, engraved on a marble slab in the vestibule of the church itself ; the catalogue of the Cluny library, the first divided according to subjects ; those of Anchin and Puy, the first in which books are regularly numbered, and so forth. But, as the proverb says, *facile est inventis addere*.

An interesting paper might be written on the exchange of manuscripts between Rome and the newly converted  inhabitants of remote provinces, especially those of Anglo-Saxon countries. In 601, Pope Gregory the Great sent to S. Austin, then preaching the gospel in the British Isles, *plurimos codices*, of which only two seem to have come down to us, namely, the two *evangeliaria* preserved, one in the Cambridge, one in the Bodleian, library. Wanley, Westwood, Goodwin, and Garrucci agree in recognizing these two volumes as unique, rather than rare, specimens of the sixth-century palæography. There is a third volume, which has long been considered as belonging to the set sent by Gregory to S. Austin, a *psalterium* now in the British Museum library, described on p. 8, Part II., of the catalogue printed in 1884. Bond, Thompson, Warner, and Delisle, however, have proved beyond dispute that the volume must have been written by an Anglo-Saxon amanuensis, towards the end of the eighth century, and is, accordingly, two hundred years younger than the *evangeliaria* of Oxford and Cambridge.

Demands for books from the Gallic, Spanish, and Alexandrine churches were not only taken into consideration at Rome, but granted as liberally as the resources of the archives and library of the Holy See would permit. Apostles and missionaries, sowing the good seed, especially in the northern regions of Europe, would constantly beg for copies of the sacred books. In 649, Amandus, Bishop of Trajectum, sent a messenger to Pope Martin I. to obtain duplicates from the pontifical library. The answer of the Pope was : " Our library is absolutely exhausted, and we could not give your messenger a single duplicate. We authorized him, however, to transcribe and copy some of them himself, but he left Rome in a hurry." The reason why no duplicates could be obtained is evident. In 649, the great Roman Council was assembled, and all available copies in the library had been distributed among the bishops, to help them in their inquiries about the heresy of the Monothelites.

The founders of monasteries in England showed a real passion for books and libraries, and in the course of the seventh century they did not spare time, labor, or money in securing rare manuscripts from Rome. Bede, in his biographies of abbots, relates how one of them, named Benedict or Biscopus, travelled the whole distance to Rome not less than five times between the years 653 and 684, for the purpose of increasing the literary supply of his abbey. And if we consider how difficult, fatiguing, disagreeable, and even dangerous a journey between the British Islands and Italy must have been in those days of anarchy and barbarism, we can appreciate the intensity of Benedict's passion for beautiful and costly volumes. From his third pilgrimage, in 671, he brought back a set of theological works *vel pretio emptos vel dono largitos*, bought of copyists or received as presents; on his fourth journey, in 678, he increased his collection with an "innumerable quantity of books in literature;" whereas the fifth journey was devoted again to the purchase of sacred and theological treatises. Even on his death-bed he could think of nothing but his library, and his last words were of earnest entreaty to his successor to preserve and enlarge his *copiosissima et nobilissima bibliotheca*, of which the *chef d'œuvre* seems to have been a codex of geography, *mirandi operis*, of marvellous workmanship, bought, like the others, in Rome.

The library contained also a valuable collection of pictures, of holy images, as Bede says, purchased during the fourth and fifth journeys. The most noticeable was a set of illustrations representing the *concordia veteris et novi testamenti*, the harmony between the old and the new testaments: for instance, Isaac carrying on his shoulder the fagots for his immolation, and our Lord carrying the cross for his crucifixion. This is, as far as we can judge, the earliest, or at least one of the earliest, records of a Bible illustrated with parallel pictures from both testaments. These Bibles, popularized at first by the work of hand and pencil, later on by the help of wood-cuts, are better known under the name of *Bibliæ pauperum*.

Rome was the centre of this sort of literary and artistic industry; and there is no doubt that the earliest fresco-paintings in Anglo - Saxon churches and cloisters, representing Christ, the Virgin Mary, the Apostles, and so forth, were copied from models sent from Rome. To this class of original drawings belongs the codex of Cambridge, already mentioned, splendidly ornamented with illustrations of evangelical history, designed in Rome.

The successor of Benedict, named Ceolfrid, shared his passion for valuable manuscripts. He brought over from Italy a "pandect" of the sacred text, of which he ordered three copies to be made; and, being already far advanced in years, he undertook another journey to Rome to offer to the library of the Holy See the best of the three copies. Death overtaking him, near Lyons, in the spring of 716, his disciples and followers pursued the journey, and presented the precious volume, containing the translation of S. Jerome, to the Pope. The volume still exists; it is preserved in the Biblioteca Laurenziana at Florence, to which it was carried from the monastery of Monte Amiata.

There is no doubt that the direct descent of Roman libraries and the transmission of classic and religious books from age to age, from generation to generation, can be followed uninterruptedly from the fall of the Empire down to the middle of the thirteenth century. We do not know how

Remains of the Turris Cartularia.

long the great library and central archives of Pope Damasus existed as a special and individual institution; we know, however, that as early as the eighth century the Lateran pontifical palace became the centre of the literary, historical, and religious libraries and archives belonging to the Holy See. There they remained undisturbed until the tenth century, in the course of which the most precious documents were transferred to a stronghold, especially built for the purpose, in the Turris Cartularia, a massive tower, to which the triumphal arch of Titus served as a buttress.[1]

The only means we possess of following the life and

---

[1] This Turris Cartularia, or "Tower of the Archives," was dismantled at the beginning of the present century. What remains of its foundations is represented in the accompanying illustration.

vicissitudes of this invaluable collection of sacred and classic books, in an age the history of which is absolutely obscure and fragmentary, are the *regesta Pontificum*; that is to say, the collection of official documents, epistles, constitutions, and canons issued by each Pope. The *regesta* are known to have existed, as a complete series and without any interruption, from the remotest ages down to the middle of the thirteenth century. Honorius III., who died in 1227, is the very last Pope who saw the volumes, who studied them carefully, and who makes express mention of them. None of his successors, so far as we can discover, mentions the library and the archives as an existing institution.

Not one of the volumes, of the documents, of the *regesta*, belonging to the incomparable collection formerly in the buildings of Damasus, then in the Lateran, and lastly in the Turris Cartularia, has escaped destruction, — not one has come down to us! Before the present learned and enterprising pontiff, Leo XIII., threw open to everybody the secret archives of the Vatican, many of us believed that the long-lost documents might be discovered there, in that mysterious den, which was inexorably closed to scholars, from the time of Pope Eugenius IV. to the time of Pope Pius IX. Our expectation has been completely disappointed: not a trace, not a particle, of the old collection has been found as yet, and most likely none ever will be. Therefore we are forced to believe that the catastrophe by which the collection was destroyed, and by which the link connecting modern with ancient libraries was severed, must have taken place soon after the death of Pope Honorius III.; but we are absolutely ignorant of the precise date, the nature, the details, of the catastrophe. The only plausible explanation which we can offer is to be found in the history of the Turris Cartularia itself. This strong-

hold, built by the Frangipani family, as a detached work
of their Palatine headquarters, and used by the Popes as
a safe receptacle for their state . documents, was handed
over to the imperial faction in 1244. Its contents were
doubtless burnt, or otherwise destroyed, out of spite and
revenge towards the Popes and their faithful supporters,
the Frangipani family.

CHAPTER VIII.

THE POLICE AND FIRE DEPARTMENT OF ANCIENT ROME.

AMONG the many points of resemblance which one discovers in comparing the leading features of life in ancient Rome and modern London, that concerning the organization of the police is perhaps the most striking. Regular troops, in the modern sense of the word, infantry as well as cavalry, were not allowed to take up permanent quarters in Rome, and so are they excluded from London; they were garrisoned within a certain distance of the metropolis, ready to answer any sudden call in case of extraordinary emergencies. The only bodies of troops tolerated in Rome were those attached to the person and to the special service of the emperor: the prætorian guard, corresponding to our European *gardes impériales et royales*, and a few select horsemen, called in ancient times *equites singulares;* in modern, *cent-gardes*, or horse-guards, or *cuirassiers du roi*. These men, however, prætorians as well as *equites singulares*, had nothing to do with the maintenance of public order; in fact, they were decidedly against it, and their barracks were nothing but hot-beds of disturbance and riot. The protection of the great metropolis was intrusted to a select body of constables, 7,500 in number; a number which corresponds very well to the 9,000 policemen of modern London. The only difference in the organization of the two bodies is that the Roman *vigiles* — this was their official name — had to perform at the same time the duties of firemen and policemen; and neither duty was a sinecure, as we shall see in the course of the present chapter.

Ancient Rome has never enjoyed a good name for its respect of private property and the personal security of citizens. The principal cause of disorder is to be found in the almost incomprehensible fact that the metropolis, in which all the wealth, luxury, and comfort of the world was concentrated, was kept in perfect darkness at night! How this could have happened in such a civilized age — why the plain, simple idea of a system of public illumination was not conceived and adopted — is a mystery hard to solve. Yet excavations at Pompeii, Ostia, and other well-preserved antique cities fully confirm the fact. Not a trace of a bracket fixed to the front of a house, or of a rope or small chain drawn across the street to support lamps or lanterns, has as yet been found, and probably none ever will be. People took advantage of moonlight when the moon illuminated the streets; but during quite half of the year, and when the silvery satellite was veiled by clouds, they made use of lanterns, the frame of which was generally of bronze, the other part of glass, or of thin plates of horn, or of oiled linen. People of the lower classes carried lanterns themselves; gentlemen and noblemen were preceded in their nocturnal strolls by a valet or slave, called by Cicero *laternarius*, and by Suetonius *servus prælucens*, who lighted their path, sometimes with a lantern, sometimes with a torch.

In consequence of this state of things, as soon as the twilight had vanished, shopmen and merchants were obliged, for safety, to lock up their premises; and the solitary streets, plunged in darkness, wore a sinister look, and became dangerous for the passer-by. The shop and house doors were closed in a very ingenious way, inwards or outwards, according to the requirements of the case. The doors were composed of three or four pieces of solid board, sometimes of a double thickness, and these pieces were made to slide, one after the other, in a groove made for the purpose in the threshold and the architrave; then a cross-bolt, the two ends of which were inserted in hollows sunk in both the door-posts, was drawn from the inside. When the door was opened and fastened from the outside, locks and keys were made use of, the arrangement of which is now perfectly well known, since Giuseppe Fiorelli, formerly director of excavations at Pompeii, and now general director of antiquities in the kingdom of Italy, conceived the happy idea of taking plaster casts of the impressions left by Pompeian doors on the soft volcanic ashes under which that lovely city was buried.

So precarious were the conditions of public security in Rome, and so great the audacity of burglars, that even windows were locked at night, as described by Pliny the elder, or else protected by railings, — a custom which has prevailed down to our own age, and which gives to the stately palaces of modern Rome the aspect of prisons. I need not say that house-doors were watched day and night, especially at night, by the *ostiarius*, or janitor, who carried a staff in his hands. The janitor, generally assisted by a dog, could be called from the outside by ringing a bell. In early times, and even during the Empire, although an exception to the ordinary rule, the attendance of the janitor was sometimes secured by fastening him by a chain to the entrance. All these precautions were not deemed super-fluous for the protection of private property.

Rome and the Campagna have been afflicted, from time immemorial, by two plagues, mendicity and brigandage, which after having infected the district with more or less violence for nearly twenty centuries, have been finally thoroughly extirpated by the Italian national government, and relegated to a place among the legends of the past.

Mendicity was practised at certain definite points as a means of dragging out an idle existence. In the city, beggars haunted chiefly the bridges and the gates; that is to say, they haunted places the narrowness of which would sometimes stop, and always slacken, traffic, and expose passers-by to the full importunity and impudence of the brotherhood. For the same reason they took up their abode on the *clivi*, or steep ascents of public roads in the Campagna, where they were sure that even the fastest horses and the lightest carriages would be obliged to slacken their speed. Famous amongst all was the Clivus Aricinus, a steep gradient of the Appian Way, just outside the gates of Aricia, fifteen miles from Rome, which is represented below. On this

The Clivus Aricinus. Showing the viaduct built by Pius IX, 1852.

ill-famed slope swarms of filthy professional beggars used to take up their station, to tax the benevolence of travellers with their importunities. They actually followed riders and drivers up the hill, harassing them with their vociferations, until the victims, to rescue themselves from such a persecution, would throw a handful of coins among the

dirty crew, which ransom would make them stop and fight
one another, and leave the traveller alone.   On these occasions wonders could be seen, — the blind recovering eyesight, the crippled and paralytic recovering the use of their
limbs, and the like, — scenes and incidents which the traveller in modern Spain, or in Italy of fifteen years ago, has
certainly witnessed.

As regards the exploits of robbers, highwaymen, and
brigands, accounts have been left by ancient writers, and
are sometimes engraved on the tombstones of the victims.
Travelling on the great consular roads of Italy was always
made disagreeable by publicans, or toll and octroi collectors, and by innkeepers insatiable of undue gain, and sometimes made dangerous on account of the precarious conditions of public security.   There were regular associations
of brigands in central and southern Italy, and also in Sardinia, against which the Emperor Tiberius dispatched bands
of Jews, who had received military drill, hoping that the
two contending parties would destroy each other.   The
geographer Strabo mentions other such associations as
flourishing in Corsica, Pamphylia, and Pisidia.   In consequence of this state of things, timid or prudent travellers
were obliged to place themselves under the protection of
the escort accompanying distinguished magistrates, ambassadors, governors, proconsuls, and other public officials.

In Italy, the greatest insecurity prevailed, as a rule, at
the end of civil wars.   Even the short journey from Rome
to Tibur was at times extremely insecure.   Augustus, at
the very beginning of his reign, attempted to stop the evil,
and covered the whole Empire with a network of military
and police stations, the number of which was largely increased by Tiberius, his successor to the throne.   The highwaymen caught by these patrols were executed on the spot,

without ceremony, or else were held prisoners to be devoured by wild beasts at the next show in the amphitheatre. The audacity of these men was such that sometimes they would ride to the very gates of the city, and make there a *razzia* of horses and beasts of burden. The Pontine marshes and the dense forest near Cumæ, called the *Silva Galli-naria*, were considered the most dangerous of all to cross. Juvenal says that the expeditions sent, under extraordinary circumstances, to chase the brigands from their haunts succeeded in restoring security for the time being; but as soon as the troops were withdrawn the hydra would again raise its head. The disturbances which usually followed the election of an emperor always caused a revival of brigandage. When Septimius Severus, in his general reform of the Roman military system, caused the prætorian soldiers, or body-guard, to be drafted from the provinces watered by the Rhine and the Danube, instead of Italy, as had been done before, Italian youths, inclined naturally to military life, gave themselves up to brigandage, as a means of enjoying their favorite sport of war. The disaffection of the younger generation, thus neglected by Septimius Severus, reached such a point that an intrepid chief, Felix Bulla, succeeded in putting the whole of Italy to ransom for two years, crossing it from end to end and from sea to sea, at the head of an army of six hundred brigands. Betrayed, finally, by the woman he loved, he was caught by the police, and ended his adventurous career in the arena, devoured by wild beasts, amidst the applause of a numberless multitude.

Ancient epitaphs very often speak of persons murdered in encounters with brigands. I have described in the third chapter the assault committed by Mauritanian robbers on Nonius Datus, an officer of the engineers of the third legion, on his way from Lambæse to Saldæ. A tombstone discovered near Oteyza, Spain, speaks of the murder of a Roman knight, only twenty years of age, named Calætus. Another, discovered on the bank of the Danube, commemorates L. Julius Bassus, president of the town council of Drobeta, and quæstor, *interfectus a latronibus*. His death was avenged by a brother, named Julius Valerianus. Three sons, likewise, in an inscription discovered in the same province of Mœsia, state that they had revenged the murder of their mother. The most interesting of these epitaphs, however, is an inscription discovered sixteen years ago, near the farm of La Magliana, six miles from Rome, on the high road to Porto. This tombstone, which belongs to the beginning of the third century of our era, describes how a schoolmaster, named Julius Timotheus, only twenty-eight years old, and held in high estimation in Rome, having gone out for an excursion on the Via Campana with seven of his pupils, fell into an ambush, and was murdered by the thieves, together with his young companions. This wholesale slaughter, accomplished almost within sight of the walls, and on the line of the great traffic between Rome and its harbor (Portus Augusti), must have created an intense excitement in the capital, and must have given occasion to some extraordinary measures towards the extirpation of the evil, inasmuch as I have not been able to find, either in books or in inscriptions, any further accounts of acts of brigandage, in the neighborhood of Rome, after the beginning of the third century.

Another source of annoyance, and, in some cases, of real personal danger, came from meeting, in the dark streets, parties of fashionable youths returning home from a late debauch. Woe to the peaceful and unoffending father of a family, who chanced to meet one of these drunken parties in the darkness! The poor man was insulted, beaten, wounded, and occasionally his clothes were torn off, so that he would have remained exposed to the full violence of the winter frost.

One peculiarity of ancient Rome, common, I dare say, to all large capitals not belonging to the Anglo-Saxon race, was the perfect accordance of all classes of citizens in evading, as much as they could, police regulations: for instance, those concerning the protection of passers from the fall of tiles and flower-pots, the free use of the city streets, and the proper construction of scaffoldings and new structures of every kind. That citizens were seriously injured and even killed by the accidental fall of pots from window-gardens, and of tiles from roofs not kept in proper order, is a fact positively asserted by Juvenal and Gaius. I shall describe in the tenth chapter the obstructions which made traffic almost impossible in the narrow and tortuous streets of Rome, in spite of edicts promulgated by the magistrates to stop this evil. As regards accidents occasioned by the fall of scaffoldings and of hurriedly-built structures, I shall quote one instance, which is connected, besides, with another source of public disturbances and riots, — the insane passion of the populace for races and jockeys, and for special horses and special jockeys, a passion which often brought on bloody encounters.

Before the reign of Domitian, the *agitatores circenses*, or charioteers of the circus, a state institution, magnificently lodged, fed, and endowed, were divided into four squadrons or *factions*, named *albata*, *prasina*, *russata*, and *veneta*, from the white, green, red, or blue color of the caps and jackets of their champions. Domitian increased the number of squadrons to six, by the addition of the *factio aurata*, the "golden," and of the *factio purpurea*, the "pur-

ple," organized and supported from the inexhaustible resources of the privy purse. The first bad example of fanaticism for a special squadron or color was set by the
emperors themselves. Tacitus says that Vitellius put the
care of riders before that of the government. Caligula was
such an ardent partisan and supporter of the squadron of
the greens that he spent the greater portion of his time in
their stables, rioting with them until a late hour of the
night. Sometimes one squadron would remain popular and
enjoy the favor and partiality of the turbulent crowds for
a period of several years. From the time of Caligula to
the end of the empire of Hadrian, the greens always maintained supremacy, never losing the confidence and affection
of the public. This fact makes us understand better the
following passage in the ninth satire of Juvenal : " The
whole of Rome has flocked to the circus to-day, and the up-
roar of the crowd can be heard miles away. I understand
from this that the greens have, as usual, won the day;
otherwise I should see the city in deep mourning, just as
if the consuls had been slain over again in the battle-field
of Cannæ." With good reason Juvenal himself asserts that
one jockey alone could make in a short time one hundred-
fold the income of a celebrated lawyer, — *centum patri-
monia causidicorum*.

They amassed their prodigious fortunes in two ways:
first, by getting the prizes established for the different races;
secondly, by taking their share in betting, and, I dare say,
by conspiring with book-makers. On May 20, 1878, we
discovered, not far from the stables of the green squadron
at S. Lorenzo in Damaso (*in prasina*), a pedestal dedicated
to a jockey of African extraction, named Crescens. According to the inscription on this pedestal, Crescens, when
only twenty-two years old, had already gained 1,558,346

MOSAIC SHOWING THE CIRCUS GAMES.

Found at Gerona, Spain, 1884.

sestertii, a sum equal to $65,000. The greatest of Roman jockeys, the William Archer of classic times, the famous Diocles, left to his son a fortune of 35,863,120 sestertii, equivalent to $1,250,000.

Horses were not less beloved than their riders. Inscriptions, mosaic pictures, bronzes, frescoes, have not only perpetuated their names and valiant deeds, but have transmitted to us even their effigies. Here is a copy of the precious mosaic discovered near Gerona, Spain, in 1884, representing a chariot-race, with the names of the champions inscribed near each group of runners. The four thoroughbreds with which the young Crescens won his first race were called Circius, Acceptor, Delicatus, Cotinus. In destroying the towers of Sixtus IV., which flanked the Porta del Popolo, we found some bas-reliefs, representing the five horses, Palmatus, Danaus, Ocean, Victor, Vindex, which bas-reliefs had been removed by the Pope from the tomb of the famous champion, Publius Ælius Gutta Calpurnianus.

Inscription from the pedestal of the jockey Crescens.

The names and effigies of these runners were cut upon various domestic utensils, objects of daily use, and even children's toys. In our storerooms in the Capitoline museum, we keep a couple of leaden wheels of a very small cart, evidently the toy of a child two or three years of age, on the circumference of which the names of famous horses and jockeys are engraved.   In Rome, in the Via Porta S. Lorenzo, and at Ostia, in the Via delle Pistrine, I have myself found two handles of pocket-knives, of bone, both ornamented with the head and name of a certain horse, Nereos, and of his jockey Euprepes, *the beautiful.*

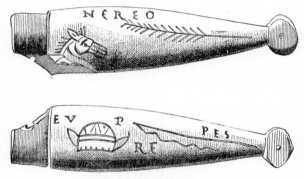

Pocket-knife of Euprepes.

Fancy what an incredible amount of labor fell upon the poor Roman policemen on race days, and generally on days of popular entertainments in theatres, amphitheatres, circuses, and the stadium.   The Circus Maximus alone could accommodate 285,000 spectators, all comfortably seated; the Circus Flaminius, 150,000, and the Colosseum, 87,000. This mania for spectacular shows, and the assemblage of these gigantic crowds, very often gave occasion to not less gigantic catastrophes, in comparison with which the recent ones of the Ring Theatre at Vienna, of Nice, Marseilles, Brooklyn, the Opéra Comique in Paris, and Exeter, sink into insignificance.   Tacitus relates that, in the year 27 after

Christ, a certain Atilius, a man sprung from the lowest classes of the city, obtained the right of building a temporary wooden amphitheatre near Fidenæ, now Castel Giubileo, five miles outside the Porta Salaria. As, under Tiberius, athletic and gladiatorial shows had become quite a rare occurrence, on account of the indifference, even antipathy which the emperor himself felt towards them, an enormous crowd met at Fidenæ, to enjoy the novelty of the exhibition, and at the same time to enjoy an excursion up the green valley of the Tiber. These spectators had scarcely taken their seats on the wooden steps, when, in a moment, and with a terrific crash, the whole structure gave way, and buried under its ruins the entire assembly. Tacitus, who had at his disposal and who consulted the official reports of the police, assures us that the number of dead and wounded amounted to 50,000. The town was struck with profound terror and amazement. Noblemen turned their palaces into hospitals. Matrons and maidens of the aristocracy took the office of nurses. "We had an example in those eventful days," says the historian, "of the fine old times, when, after a great battle, the town was turned into one affectionate family, in which the able portion gave up all their time and attention to the disabled." The Senate made new regulations for the safety of public places of entertainment; generous subscriptions came to the relief of the sufferers; and, to make the similarity with modern cases more perfect, just as the author of the Marseilles catastrophe was fined only a few hundred francs, so Atilius, the author of the Fidenæ slaughter, was only banished from Rome and from Italy.

There is no doubt that all the evils and accidents I have described must have kept the vigiles constantly on the *qui vive ;* still, I have not yet mentioned their principal duty and labor, as firemen. I do not think there has ever been a town so often and so thoroughly purified by fire as ancient Rome was. That conflagrations on a large scale should have occurred in the first two or three centuries of its life was natural enough, since its houses were mostly of timber and covered with thatched roofs. I admit also the possibility of great fires after the city, burnt down and destroyed by the Gauls A. U. C. 364, was reconstructed with stone and brick, because, as soon as those barbaric hordes were swept from the region of the Seven Hills by Camillus, the only care and solicitude of the *patres patriæ* was that the city should be rebuilt quickly, not that it should be rebuilt regularly and well. Livy relates that as soon as the decisive words of the centurio, *hic manebimus optime,* were heard through the Forum, the populace at once gave up the idea of migrating to Veii, and that *antiquata lege promiscue urbs ædificari cœpta ;* they began to rebuild their houses, with no consideration whatever for regularity, for the straight line, or for æsthetic and sanitary laws. Bricks and tiles were distributed gratuitously ; every one was allowed to quarry stones wherever they could be obtained, and to establish lime-kilns in the very heart of the city. The eagerness to gain the prize promised to those who would complete their constructions in twelve months' time made them despise the straight line in the new streets and lanes ; and the desire of gaining more ground caused them to increase the size of the houses at the expense of that of the streets. "This is the reason," Livy concludes, "why the drains, which before the fire of the Gauls ran under public land, now run irregularly under private property ; this is also the reason why the plan of Rome is more erratic than that of any other great city."

No wonder that, under such adverse circumstances, we hear of fires sweeping periodically over whole quarters of the capital. Such was the fire described by Livy in chapter twenty-seven of the twenty-sixth book, by which all the shops and houses surrounding the Forum, the palace of the high-priest, the fish-market, and the region of the Lautumiæ, were levelled to the ground; such also was the fire described by Livy in chapter twenty-six of his forty-seventh book, a fire by which the region of the Forum Boarium, from the modern Piazza Montanara to the foot of the Aventine, was totally devastated. I need not speak of the most fearful of all conflagrations, — of the conflagration which, under Nero, in the year 65 of our era, annihilated two thirds of the great metropolis, — because I have had occasion to describe it in my fifth chapter, on "The Palace of the Cæsars."

In all these reports of fires, however, there is one thing which I fail to understand, and that is how fire could have attacked, injured, or altogether destroyed edifices built of marble and bronze, without a particle of timber or other combustible matter. Take, for instance, the Pantheon of Agrippa, which ancient writers assert was twice burnt, — once under Titus, once under Trajan. There is not an atom of it capable of catching fire; not even French *pétroleurs* could do the slightest harm to it. It is also a mystery to me how the Colosseum could have been set into a blaze by a thunderbolt, on August 23, A. D. 217, and that it should have taken not less than six years to repair the damage. Still, the fact is proved by the testimony of Dion Cassius (lxxviii. 25), by the coins of Severus Alexander, showing the view of the restored amphitheatre, and by the amphitheatre itself, the upper tiers of which appear to have been rebuilt in haste, with materials taken from other edifices.

As to smaller fires, of single houses and premises, they were almost a daily occurrence. In fact, they broke out

Upper part of the Colosseum.

so often and so unexpectedly that there sometimes arose suspicion of the owners themselves having set the property on fire; because, although the Romans did not possess, as far as we can judge, fire insurance companies, yet such munificent contributions were made by friends and clients to the sufferers that it was in many cases a fortunate thing to be burned down. Martial, in the fifty-second epigram of the third book, speaks of a certain Tongilianus, whose house, worth two hundred sesterces, had been rebuilt, after a suspicious fire, at a cost of ten thousand, raised by the subscriptions of friends. Juvenal, in the third satire, describes the zeal of those who, not satisfied with rendering pecuniary help to the sufferers, made them also presents of statues, pictures, books, and furniture.

Let us see now in what way Rome tried to protect itself from so many perils, risks, and casualties.

At a very remote age the direction of the police was intrusted to three magistrates, called *triumviri nocturni,* because their principal duty was to watch for the safety of the city at night. Valerius Maximus speaks of one of them, P. Villius, being fined *quia vigilias neglegentius circumi- erat* (for not having kept with diligence his nocturnal watch), and of other triumviri who were punished because they had not run with proper speed to extinguish a fire which had broken out in a jeweller's shop on the Sacra Via.

The *triumviri capitales* was composed of a body of men belonging to the *familia publica,* " servants of the com- monwealth," stationed in groups of twenty or thirty in the neighborhood of the gates of the town, and furnished with the most elementary instruments known to our firemen, such as ladders, saws, pickaxes, and ropes. In process of time, these *servi publici* having become insufficient to meet the requirements of a largely increased population, compa- nies of volunteers were formed for the extinction of fires, and for helping the triumviri gratuitously in the accom- plishment of their duties. These companies, however, did not enjoy particularly the favor of the government, whether republican or imperial. In the thirty-third letter addressed by Pliny the younger, when governor of Bithynia, to the wise Emperor Trajan, permission is asked to form a body of one hundred and fifty volunteer firemen at Nicomedia. The answer of the emperor is not favorable to Pliny's pro- posal, because, he remarks, societies originated with a praiseworthy idea often degenerate into political sects, and become a permanent source of disturbance and danger to state institutions.

In the year 6 B. C., a fire having destroyed a large district of Rome under the eyes of Augustus, that emperor at once decided to reform the service, and enrolled for this purpose a body of freedmen, seven thousand strong, which was divided into seven battalions, or *cohortes,* and placed under the command of an officer of the equestrian order. The body was distributed and lodged throughout the city, so that each battalion could watch two of the fourteen regions, or wards, into which the city itself had been divided by Augustus. The seven companies of each battalion were placed under the orders of *centuriones,* or captains; each battalion under the orders of a colonel, or *tribunus;* and the whole body under a general or prefect of police, called *præfectus vigilum.* The cost of the maintenance of the corps was charged against the public treasury; and as the state of the public treasury was not very flourishing at the time, Augustus not only suppressed unnecessary outlays, such as the subsidy which used to be allowed to magistrates who gave, in their own private name, gladiatorial shows, but also increased the public revenue by instituting a new contribution, called the *vicesima quinta venalium* (twenty-five per cent. on the sale of slaves).

Every time a fire took place the prefect of the vigiles was obliged to open an official inquiry, and judge of the case, sitting in court. Of course no penalty was inflicted in case of a pure accident; but if the fire had been caused by negligence, the culprit was punished either by a solemn public admonition, or, in the worst cases, with castigation, the number of strokes being fixed according to the degree of the culprit's responsibility duly ascertained. Incendiaries were handed over to the higher court of the prefect of the city, and sentenced to death. However, as the spirit of the police regulations of Rome was rather to prevent than to punish, the prefect of the vigiles was authorized to watch and examine kitchens in every house, and state whether the supply of water in the kitchen corresponded to the impor tance and size of the house, and whether the furnaces and heating apparatus worked properly. Another of his duties was to supervise wardrobes at the entrance of the great *thermæ*, and to pass judgment upon the wardrobe-keepers, or *capsarii*, every time the loss of wraps or overcoats was complained of by a customer. Imagine what the life of these poor magistrates must have been, if they put any particle of zeal into the accomplishment of their functions, obliged as they were *per totam noctem vigilare*, and to sit the whole day in court, dealing with the worst class of roughs and vagabonds. Some of the cases brought before them were discussed for eighteen years; that is to say, for a space of time considerably longer than that occupied by the famous Tichborne case. Near the church of S. Antony, on the Esquiline, inscriptions have been discovered relating to a process instituted in the year 226 of our era by the *collegium fullonum*, the corporation of washermen, against the *curator aquarum*, or superintendent of public aqueducts, on account of a certain supply of water to which the corporation claimed to be gratuitously entitled. The controversy lasted from the year 226 to 244, and was finally settled by an elaborate sentence of the prefect of police, the very text of which, engraved on a marble pedestal, has been discovered in the above-mentioned place.

The policemen themselves, whom Augustus at first enrolled among freedmen, did not enjoy, as usual in European cities, the favor of the populace; and as in modern Rome the *guardie di publica sicurezza* are called all sorts of names by the roughs and their sympathizers, so the classic vigiles were nicknamed *sparteoli* by our forefathers. Yet this ludicrous and sarcastic denomination is not devoid of interest for the archæologist, because it is evidently derived from *spartum;* in other words, it shows that the firemen used to carry water in buckets of *spartum,* made watertight with a coating of pitch or tar.   To console them for the want of public sympathy, the emperors increased periodically their privileges and their accommodations, and conceded to them the rights of Roman citizenship, not after the expiration of their term of service, as was customary, but after only three years of good service.   The captains, in case of promotion, had the right of serving in the prætorian guard; and their prefect usually exchanged the department of police first for that of the *annona,* then for the governorship of Egypt, to end his career as prefect of the prætorium, the highest dignity which a Roman knight could reach.

In my opinion there is no single instance better adapted to show the difference in the accommodations of ancient and modern police than the comparative study of their lodgings or barracks.   In Rome there were seven main barracks, called *stationes,* and fourteen *corps de garde,* or detached posts, called *excubitoria.*   Of the seven stations, four have been discovered; of the fourteen *excubitoria,* only two.   The barracks of the first battalion, which contained also the headquarters of the whole corps and the offices of the commander-in-chief, were found during the pontificate of Pope Urban VIII., Barberini, in 1644, at the northern extremity of the Piazza dei SS. Apostoli, in the foundations of the Palazzo Muti-Savorelli, now Balestra. Their remains were examined and described by Lucas Holstenius. He speaks of huge halls, ornamented with columns, pedestals, statues, marble incrustations, mosaic pavements, and of waiting-rooms and offices, having marble seats around the walls, which were covered with finely designed frescoes. Amongst the statues raised to gods and emperors in the vestibule and in the atrium of the barracks, only eight were discovered, in a more or less fragmentary state; they represented the *Genius cohortis primæ vigilum*, Caracalla, Gordianus Pius, Furia Sabinia Tranquillina (his empress), Constantine, Constans, Valentinian, and Gratianus. If the site occupied by these barracks were not actually covered with palatial and costly structures, such as the Palazzo Muti-Savorelli and the convent of S. Marcello, it would be well worth while to excavate it again, for I have come across documents proving the existence there of some remarkable works of art. In the archæological memoirs of Pietro Santi Bartoli, imperfectly published by Fea, are the following memoranda : —

" Amongst the many exquisite works of leading Greek chisels discovered by Cavaliere Giovanni Battista Muti in rebuilding the foundations of his palace, at the northern end of the Piazza dei SS. Apostoli, there was the bas-relief representing Perseus and Andromeda (now preserved in the Casino of the Villa Doria-Pamphili). Two more bas-reliefs were brought to light, of the same perfect workmanship; but by order of the Cavaliere Muti they were broken in pieces, and buried again under the foundations of the palace."

As regards the adjoining convent of S. Marcello, Pietro Santi Bartoli says : " In laying the foundations of that wing of the convent which lies toward the Palazzo Muti, and overlooks the same Piazza dei SS. Apostoli, many columns and ancient marbles were discovered, and among them a fine statue of colossal size and in perfect preservation. By order of the monks, it was buried again." It is worthy of consideration how, in my native city, even fate seems to be inspired by archæological instincts. Who in modern times has taken possession of this convent of S. Marcello, built on the site of the barracks and headquarters of the ancient Vigiles? The superintendent of police himself, the *Questore di Roma*, with his staff of *Guardie di Publica Sicurezza*.

The barracks of the second battalion were discovered during the pontificate of Clement XII., on the road leading (at that time) from the Esquiline to the Porta Maggiore, and corresponding to the ancient Via Labicana. Affixed to the walls of the edifice were inscriptions commemorating the dedication of a tetrastyle temple in honor of Jupiter Dolichenus, and of a *Nymphæum*, by Claudius Catullus, prefect of the Vigiles in the year 191, together with some of the officers of the second battalion. The site of the barracks of the third battalion is unknown.

The site of the fourth *Statio*, in the neighborhood of the church of S. Saba, on the so-called Pseudo-Aventine, was revealed, as early as the beginning of the fifteenth century, by the discovery of a pedestal dedicated in the year 205 to the emperor Caracalla. On the left side of this pedestal the following remarkable document was inscribed:

" Severus and Caracalla emperors, to Junius Rufinus, prefect of the Vigiles, greeting. You are hereby authorized to punish with the rod or with the cat-o'-nine-tails (*fustibus vel flagellis*) the janitor or any of the inhabitants of a house, in which fire has broken out through negligence. In case the fire should be occasioned not by negligence but by crime, you must hand over the incendiaries to our friend Fabius (Septimianus) Cilo, prefect of the city. Remember also that one of your duties is to discover runaway slaves and to return them to their masters."

We have now reached the barracks of the fifth battalion, which occupied, as I shall presently show, the higher plat-

Entrance to the Villa Mattei.   Site of the Barracks of the Fifth Battalion of Police.

form of the Villa Celimontana, formerly belonging to the ducal family of the Mattei di Giove, and now the property of Baron Richard von Hoffman.   An inscription was found in that part of the villa which overlooks the church of S. Stefano Rotondo, describing how a shrine, dedicated A. D. 111 to the Genius of the fifth battalion, had been restored forty-five years later, in 156.   Another inscription, discovered in the same place in 1735, speaks of another *ædiculum* dedicated to the same Genius in the year 113.   The shrine itself, or, at any rate, one of the many shrines of the barracks, seems to have been found and brought to light in the sixteenth century in this neighborhood, more precisely in the garden then belonging to Uberto Strozzi of Mantua.   I describe it to show what an extraordinary display of art and luxury there was in a chapel belonging to ordinary police barracks. The shrine was built in the shape of a small temple, circular outside, octagonal inside, and was surrounded by a colonnade. of the Corinthian order, with shafts of porphyry, capitals, frieze, and cornice of Carrara marble. Each of the eight sides of the interior was ornamented with a niche for statues, of which niches four were semicircular, four square. One of these last served as a door. In the corners of the octagon there were eight columns of porphyry, supporting an exquisitely carved frieze.

The discoveries I have described were cast into the shade by those made in January, 1820, a little to the left of the main gate of the same Villa Mattei, or von Hoffman. At a depth of thirteen feet, two marble pedestals, five feet high, were dug up ; they were found standing in their original position, on a tessellated pavement, and bore the complete rolls of the battalion. The first pedestal had no dedicatory inscription, but began at once with the rolls of the first company, commanded by Captain Cæsernius Senecio. The inscription on the second pedestal began with the following words, which I translate freely : —

" To the Emperor Cæsar M. Aurelius Antoninus Caracalla, the pious, the fortunate, consul for the third time, son of the late Emperor L. Septimius Severus Pius Pertinax, this pedestal and this statue have been raised by the officers and men of the fifth battalion of police on July 6th, under the consulship of Faustinus and Rufinus " (the year 210 A. D.). Then follow the names of the superior officers, of C. Julius Quintilianus, prefect of police and general commanding the corps ; of M. Firmius, adjutant-general ; of L. Speratius Justus, colonel of the fifth battalion ; of the captains commanding the seven companies ;

of the four physicians and surgeons attached to the barracks ; and lastly, of the two officers to whom the care of erecting the statue had been intrusted, namely, the captain and the standard-bearer of the first company.

The importance of these two documents, however, is far greater if we take into consideration the rolls of the men. In the year 105, which is the approximate date of the first pedestal, the battalion numbered 115 officers and sub-officers, and 930 men. In the year 110 the number of the former had decreased to 109, the number of the latter had increased to 1,013. Taking as the average strength of a battalion, 1,033 men all told, the whole police corps of imperial Rome must have numbered 7,231 men. The strength of each of the seven companies varies from a minimum of 125 to a maximum of 173, the seventh or last company excepted, which numbers scarcely 94 men, probably *tirones* or recruits in course of training.

The sites of the sixth and seventh barracks have not yet been ascertained.

Before leaving the subject of police and firemen I must add a few words on the comparatively recent discovery of one of the detached posts or *corps-de-garde*. The discovery of the *excubitorium*, or outpost, of the seventh battalion, stationed in the fourteenth region, Trastevere, took place in 1868 near the church of S. Crisogono. It appears that the police authorities established outposts according to circumstances, at special points of the district where disturbances were most likely to take place. For this purpose they rented a private house, or portion of a private house, and stationed men in it, until the requirements of public security made a further move necessary. The house discovered in 1868 seems to have been rented by the police for a long term, at least from the reign of Cara-

calla to that of Philip the Arab ; in other words, for more
than thirty years. It is an elegant structure, with mosaic
pavements, fresco paintings, marble fountains, baths, and
heating apparatus. The importance of the discovery, however, does not come from the beauty of the building, but
from the many inscriptions scratched in the plaster by the
policemen themselves, during the hours of indoor rest,
which inscriptions admit us into the most intimate secrets
of barrack life, and reveal to us every minute detail of the
daily routine of the men, their own feelings towards their
emperors and officers, and other items of police life. The
language they use in scrawling their sentiments is always
direct and plain, very often profane. I refer those of my
readers who wish to know more on this subject to the essay
by the late Dr. Wilhelm Henzen (*L' escubitorio della set-
tima coorte dei Vigili*), published in the " Annali dell'
Instituto, 1869."

THE EXCUBITORIUM OF THE SEVENTH BATTALION OF
POLICE.

CHAPTER IX.

THE TIBER AND THE CLAUDIAN HARBOR.

THE subject which I have selected for this chapter, the archæology of the Tiber, is so comprehensive, and covers such a vast space in the field of Roman antiquities, that it gives the writer an *embarras du choix*, and makes it a difficult task to concentrate the whole subject within prescribed limits. In the Essay on the Bibliography of the Tiber, published by Enrico Narducci in 1876, not less than four hundred special works are registered, perhaps two thirds of the whole number on this subject. If the publications of the last twelve years were added to the list, we may be sure that a special library on the famous river of Rome would contain about eight hundred volumes. There is probably no other river in the world which has been discussed so exhaustively.

The principal springs of the Tiber are located in a gorge of Monte Coronaro, in the Apennines of Tuscany, at the height of 3,600 feet above the sea. The river runs through the lowlands of Etruria, Umbria, Sabina, and Latium for a distance of 249 miles, of which nearly 80 are navigable even by steamers of moderate size. Between Rome and the sea, it expands into a beautiful channel some 400 feet wide, and is navigated by steamers and barges of nearly 100 tons register. Nothing can be more charming than a sail down the river from Rome to the sea, not only on account of the historical associations of the river itself, but more especially on account of its natural beauty. Let us recall the magnificent verses in which Virgil describes how Æneas, sailing along the Latin coast, discovered the mouth of the Tiber and entered the unknown waters, wondering at the lovely scene which opened before his eyes, and at the feeling of rest and tranquillity which pervaded all his being, after a long and eventful voyage, —

> " Atque hic Æneas ingentem ex æquore lucum
> Prospicit : hunc inter fluvio Tiberinus amœno,
> Vorticibus rapidis, et multâ flavus arenâ,
> In mare prorumpit.   Variæ circumque supraque
> Assuetæ ripis volucres et fluminis alveo,
> Æthera mulcebant cantu lucoque volabant."

The fidelity of this picture is astonishing ; at least it was so, until two or three years ago, before the appearance in this remote region of peace and enchantment of so-called civilization, with its pretence of making the air healthier, and of banishing malaria from the lowlands of the delta. The trees sung by Virgil have been cut down ; the sandbanks, a favorite resort of flamingoes and pelicans, have been dredged away ; and to make the profanation complete, a cast-iron bridge is to be thrown across the river, in place of the picturesque old boat which for centuries has ferried passengers across from Ostia to Fiumicino.

The special characteristics of the river are three : first, the wholesome quality of its waters ; second, the considerable amount of solid matter it carries down to the sea, which, deposited on each side of the bar, makes the coast advance at a considerable rate ; and, third, the abundance of the springs that feed the river, in consequence of which its normal level never varies by an inch, summer or winter. Of the first characteristic, I have spoken in the third chapter ; of the second, I shall have occasion to speak at length in this.   For the third, I may observe that the

Tiber, as regards volume and level of water, has never changed within historical times. One may read, even in books of sound archæological value, that the Tiber was much lower in ancient times than it is now. Even Bonini, one of our best engineers, has stated the difference of level at eighteen feet. His great argument, repeated so often, is drawn from the passage in Pliny which describes how Agrippa once rowed into the Cloaca Maxima, the mouth of which is not high enough above the water now to admit the possibility of any such anti-hygienic sport. But from a series of observations taken in the course of the present works of embankment, it appears that for the last twenty-one centuries the level of the water, and consequently the bed of the river, has risen only two feet and two or three inches.

There is an important work, written in Latin by Paolo Giovio on the fish belonging to the Tiber. The most famous and costly in ancient times was the *lupus*, a fish described and praised by Macrobius, Pliny the elder, and Juvenal. The best in quality, the ones reserved for imperial and aristocratic tables, were caught *inter duos pontes*, near the island of S. Bartolomeo and near the mouth of the Cloaca Maxima. The sturgeon also was highly appreciated. In the Conservatori Palace, on the Capitol, there is still to be seen a marble bas-relief, representing a sturgeon forty-six inches long, and underneath it is engraved the text of a law passed by the *Senatus populusque Romanus*, in the year 1581, according to which any sturgeon caught in Roman waters, equalling or exceeding the statute size, as represented in the bas-relief, must be considered public property, and placed at the disposal of the city authorities. As far as I know, the city authorities have never feasted on a sturgeon since the promulgation of that strange decree.

As regards inundations, the Tiber ranks among the proudest rivers in the world. That of December, 1870, will never fade from the memory of the living generation; and I fear that this impressive and picturesque spectacle will never again be seen, since civilization has taken up the matter, and by means of lofty embankments, of locks and gates, will succeed, I am sure, in keeping the river confined hereafter within its two parallel walls.

In the second century after the foundation of Rome, King Ancus Marcius, feeling the safety of the kingdom well insured on the land side, turned his eyes towards the Mediterranean, the waters of which he could see glistening under the rays of the setting sun, within a few miles of the city, and in order to open a *débouché* for international trade, occupied the mouth of the Tiber, and founded a colony by it, which was named Ostia Tiberina, from its position near the bar of the river. At that remote age, however, very little seems to have been done to secure safety of navigation; and when we hear the harbor of Ostia mentioned by writers of the republican and early imperial periods, we must not think of a real basin of water with piers, and jetties, and breakwaters, but only of the natural channel of the river, which shoals, moving sands, and an almost complete absence of tide made exceedingly difficult and dangerous for sailing vessels.

To these natural defects, common to all river harbors on the coast of the Mediterranean, another must be added, resulting from exceptional local causes, — the enormous yearly enlargement of the coast, by means of the sand carried down to the sea by the Tiber, and deposited on each side of the river's mouth. I have already stated in the third chapter that the *flavus Tiberis* washes down every year eight and one half million tons of sand, cor-

responding to a volume of more than four million cubic
metres. No wonder that, in such extraordinary circumstances, ancient Ostia, the Ostia of King Ancus Marcius, is at the present day fully four miles distant from the
bar; that the tower built by Michael Angelo in 1567,
on the very edge of the coast, and named Torre S. Michele
(now used as a light-house), is 2,250 yards inland; and that
the tower built by Clement XII. at Fiumicino, *in ipso
maris supercilio*, as the dedicatory inscription says, is now
separated from the sea by a line of sand-hills 970 yards
wide. From careful measurements taken by the astronomer
Angelo Secchi and by myself, the average yearly increase
of the coast along the delta of the Tiber has been determined at nineteen feet, from a maximum of twenty-eight at
Ostia, to a minimum of ten at Fiumicino. I may here mention a fact, highly illustrative of this singular state of
things. The sacred island surrounded by the two arms of
the Tiber was sold in 1830 by the pontifical government to
the Marchese Guglielmi, of Civita Vecchia, with no stipu-
lation whatever, except the payment, once and for ever,
of a fixed amount of money. It was only two years ago
that the fiscal authorities opened their eyes to the ir-
regularity of the bargain. It has been ascertained that
since the day the property was bought, fifty-six years ago,
its surface has been nearly doubled by the addition of 648
acres of ground, which should have been added, of course,
not to the patrimony of the Marchese Guglielmi, but to
that of the nation.

In spite of so many adverse circumstances, a very brisk
trade began to be carried on between Rome, Ostia, and the
Mediterranean very soon after the foundation of Ostia.
The vessels sailing to it, if men-of-war, could easily get
over the bar, on account of their light draught, and also

on account of the considerable propelling power they derived from a numerous and well-ordered crew. If mer-
chantmen, they had to steer a different course, according to their capacity and size. Vessels under 3,000 *modii*,
that is to say, under thirty or thirty-five tons register,
could sail up the mouth of the river easily. Vessels of
larger tonnage were obliged to cast anchor at a certain distance from the bar, and to diminish their draught by trans-
ferring part of their cargo to barges and lighters. These
particulars show that the Romans of the republic never
tried to improve the approach to their only harbor by
skilful engineering. By the help of two palisades, or jetties, which have been built at Fiumicino, vessels and steamers of one hundred and fifty tons are now able to reach
Rome with perfect ease.

With regard to the navigation of the river from Ostia to
Rome in ancient times, we must again make a distinction
between war and trading vessels. War vessels could easily
overcome the force of the current with their powerfully-
manned oars; trading vessels had to be towed up-stream
by oxen and buffaloes, for which purpose tow-paths on
each bank of the river were opened and carefully paved.
Navigation was suspended at nightfall, when every ship
was obliged to moor at the nearest station. There must
have been at least thirty of these stations between Rome
and the sea.

In view of the fact that the quantity of shipping moored
at night along the banks must have been enormous, and
that the crews of those days were certainly not better nor
quieter than those of our own, we need not wonder that
special police precautions had to be taken to insure order,
and to protect neighboring property from the nocturnal
inroads of marauding sailors. Vigiles, that is to say, a

special body of constables and firemen, were stationed from point to point along the banks; but the expense of this night watch, and of keeping their stations in due repair, had to be met by the owners of property facing the river, who were subject accordingly to an extra tax, called *onus vigiliarium.*

The Tiber was not always navigable : in winter, because its water would sometimes freeze ; in summer, on account of shoals and sand-banks. Of course I am speaking of re-publican times, during which the river was left absolutely to itself, and to its own caprices, with no check or im-provement by hydraulic means.

The best season for navigation along the coast of Ostia was from the beginning of March to the middle of Septem-ber; but there were captains and merchants daring enough to run the risk in winter. Vessels would generally sail into the harbor in the afternoon, and sail out in the morn-ing, a practice due entirely to the regularity with which the breeze blows from the sea in the afternoon, and from the land in the morning.

I may add that, under favorable circumstances, vessels sailing from the mouth of the Tiber could reach Alexan-dria and the Nile in eleven days ; the Straits of Gibraltar in seven ; the Straits of Messina and even the Albanian coast in five : the coast of Barcelona in four ; the Gulf of Marseilles in three ; the coast of Africa in less than two.

At the beginning of the empire, when Rome had become the centre of the trade of the world, and had gained a population of over a million souls, for whose maintenance, comfort, and luxury the produce of the whole world was scarcely deemed sufficient, the necessity of building a large and safe harbor forced itself upon the government. So shallow had the waters become at the bar of the river, that

Caligula was obliged to resort to a simple *biremis*, the smallest kind of war sloop, to convey to Rome, from the island of Ponza, the ashes of his mother and brother. We know also that the Emperor Claudius made an unsuccessful attempt to land, after a cruise, and was obliged to ride at anchor until boats could be sent from Ostia to his rescue. This explains why large ships laden with grain, such as the one mentioned in the Acts of the Apostles as having on board, besides its heavy cargo, two hundred and fifty souls, were obliged to avoid Ostia, and to land either at Brindisi or Pozzuoli.

Julius Cæsar was the first statesman who proposed the construction of a spacious harbor, not at, but near, the mouth of the Tiber; his project was *propter difficultatem omissus* (given up on account of its difficulties), as well as that other curious plan of his for opening a deep canal from Rome to Terracina, to save vessels the danger of rounding Cape Circeum. The honor of the great undertaking was reserved to Claudius, the prince famous for his gigantic hydraulic enterprises, such as the aqueducts of the Aqua Claudia and of Anio Novus, eighty-nine miles long in all, and the drainage of the Lake of Fucino. I shall not describe the harbor two miles west of Ostia, which he succeeded in building, in spite of untold natural difficulties, and in spite of the opposition of the supreme council of government engineers. It was inclosed by two jetties, each 809 yards long. The area of the harbor amounted to 691,000 square yards, the depth from 15 to 18 feet, with an aggregate length of quays amounting to 2,600 yards. This colossal work necessitated the removal of 112,000,000 cubic feet of sand. Its only defect was the faulty position of the breakwater, which had been built, not far out at sea, so as to shelter the entrance to the harbor, but on the line connecting the ends of the jetties, leaving the two entrances exposed to the full force of the high sea. Tacitus informs us that, during a fierce gale in the time of Nero, not less than two hundred vessels were lost in the roads. I might add that this breakwater, in spite of its defective position, is one of the best, if not the very best example in ancient times of successful construction in deep water by means of caissons.

Claudius managed the enterprise in this way: There was moored at the time — I do not know whether at Rome or at Ostia — the huge ship by which the great Vatican obelisk had been brought over from Egypt. To give an idea of its size I will say, that, besides the obelisk itself, weighing many hundred tons, the vessel was laden with a ballast of 120,000 *modii* of lentils, corresponding to one thousand tons. Claudius caused the ship to be moored at the place designed for the breakwater, and to be filled with concrete until the weight of the masonry made it sink. This foundation was then strengthened by a girdle of rocks on the weather side, and in due time it grew above the water-level, and was crowned with a lighthouse nearly two hundred feet high, built in imitation of the celebrated Pharos of Alexandria.

Relief on a Sarcophagus showing the Claudian Harbor.

Nero, the successor of Claudius, conceived the grand idea of making Rome itself a seaport, by dredging a deep canal between the metropolis and the Claudian harbor. The idea does not seem to have been carried into execution. The same emperor, acting on the advice of his favorite engineers, Severus and Celer, began another canal between the harbor of Misenum, on the Bay of Naples, and Rome. If it had been completed, this canal would have been one hundred and sixty miles long, and wide enough to allow the passage of two lines of *quinqueremes* abreast, the *quinqueremis* being the largest kind of man-of-war used in the Roman navy. The cutting was begun in that district of Campania Felix, near Amyclæ and near the gulf of Gaeta, where the famous Cæcubus was grown, the wine which, according to Pliny, had held the first rank among Italian brands from remotest antiquity. The only result of Nero's undertaking was to ruin forever this noble wine-growing district. The place of the lost Cæcubus on the tables of the Roman aristocracy was henceforth to be taken by the Setinian, a wine which Augustus first brought to the notice of connoisseurs, and which was grown on the slopes of the Lepini mountains, facing the Pontine marshes.

Medallion showing the Harbor of Trajan.

The harbor system at Ostia was brought to absolute perfection under Trajan, who, like Claudius, was devoted to grand hydraulic enterprises, as shown by the bridge thrown across the Danube in its widest part; by the harbors of Ancona and Civita Vecchia, still among the best and safest in the Mediterranean, and by the Trajan aqueduct which still supplies one fifth of the city. The fact is that the Claudian or outer harbor had long been insufficient for the trade of the metropolis. Everything which taste or luxury required, and all the supplies necessary to feed a population which had increased to nearly two millions of souls, had to be landed and stored at Ostia. Egypt alone every year shipped nearly one hundred and ninety million bushels of wheat and grain. A far larger supply was imported from Sicily, Sardinia, Africa, Numidia, Mauretania, and from the provinces bordering on the Danube and the Black Sea.

To the commercial transactions we must add the trade in building stone, so brisk and active that even Tibullus complained that the streets of the metropolis were always obstructed by enormous carts, loaded with transmarine columns and blocks : columns measuring, sometimes, six feet in diameter [and fifty-five in height], like the one discovered in May, 1887, among the ruins of Trajan's temple ; blocks weighing, sometimes, twenty-seven tons, like the one belonging to the temple of the Sun, now lying

The largest Block of Marble in Rome.

in the Colonna gardens on the Quirinal. This mania for rare and costly products of quarries, thousands of miles

distant, began in the year 610 of Rome.   Q. Metellus
Macedonicus is said to have been the first Roman citizen
to bring into fashion foreign building stones ; and, accordingly, he is reproached by Velleius Paterculus as the
first corrupter of republican simplicity.   Pliny relates that
when Lucius Crassus, fifty-two years later, decorated his
house on the Palatine with six columns wholly of Sicilian
marble, and only twelve feet high, he was nicknamed the
Palatine Venus.   Four years later, M. Lepidus imported
for the first time columns of Numidian marble (*giallo
antico*), and was publicly censured for having cut a threshold out of the same valuable material.   Lucius Lucullus
brought over from Egypt the first samples of black marble
(*nero antico*), called *marmor Lucullanum* on his account.
Sulla, the dictator, stole from the Olympeion at Athens
many columns of Pentelic marble.   Marcus Æmilius Scaurus, to celebrate his nomination as Ædile, built a temporary stage and decorated it with 370 columns of Lucul-
læan marble, 33 feet high.   About the same time, Mamurra
was adorning his house on the Cœlian porticoes with
shafts of *cipollino* and Carrara marble.   No wonder that,
at this stage of luxury, the price of elegant private mansions should have reached fabulous sums.   Messala bought
the house of Antonius for a sum corresponding to $165,000.
Cicero gave for the house of Crassus $155,000 ; the house
of Claudius had cost $655,000 ; that of Scaurus was valued
at $4,425,000 ; and I am speaking of republican times !   No
wonder that the contractor for the maintenance of public
drains should have required from M. Scaurus a security
against any possible danger of the sinking of streets in
the transportation of his columns and blocks of marble,
so heavy were they.   A gentleman possessed of great perseverance, Sig. Faustino Corsi, counted in Rome, forty-one

years ago, 7,012 ancient columns, or important pieces of ancient columns, which had escaped destruction. The number has been increased through recent discoveries and excavations to nearly 9,000. I have brought to light, in the excavations intrusted to my care, 390 of them. Considering what an amount of destruction, of breaking up, of burning into lime, has been accomplished in Rome since the fall of the empire, there is no danger of exaggerating if we place the total number of columns landed at Ostia at 50,000 at least; and columns represent but a small item in the marble trade of ancient Rome.

The Claudian harbor was not only a commercial, but also a military station, from which emperors and admirals were wont to sail, escorted by powerful fleets, on their expeditions to the far-away border lands of the empire. The same harbor contained a central post office for correspondence with the provinces beyond the sea, the existence of which office was revealed for the first time in 1874. Our late King Victor Emmanuel, when undertaking, near the end of that year, some excavations on his hunting estate of Castel Porziano, between Ostia and Torre Paterno, discovered the public square or *forum* of a village, named Vicus Augustanus Laurentium, mentioned by Pliny the younger as adjoining his famous Laurentine villa. In the centre of the square stood the marble pedestal of a statue, raised by the worthy inhabitants of the village in memory of a local benefactor, named P. Ælius Liberalis, a freedman of the Emperor Hadrian. As usual, the career of the gentleman so highly esteemed by his fellow-citizens is described in the legend on the pedestal. We are told by it how Liberalis began his career in the finance department, as *præpositus mensæ nummulariæ fisci frumentarii Ostiensis*, that is to say, as cashier of the branch office for the importation of breadstuffs, which had been established at Ostia as the landing-place of the fleets laden with the harvest of all the provinces of the empire. In course of time he was elected to another office, *procurator pugillationis et ad naves vagas,* — postmaster of Ostia and superintendent of the fleet of despatch boats.

Postal institutions, in the modern sense of the word, were not unknown in Roman times. To secure quick and accurate intelligence, even from the remotest provinces, Augustus established, all along the great highways, a system of couriers mounted on swift horses, and stationed at an average distance of seven miles from one another. Later on, he organized a regular service of mail coaches, which seems to have been brought to a higher point of perfection by the Emperor Trajan. These accommodations, however, were reserved for the benefit of government employees, — such as cabinet messengers, military officers, governors, and so on, — and very seldom were for the benefit of private individuals, to whom the privilege of using mail coaches was granted only by the emperor himself, or by the governor of a province. At the same time, all the burden of the institution had to be borne by the inhabitants of the villages and towns crossed or approached by the high road : they were compelled to supply horses, mules, and oxen, and to keep the stations in proper repair ; in other words, they had to pay all the expenses of an organization from which they did not reap any advantage, except the manure from the stables, graciously left them by the generosity of the government. Good, humane emperors did their best to relieve the populace from this indirect heavy taxation. There is a coin struck in honor of Nerva, with the legend, *vehiculatione Italiæ remissa,* which signifies that the inhabitants of the Peninsula at least had been exempted from

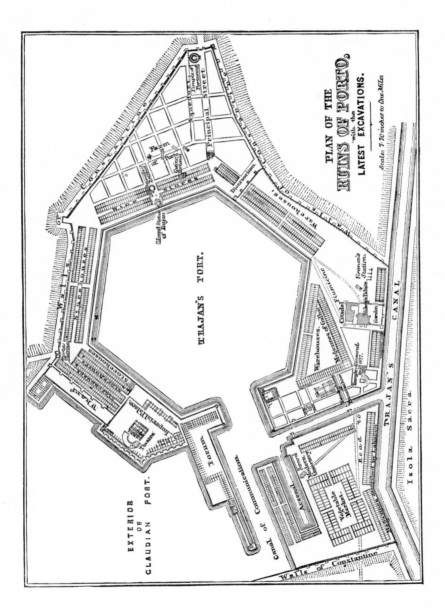

PLAN OF THE
RUINS OF PORTO,
with the
LATEST EXCAVATIONS.

Scale: 7.70 inches to One Mile.

TRAJAN'S PORT.

EXTERIOR
OF
CLAUDIAN PORT.

Principal Street

Walls of Constantine

Canal of Communication

TRAJAN'S CANAL

Isola Sacra

compulsory supply of horses. Hadrian and Antoninus seem
to have met the exigencies of the service with their own
purse; and, finally, Severus Alexander transferred permanently the burden from the people to the imperial treasury. The postmaster-general, styled *præfectus vehiculo-
rum*, of equestrian rank, was selected generally from among
retired cavalry officers: he had under his orders provincial
postmasters of inferior rank.

Such was the state of things as regards the over-land
post; regarding the maritime post nothing was known until
the inscription of P. Ælius Liberalis was brought to light.
His double office of postmaster and master of despatch
boats makes it evident that the two things were connected
as two branches of the same department. There is no
doubt that the *naves vagæ* of the inscription were something like the *naves tabellariæ* mentioned by Seneca as
running in front of the fleet laden with grain from Egypt,
to announce its arrival at Pozzuoli, or like the *naves spe-
culatoriæ*, corresponding to the *avisos* of the modern
navy. There is no doubt that, with the combined action
of canvas and oars, finely-modelled ships could accomplish as quick a passage across the sea as was usually
made in the first quarter of the present century. This
is proved, to quote only one argument, by the remarkable instance related by Plutarch, in chapter sixteen of
his life of Cato, when, to impress the Senate with the necessity *delendæ Carthaginis*, he unfolded his mantle, and
showed the astonished assembly a batch of fresh figs which
had been gathered on the African coast only two days
before.

I have already said that the harbor system at Ostia was
brought to absolute perfection by Trajan. He was the
builder of that magnificent inner dock, which, although

left fully two miles inland by the filling up of the estuary, still exists in its integrity, and is known, especially among wild-duck shooters, as the *Lago Trajano*, the Lake of Trajan. It had the form of a regular hexagon, 393,000 square yards in extent, with a line of quays 2,156 yards long, and with a constant depth of 18 feet. The construction of Trajan's dock required the excavation and removal of 85,000,000 cubic feet of sand, and the construction of 1,940,000 cubic feet of masonry.

In modern times undertakings of the same kind have been accomplished successfully even on a larger scale; but for beauty of construction, richness of decoration, and splendor of materials, these will not bear comparison with the work of Claudius and Trajan. We can see with our own eyes the perfection of Trajan's dock, and I better than any one else, because I have been the only archæologist allowed to follow the excavations which Prince Alexander Torlonia, the owner of the ruins, has carried on for five consecutive years, doing more harm to the place in this short time than had been done in fifteen centuries of abandonment and desolation.

Medallion of Claudius.

Of the outer harbor, built by Claudius, and now inaccessible b e c a u s e of the pestilential marshes, we possess three genuine and perfect representations; one in bronze, one in colors, and one in marble. The bronze one is a large medallion in alto-rilievo struck by Nero, with his own portrait on one side and a bird's-eye view of the harbor on the other, reproduced by Donaldson in Plate No. 89 of

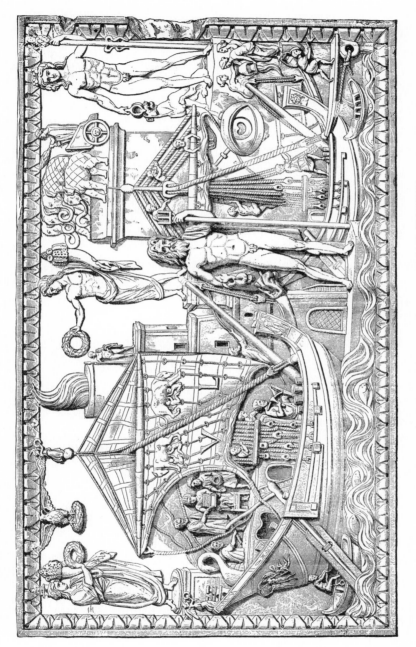

BAS-RELIEF SHOWING THE CLAUDIAN HARBOR.

his " Architectura Numismatica." The painted view was discovered some three centuries ago on the walls of a Roman house near the Subura, and has been reproduced

Mooring Rings on the Tiber.

and illustrated by Bellori, Falconieri, Canina, Mercklin, and De Rossi. The marble representation was discovered by Prince Torlonia in the spring of 1863. It is a bas-relief, of exquisite workmanship, four feet six inches long, two feet six inches high, showing the inside of the harbor, with its jetties, breakwater, light-house, colossal statues, triumphal arches, and the like, and two large ships, one named the " She-Wolf," the other the " Lynx ": the first sailing for an expedition on the high seas; the second furling her canvas as she approaches the quay.

There is no doubt that, in ancient times, no hydraulic work was considered perfect unless it joined to the skill of engineering the beauty of architcture. What I mean is this: we are satisfied, for instance, with fixing to our wharves iron rings and old guns as moorings : in ancient times, the rings (*dactylia*) were cut in stone or marble, in the shape of a lion's head, or dolphin (see previous page) ; — and the columns were costly marbles, and bore inscriptions in praise of the constructor of the harbor. We fence the space alloted to commercial transactions with iron railings ; the ancients enclosed it with colonnades of Oriental marble. We enter the docks, or the line of customs, through an iron gate ; the ancients entered through triumphal arches, such as the well-known Arch of Trajan on the eastern pier of the harbor of Ancona. For the storing of merchandise, we make use of wooden and iron sheds, and, in exceptional cases, when we want to impress the stranger with our magnificence, we build brick warehouses. I wish the reader could see, as it has been my privilege to see, the beauty of the docks and warehouses of Porto, the perfection of their reticulated masonry, their cornices and entablatures, carved and moulded in terracotta, their mosaic pavements, their system of drainage and ventilation !

The aggregate length of the warehouses around Trajan's dock amounts to 17,500 feet. At Ostia, a town nearly two miles long by one wide, they cover one half of the area. In Rome the statistics are even more wonderful. We are now engaged in building a new quarter in the so-called " Prati di Testaccio," that is to say, in the plain stretching from the foot of the Aventine hill to the left bank of the Tiber, and surrounding the artificial hill called Monte Testaccio. This enormous extent of ground, amounting to 800,000 square yards, was entirely occupied by imperial warehouses, denominated *Horrea Galbana*, from the family of Sulpicius Galba, who owned the greater portion of them before they were incorporated in the imperial domain. Of

THE WAREHOUSES AT OSTIA.

these public warehouses, there were in Rome 290 : this, at least, is the number registered in the official almanac of the empire, in the original edition of the year 312 of our era.

Ruins of the Horrea Galbana.

Of course, not all of them equalled, or even approached in extent and importance, the *Horrea Galbana ;* but we must bear in mind that more than one half of the population of Rome was fed directly by the emperor, from his own private treasury.   Imagine what precautions must have been taken to avoid even the slightest suspicion of famine, which would have brought with it revolution and disorder.   Aurelius Victor says that, under Augustus, at the beginning of the imperial period, not less than 48,115,000 bushels of grain (of our standard) were imported from Egypt, but that this quantity was sufficient for four months only :

144,345,000 bushels were thus required for the whole year, and for a population which had not yet reached its maximum of nearly two million souls.

The *Horrea Galbana*, in imitation of which all Roman storehouses were built, was composed of a certain number of courts, surrounded by porticoes wide enough to allow the free circulation of carts, and the unloading of merchandise under shelter. The magazines themselves opened upon these porticoes, and were usually two stories high. The lower floor generally was reserved for heavy and common merchandise, — timber, fuel, lead, iron, tin, marble, wine, oil, grain, honey, dried fruit, dried fish; the upper floor for rare and costly merchandise and for offices of adminis-

Monte Testaccio from the Tiber. (In the foreground the quay at which marbles were landed, as it appeared during the excavations of 1868.)

tration. Not long ago, I watched the excavation of one wing of the *horrea* which some workmen were uncovering: of the four storerooms searched under my direction, the first contained huge tusks of ivory, forming a total volume of 675 cubic feet; the second contained a few bushels of lentils; the third, a bed of crystalline sand, used by stone-cutters; the fourth was filled up with amphoræ of various sizes.

I have mentioned the Monte Testaccio two or three times. This singular hill, unique of its kind, rises from amidst the plain occupied by the imperial warehouses to the height of one hundred and forty feet, and covers an area of nearly sixteen acres. Its singularity arises from the fact that it is not the work of nature, but the mysterious work of man, composed of millions and millions of broken amphoræ, and terra-cotta jars, piled up in regular layers, in imitation of geological strata. Many conjectural explanations have been made of its origin and character. Commendatore de Rossi has suggested one which is worth consideration. On the quay of the Tiber, near the foot of the Monte Testaccio, where the grain and wine-laden ships and barges were moored, there was a large marble slab inscribed with the following notice : *Quidquid usuarium invehitur, ansarium non debet,* — " Whatever is imported of first necessity for the subsistence of the population is not subject to the octroi." The word used for octroi is *ansarium,* and the root of the singular word is *ansa,* " handle," evidently the handles of amphoræ, in which wine, oil, dried fruit, caviar, and salt fish were shipped over. Considering now that nearly one half of the whole mass of Monte Testaccio is composed of handles, or *ansæ,* Rossi supposes that the customs officers, to mark out the amphoræ for which duty (*ansarium*) had been regularly paid, would knock away one of the handles with a wooden hammer. In other words the Monte Testaccio would be nothing but a gigantic heap of receipts of the import duty from the custom-house of Rome. This explanation, however ingenious and impressive it may seem, cannot

Handle of an Amphora, from the Monte Testaccio.

be regarded as satisfactory. There is no doubt, I admit, that a large part of the provisions for Rome was shipped in amphoræ. The amphora is the unit, the standard measure, by which the capacity of a merchant vessel was calculated. In the Torlonia Museum there is a bas-relief representing the unloading of a ship, moored alongside the quay in the Claudian harbor. There is a plank connecting the ship with the quay, and upon this plank a line of sailors and porters, each carrying a laden amphora upon the left shoulder, and a *tessera* or ticket in the right hand. On the jetty, there is a *commissionaire*, or, perhaps, customs officer sitting at a desk, with a large book before him; each of the sailors and porters, in passing by on his way to the warehouse, throws the *tessera* or ticket on the desk. Thus the scribe or customs officer, whichever he may have been, had no trouble whatever in keeping his accounts; he had simply to see that, for every amphora landed and removed to the shed, a mark was left on his table, and, at the end of the operation, sum up the marks, and compare their number with the bill of lading declared by the captain of the ship.

An interesting instance of shipment by amphoræ in ancient times came to light in the spring of 1885, when I was residing at Sorrento. Some amphoræ were shown to me which evidently had remained at the bottom of the sea for centuries, for they were covered with the most wonderful incrustations of shells and corals, of zoöphytes and mollusks. On inquiring about their origin and discovery, I was told that they had been found under water, near the Promontorium Minervæ, now Capo della Campanella, and that they belonged to a wreck many centuries old. I had not then the means or the opportunity of verifying the accuracy of this account. But about a month later, at Porto d' Anzio, a delightful little harbor thirty-six miles from Rome, amphoræ of the same kind, I mean with the same beautiful incrustations, were offered for sale to some of the noble owners of villas on the coast. This time I was more fortunate in tracing the origin and real nature of the discovery. About two miles west of the castle and harbor of Astura, a place well known in the history of Cicero, Augustus, and Conradin von Hohenstaufen, and about fifty yards from the shore, which is there exceedingly shallow, a fisherman had discovered the wreck of an ancient Roman trading ship, of no considerable size, the hull of which was filled with amphoræ. The incrustations, a work of centuries, had cemented, as it were, the whole mass into a kind of coralliferous rock, from which it was very difficult to extricate an amphora without breaking it. Still, by perseverance and skill in diving, the fisherman had succeeded in removing the four or five beautiful specimens which I had admired at Porto d' Anzio.

But to come back to Commendatore de Rossi's explanation of the origin of Monte Testaccio; I cannot admit that customs officers would be allowed to knock away the handles of amphoræ, because the amphora was a costly receptacle, and without *ansæ* could not be used any longer. If handles enter in a large proportion into the composition of the mysterious hill, this is due to the fact that they were the most solid and heavy portion of the vase, and could not, like the thin body of the receptacle itself, be broken into atoms.

The true explanation has been given by Professor Heinrich Dressel in a memoir, " Ricerche sul Monte Testaccio," published in the " Annali " of the German Institute, 1878. It appears that, when the trade between Rome and the provinces began to assume a certain amount of importance, the authorities of the Tiber set aside a space of ground in the vicinity of the landing-place, in which the fragments of amphoræ broken during the journey, or in the act of unloading, could be thrown. These fragments were piled up, heap after heap, of the same height, until the whole surface allotted by the magistrates was covered with a stratum, four or five feet high. The horizontal space having been thus all occupied, the deposit began to increase in height; and so layer after layer was superimposed, until a real hill, at least 150 feet high, and nearly 4,000 in circumference was formed. I say at least 150 feet high, because we must remember that it has been for centuries a quarry for building materials, and must have lost a considerable percentage of its former volume. Professor Dressel has been able to investigate the surface only; he examined nearly 3,000 fabric-stamps, impressed on handles of amphoræ before they were baked in the kiln, and nearly

Amphora from the Monte Testaccio, showing inscriptions.

1,000 inscriptions, written in pencil and in red or black tint on the body of the amphoræ by the producers or under-writers, of ship-captains or customs officers; and the results of his examination prove that the mountain reached its actual height and size at the following dates: on the north side between the years 140 and 149 of our era; on the east side between 150 and 160; on the west side between 174 and 230.

The latest date, 251, was discovered not far from the summit, on the east side, but evidently out of its original place.

I come now to the most important question connected with the archæology of the Tiber, to the question of the treasures which are said to be buried in its bed. The question may be treated from a theoretical point of view, or, practically, from the point of view of discoveries actually made in the river. The idea that the river contains an untold amount of wealth, buried at great depth in its soft, yellowish sand, has been generally held since the Middle Ages. Familiar among the mistaken beliefs is that concerning the golden plate and the seven-branched candlestick, which Titus brought over from Jerusalem, and which are commonly supposed to have been thrown into the Tiber. No such plate and no such candlestick ever were thrown into the river; the story has no more foundation than the parallel one of the wealthy banker Agostino Chigi. But setting aside all information which is not based upon solid evidence, I must declare that the number and the importance of discoveries, made in the bed or on the banks of the Tiber before the present age, and registered in archæological books, are not such as to make us believe in the existence there of any extraordinary amount of riches. One or two marble statues, one or two busts, and some blocks of rare marbles, very likely fallen overboard in the act of unloading, were, before 1875, the most noticeable objects discovered in the river. With such scanty evidence at our disposal, we came to the conclusion that any regular search of the stream would prove, if not fruitless, certainly not particularly remunerative. Our judgment was confirmed by a strange occurrence, which took place in 1866. A freight train having been carelessly coupled on the gradient which leads from the railway bridge at S. Paolo to the station of Porta Portese, fourteen trucks began to descend the steep incline towards the bridge with such velocity that the central span, which was open for the passage of a steamer, could not be closed in time, in spite of the desperate efforts of the guardsmen. The fourteen trucks fell through the gap in mid-stream and were heaped up to the height of some twenty feet above water. It took the government engineers a little more than two weeks to make the necessary arrangements for the removal of the wreck ; but they had scarcely completed these when they found, much to their astonishment, that the whole mass had disappeared without leaving a single trace of the catastrophe. The fourteen cars had been swallowed, as it were, by the quicksands which fill the bed to a depth of some thirty feet.

From this fact it appeared evident that the power of absorption of the Tiber was such as to leave no hope of the recovery of heavy objects sunk in its waters. As regards lighter objects, we were of the opinion that a stream running occasionally at the rate of six feet per second must have carried them to such a distance from the town as to make a search for them almost useless.

It is with deep satisfaction that I acknowledge that I was deceived this time by false appearances, and by false deductions. The work on the embankment of the Tiber, carried on in the course of the last ten years, has proved beyond a doubt, that never has such an abundant mine of valuable antiquities been open to science before our age ; that the bed of the river has power of absorption enough to keep works of art firmly and softly embedded in its sands, but not so deeply hidden as to escape the reach of man ; that smaller articles have not been carried far away by the violence of the stream ; and lastly, that if we were to collect in a special museum the contents of the Tiber, this museum, arranged in chronological sections from the early ages of

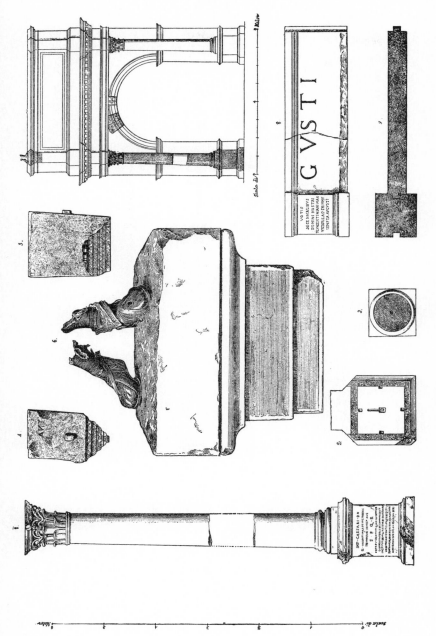

REMAINS OF A TRIUMPHAL ARCH.

Discovered in the Bed of the Tiber, 1878.

stone, of brass, of iron, to the pontificate of Pius IX., would be absolutely without parallel in the world.

To those who may find my assertions slightly extravagant, or think that the works of art and miscellaneous antiquities, found lately in the Tiber, do not correspond in number and value with the brilliant prospect above referred to, I must reply that a regular search of the river has not yet been commenced; and that the considerable amount of Tiberine antiquities already put aside by us has been brought to light quite accidentally, during the construction of the embankment. Fancy what would happen if a truly scientific investigation, amply furnished with the proper contrivances, should be undertaken!

Twice only has the bottom of the river been explored more or less regularly, although in an exceedingly small space, and twice have we gathered a surprising mass of scientific and artistic objects. The first search was made in October, 1878, under the first arch of the Ponte Sisto, on the left (or cis-tiberine) side, in an area sixty feet long by fifty wide. There we discovered the remains of a triumphal arch, raised A. D. 367, in honor of the emperors Valentinian and Valens, together with pieces of one of the bronze colossal statues which stood on the top of the monument. We found, also, an historical inscription describing how the banks of the Tiber had been surveyed and enclosed within a line of stone *cippi*, under the rule of Vespasian, by Cæcina Pætus, chief commissioner of the river, A. D. 71; another inscription, describing how the bridge, now called Ponte Sisto, had been rebuilt under the rule of Valentinian and Valens, between 366 and 367, by L. Aurelius Avianius Symmachus, præfect of the city; and then, coins, terra-cottas, fragments of marble statues and bas-reliefs; fragments of a third inscription which must have measured 320 feet in length ; and many architectural pieces belonging to the decoration of the old bridge.

The second search took place in the summer of 1885, right in mid-stream, and about 250 feet above the island of S. Bartolomeo. In sinking the compressed air caissons, for the foundations of the central pier of the new bridge (Ponte Garibaldi), a lovely bronze statue was discovered, lying head downwards at a depth of some thirty-five feet below the bottom of the river, described and illustrated in Chapter XI. ; a *patera* of gilt bronze, in *repoussé* work, two feet in diameter ; an inscription mentioning a land survey made under Agrippa ; and then the usual prodigious mass of smaller objects, from the family coins of the seventh century of Rome, to the medals of devotion struck under Gregory XVI. and Pius IX.

CHAPTER X.

THE CAMPAGNA.

MANY of my readers must have seen districts of the Roman Campagna, either when walking, riding, or gliding swiftly by in the railway carriage ; many must have read descriptions of it in historical works, or in works of fiction ; but I wonder if a passing view only, in some particular season of the year, or a more or less imaginary description, has placed before them a true picture. In a letter addressed to his friend M. de Fontanes, the charming writer Comte de Chateaubriand speaks of the famous district in the following terms : —

"Imagine something like the desolation of Tyre and Babylon, of which the Holy Scripture speaks : a silence and a solitude as vast as the noise and tumult of the men who formerly occupied the same soil. One imagines that he hears again the malediction of the prophet : *'Venient tibi duo hæc in die uno, sterilitas et viduitas,'* — 'Two things shall come to thee in the same day, sterility and widowhood.' One can see here and there remnants of old Roman roads in places where now no one passes ; one can see here and there dried-up beds of winter torrents, which, at a certain distance, have the aspect of roads well beaten and frequented, and in reality are only the furrows excavated by a passing wave. One hardly meets with a tree ; but everywhere, in whatever direction one gazes, are ruins of tombs and aqueducts, — ruins which appear like a forest of indigenous plants, the growth of an earth composed of the dust of the dead.   Sometimes, in the large plain yonder, one seems to discover rich, luxuriant harvests ; one approaches : burnt grass and dry herbs have deceived the eye.   On examining these sterile harvests traces of ancient cultivation are discovered.   No birds, no laborers, no happy country sounds, no activity, no bleating of flocks ; no villages clustered around the antique church.   A small number of dilapidated farm-houses rise from the midst of the plain : the windows and doors are closed ; no smoke rises in graceful curls from the chimney ; one hears no noise ; in fact there are no inhabitants, — a sort of savage, pale and trembling with the chill of evening dew, gazes at these dens of fever, like the spectres who in Gothic ballads defend the entrance to an abandoned château.   In fact, one would say that no nation has dared to succeed the great masters of the world on their native soil ; and that the fields of Latium are as they were left by the iron spade of Cincinnatus, and by the last Roman plough."

After this impressive description you might be led to believe that there is nothing worse to behold than the Roman Campagna.   You would be greatly mistaken.   The Campagna has an inconceivable grandeur of its own ; one is always ready, in contemplating its wonderful aspect, to exclaim : *Salve, magna parens frugum, Saturnia tellus, magna virum !* — Hail, land of fecundity, land of Saturn, mother of great men !   If you look at it from an economic point of view, it will completely discourage you ; if you contemplate it as an artist, as a poet, even as a philosopher, you would not wish, perhaps, to have it different from what it is.   The view of an undulating field of grain, or of a luxuriant vineyard, cannot give you a stronger emotion than the aspect of this Campagna, the soil of which has not been rejuvenated by a modern cultivator, and has

THE APPIAN WAY.

remained as ancient as the ruins which cover it. Nothing can equal, or be compared with the lines of the Roman horizon, the gentle inclination of its plains, the soft and fugitive outlines of the mountains which surround it. Often the valleys in the Campagna have been shaped by nature like arenas, circuses, and hippodromes; their slopes are cut in steps and terraces, as if the powerful hand of the Romans had up-turned and moulded all this land. A peculiar kind of vapor, rising in the distance, softens all objects, and hides those that might be hard or ungainly in their outlines; the shadows are never heavy or black; there are never masses of rock or foliage so dense or obscure that some little ray of light does not penetrate them. A singularly harmonious tint unites the earth, the heavens, the sea: by means of an insensible gradation of color, the lines of contact melt so that one cannot determine where one shade begins and the other finishes.

Doubtless every one has admired in the landscapes of Claude de Lorraine and Gaspard Poussin that seemingly ideal light, more beautiful almost than nature itself. Well, this is the light, this is the atmosphere of Rome. I never tire of looking from some lofty point — for instance, from the Parnassus or Belvedere of the Villa Medici on the Pincian — at the sun setting behind the stately cypresses of Monte Mario, or behind the pines of the Villa Pamphili, planted by Le Nôtre. Often I have sailed up the Tiber, as far as its junction with the Anio under the hill of Antemnæ, in order to enjoy the grand scene of the declining day. The summits of the Sabine Mountains appear as if they were melted in lapis lazuli and opals, while their slopes and bases are steeped in a violet or purple tint. Sometimes beautiful clouds, resembling light chariots of gods borne along with inimitable grace and swiftness by the wind, make one almost believe in former apparitions of the inhabitants of Olympus, under this mythological sky. Sometimes ancient Rome seems to have spread on the western horizon, under the last steps of the god of day, all the purple robes of her consuls and of her Cæsars. This rich and powerful effect does not fade as quickly as in northern climates; when you think that the last tints are dying away, they suddenly light up again in some other part of the horizon; one twilight follows another, and the magical effect of sunset is thus indefinitely prolonged. It is true that at this hour the Campagna rests in deep repose : one hears no pastoral songs; the laborers have migrated to other climates : *dulcia linquimus arva !* But one still can see the gigantic white oxen, raised on the banks of the Clitumnus, or herds of half-wild horses, descending to the bed of the Tiber, to refresh themselves in its cool waters. One imagines one's self transported to the time of the old Sabines; to the age of Evander the Arcadian, when the river was called Albula; to the age of the pious Æneas, sailing up the unknown waters to moor his ship at the foot of the Palatine.

I admit that the views of Naples, of Rio de Janeiro, of Constantinople, are more dazzling than that of Rome. For instance, when the brilliant sun or our own satellite rises above Vesuvius, like a ball of fire thrown up by the volcano, the bay of Naples, with its banks fringed with blooming groves of lemon and orange trees; with its island of Capri, rising in snowy whiteness from the sapphire waters of the Tyrrhenian; with the hills of Posilippo clothed in myrtle, stretching towards Baiæ and Miseno; all this land sung by Virgil presents, no doubt, a truly magic aspect. But, in my opinion, it has not the grandeur of the Roman Campagna. However that may be, one soon becomes prodigiously attached to this famous soil.

Has the Campagna always been in its present state of fascinating desolation? By no means. It is sufficient to take a ride across its fields and valleys in any direction you may choose, to meet at every step with remains of villas and farms which in ancient times must have been teeming with life. These villas are all modelled on a uniform pattern, rising in steps and terraces from the foot of the hill, each terrace supported by huge foundation walls, ornamented with niches, and nymphæa. The lower terraces

The Nymphæum in Hadrian's Villa.

never contain buildings; they were simply laid out in gardens, and less frequently in an orchard: the mansion of the landlord is perched on the very top of the hill, and within the area of the highest terrace. This general type of a Latin villa was praiseworthy for two reasons: first, because from the edge of each platform the eye could freely command every point of the horizon; secondly, because, with a comparatively small quantity of water, many fountains and nymphæa could be supplied, by taking advantage of the surplus of every basin, and making as many shows of it as there were steps and terraces. But it is incredible how ingenious and clever ancient architects proved themselves to be, in adapting the general type of villa to the natural conditions of the special tract of land which had been selected for its establishment; and equally surprising was their skill in exposing palace and gardens to the north, or to the mid-day sun, according as their patron wished to have a winter or a summer country residence.

From the last century of the republic, and on a much larger scale under the imperial rule, the wealthiest patrician families owned not one but several villas, planned and arranged on a different principle, in accordance with their destination of winter, spring, or summer residences. The two ill-fated brothers, Quintilius Condianus and Quintilius Maximus, owned a magnificent winter seat at the fifth milestone of the Appian Way; indeed, so magnificent that the Emperor Commodus caused both brothers to be murdered, to secure by confiscation what he had failed to secure by direct purchase. This villa, the ruins of which cover an area of nearly a square mile, was only seven miles distant from another, built by the same family on the slopes of Tusculum, as a summer resort. The Valerii, likewise, owned a line of villas, beginning at the second milestone of the Via Latina, and ending near the Castrimœnium, the modern Marino, which was adaptable to the various seasons of the year. The same practice is known to have prevailed in the Servilian, the Flavian, the Claudian, and other families of the old aristocracy.

We must not consider, however, this abundance and variety of country seats as an extravagant display of luxury. The old Roman aristocracy was educated under the same principles as the English aristocracy is at the present time. Latin gentlemen of the republic and of the empire, as English gentlemen of nowadays, were not brought up in laziness and inactivity, but served their country with their intelligence and their strength, fighting gallantly in their youth against the foes of the commonwealth, and sharing the cares of government in their mature age. From identity in the education and principles of the two aristocracies came identity in their systems of life. Our patricians, like the English, had houses in town, in keeping with the rank of the owners, in which hospitality was practised during the winter, as it is now during the London season; though in Rome the season was, so far as I can judge, exceedingly short. As soon as spring began to appear, with its tepid breezes and brilliant sunshine, the aristocracy dispersed at once to their country seats; I mean to those the average distance of which did not exceed six or seven miles from the outskirts of the metropolis. So short a distance, which they could cover with their swift Numidian ponies in less than an hour, allowed them to attend daily, and without inconvenience, to their official duties, — to the administration of public waters and granaries; to the *préfecture* of the Tiber and its docks and harbors; to the government of the city, and of the prætorium; to the administration of justice; to court duties; to the sittings of Parliament. At the same time, the comparative quiet of their delicious dwellings, half urban, half rustic, helped them wonderfully to recover the peace broken or lost among the vicissitudes of political life, to shelter themselves from court intrigues; to regain strength and vigor, after the hardships of long journeys, made through the military outposts, along the far-away frontiers, and through the provinces beyond the sea. How like the Roman aristocracy of the present day !

We must attribute to the state of things which I have described the origin of that circle of villas which surrounded the Capitol within a radius of four to ten miles from the *umbilicus Romæ ;* otherwise it would be impossible to explain why the Romans should have spent fortunes for building-sites which could not be inhabited in summer, as they were at that season hotter and less salubrious than the town itself. The number of these villas is really incredible : one must have scoured the Campagna as I have for twenty years ; one must have explored every remotest corner, on each side of the Tiber and of the Anio, as I have done, to recognize how near to truth comes the theory of those who extend the surface of Rome as far as the neighboring territories of Ostia, Bovillæ, Tusculum, Tibur, and Veii. In the golden age of the empire, before the transformation of Rome into an intrenched camp, accomplished by Aurelian, it was impossible to define, even approximately, its extent. To the thick nucleus of the fourteen regions into which Augustus had divided the city, to the houses adjoining one another succeeded a second ring of houses separated by small gardens ; a third, of houses separated by larger estates ; and lastly, a fourth ring of great villas and huge *latifundia,* each one constituting a populous and flourishing village. These groups of rustic dwellings were laid out in the town fashion, with the shrines of the compital or domestic gods at the street corners, and with local festivities and solemnities, registered in the Calendars discovered by Colocci and by Della Valle. One who attempts in our days to cross the wilderness of Fiorano, for instance, and of Capobianco on the Via Appia and on

the Via Nomentana, finds it difficult to believe that, in bygone days, these very solitudes could have resounded with
the joyful mirth of large gatherings of the peasantry; but
of those meetings, festivities, and games, we possess records
engraved on stones discovered on the spot. To this radiation of life from the city, decreasing, it is true, in direct
proportion with the distance, but decreasing little by little,
without the sudden transition of the present day, — to this
radiation of life, I say, let us add the intensity of traffic on
the high-roads, on the cross-lanes, on the flood and on the
banks of the Tiber; let us think of the aqueducts, running on triumphal arcades through the inhabited centres
of the district, distributing everywhere life and health; let
us mould again those shapeless ruins into temples, shrines,
and sanctuaries, lining at short intervals the banks of the
high-roads with roofs of bronze, glistening under the rays
of the sun; let us picture to the mind those endless marble
cemeteries, shaded by the ilexes of the villa, and by the
olive-trees of the farm; let us animate the brilliant scene
with groups of countrymen carrying into town the produce
of the fertile soil, with pious pilgrims offering libations and
flowers on the tombs of dear ones, and with travellers carried on the *lectica* or driving the *rheda* or the *petorritum*,—
and we shall thus gain a faint idea of the aspect of the
Roman Campagna in bygone times.

The picture which I have endeavored to sketch is not
imaginary; it represents with exactness the state of things
under the first three centuries of the empire, as I have been
able to reconstruct it, by the aid of daily discoveries, and
on the evidence of many thousand published and unpub-
lished documents which I have collected. Wherever, since
1867, I have seen excavations made in the Campagna,
always and everywhere, even in the most remote and se-

cluded corners, they have brought to light traces of the work of man, — roads, bridges, aqueducts, drains, rustic houses, patrician villas, mosaic pavements, enclosure walls, tombs, granaries, wine cellars, oil presses, and besides, amphoræ, oil jars, coins, utensils, bricks, water-pipes, building materials, sculptured marbles, busts, statues, inscriptions, and so forth. Totally unknown, I am sure, to my foreign readers, and, I dare say, to my countrymen also, are the names of the "tenuta (farm) di Benzone," lost in the wilderness crossed by the Via Prænestina ; of the "tenuta delle Casaccie," lost in the woodlands crossed by the Via Clodia ; or the savage glen of Monte Oliviero on the Flaminia ; desolate places, miles distant from the nearest inhabited house. And yet the excavations made under my personal supervision in these three places, in 1873, 1878, and 1883, seemed like excavations made in Rome itself, so grand was the extent and the magnificence of the buildings, the perfection of roads and drains, the abundance of works of statuary. If any one supposes the tints of my picture too enthusiastic, let him examine *de visu*, or at least let him read the official account of the excavations which my learned friends, the brothers Lugari, are carrying on, in their farm of Tor Carbone, at the fourth milestone of the Appian Way, with a view to laying open permanently a district of the ancient Campagna. Although these researches are far from being completed, the work accomplished in the last five years by the Lugaris is enough to convey to the visitor the true idea of the perfection to which the suburban districts were brought under the empire. The ground is crossed at right angles by roads, as frequent as they would be in the city itself ; and these roads are so neatly levelled and paved, and their sidewalks so cleverly arranged, that one would scarcely believe them to be country roads. Some cross-lanes were on private property, and were closed accordingly with gates at each end. You can see still the very walls, or *maceriæ*, as they were styled in ancient times, enclosing the fields; and in these fields, remains of rustic dwellings, of a modest appearance, but wonderfully well adapted to their purpose. They show what care Roman landlords took of the hygiene and welfare of their peasants. The ground-floor rooms are provided with double pavements, for the circulation of the hot air, or vapor, in the interstices, — a precaution most commendable in damp, low lands. Great care was bestowed on the drainage of the house, which was always carried to a great distance, and forced through its channel by a permanent jet of water. Remarkable, also, were the arrangements for the supply of water; which, when not actually needed for drinking, bathing, or irrigating purposes, was stored in huge reservoirs and cisterns, ready for any extraordinary emergency. At the crossing of the roads, or *quadrivia*, there were fountains for the accommodation of travellers and of their horses ; in fact, the gentleness and kindness of those happy generations went so far as to provide the weary pilgrim with seats, shaded by trees, where he could rest during the hottest hours of the day.

The starting of a patrician family for its country manor (I quote Becker and Friedländer almost verbatim) was always an event of great importance, witnessed by idlers with curiosity and admiration. Driving in a carriage was forbidden in Rome, at least during the first century of the empire, on account of the narrowness and crookedness of the streets, filled as they were with a motley, bustling crowd, especially about the sixth hour of the day, when there was a general cessation from business, and people were wont to take their morning meal. Great annoyance was created by sellers of matches (*sulphurata*) and of boiled peas, who would sometimes take in exchange broken glass instead of money. The abode of these miserable street pedlars was Trastevere, from which quarter they dispersed every morning through the whole city, but especially in the direction of the infamous Subura. The streets were choked, too, with clusters of disagreeable shops, built, in spite of municipal regulations, by hucksters and merchants of all sorts, barbers and salve - sellers, butchers and pastry cooks, but chiefly by wine-sellers, whose tables, protruding far into the street, were covered with bottles which were fastened by little chains, lest they might be stolen by some passer-by.

To gain the outskirts of the city, ladies and gentlemen of fashion made use of litters. These litters were manned by six powerful slaves in bright liveries; the rest of the escort were dressed in brown travelling suits. Numbers of slaves were despatched in advance with the baggage, while others followed in the rear, the lord and the lady being accompanied by those only whose services were deemed absolutely indispensable. The carriage which awaited the travellers outside the gate was the *rheda*, a sort of light vehicle drawn by a couple of swift ponies. The body of the carriage was ornamented with beautifully wrought foliage in metal, and Medusa heads. The hood of leather served as a protection against the hot rays of the midday sun, whilst the purple hangings, half fastened, admitted an agreeable current of cool air, and protected the inmates from being incessantly seized by the hands, addressed, or kissed, by passers-by. This exceedingly disagreeable fashion, which began to prevail under Augustus, is ridiculed in several humorous epigrams by Martial. Not merely at the official morning salutation, but at every meeting in the streets, a person was exposed to a shower of kisses, from friends and acquaintances, in fact from any one who desired to show his attachment, whether farmer, tailor, barber, shoemaker, or what not. The misanthrope Tiberius, who was unwilling to be humbled by this custom, issued an imperial decree

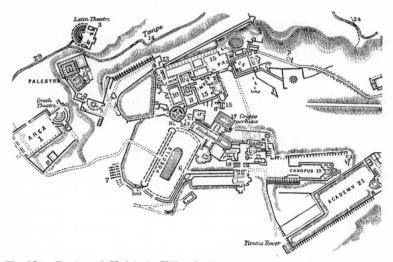

The Main Portion of Hadrian's Villa, showing to what excess the buildings and architectural decorations were carried in ancient villas, and how little space was left for landscape effects.

against it ; but it does not seem to have done much good, as the jokes of the poet above alluded to prove. In winter only was it improper to annoy another with one's cold lips.

Roman villas, as a general rule, but especially those of the Campagna, were divided into two distinct and independent portions. The first comprised the lord's manor, with more or less spacious gardens surrounding it : the second comprised the farmer's house, the various stables and barns, the dwelling of the slaves, orchards, olive-yards, vine-yards, cornfields, woodlands, and so forth.

The characteristic of an ornamental Roman garden was the entire absence of natural beauty. Its style can be compared, to a certain extent, to the French and Italian villas

of the sixteenth century.   No tree or shrub dared to grow
in its own natural fashion, for the *topiarius*, or head gar-
dener, was ready instantly to force it into the prescribed
form.   The *allées* were shut in by walls of green box or
laurel, with windows, doors, and niches imitating the architecture of palaces.   Here and there appeared threatening
forms of wild beasts, bears and lions, serpents winding
themselves round the trees, all cut by the skilful hand of
the *topiarius* out of the green cypress, box, yew-tree, myrtle, and laurel.   The reluctant foliage was compelled to
imitate letters, indicating in one part the name of the
owner, in another the name of the artist to whose invention
the garden owed its present appearance.   Grounds laid out
in this style, in which vegetation is forced into stiff geomet-
rical figures, and every vestige of nature's free dominion
annihilated, are not only described by ancient writers, especially in the famous letter of Pliny the younger, on his
Laurentine estate, but actually painted, I might almost say
photographed, in the frescoes of Pompeian dining-rooms, in
those of the greenhouse in the gardens of Mæcenas on the
Esquiline, and in those found in the villa of Livia, *ad Gal-
linas Albas*, near the eighth milestone of the Via Flaminia.
An excuse for such absurdities can be found in the fact
that the means afforded by nature in those days were but
small in comparison with the abundant resources of our
time.   Foreign countries had not as yet unfolded their rich
treasures of rare and splendid vegetation, nor their thousand shrubs and flowers : restricted to a barren flora, but
little improved by culture, the Romans sought to create, by
artificial means, a striking contrast to the free forms of nature.   This is, at all events, the excuse given by Becker.

  The trees represented in the magnificent paintings of the
villa of Livia are the laurel, the pomegranate, the stone

pine, three different kinds of firs, *corbezzoli*, popularly called *sea* cherries, ilexes, plane trees, myrtles, and cypresses. Great ingenuity was displayed in training ivy, evergreens, and acanthus upon the walls, the trees, and the terraces. Paths were usually covered with trellises and green arbors, constructed of canes and vines; and their floors were spread with yellow golden sand. Windows were generally lined with flower pots.

Greenhouses were very common; winter grapes, asparagus, gherkins, watermelons, and flowers were forced, by the proper exposure of the conservatories to the mid-day sun, and by a proper shelter of glass. Much might be said concerning the flowers known to the Romans; for, though the flora of those days was but poor in comparison with ours, still there is no truth in the assertion that the Romans contented themselves solely with wild plants, and neither laid out flower gardens, nor cultivated any exotics. Violets and roses were certainly the main ornament of pleasure grounds. Next came the bulbous roots, the crocus, narcissus, lilies of more than one sort, iris, hyacinth, poppy, amarynth, and so on. The Roman flower, however, the flower par excellence, was the rose. So excessive was the demand for roses in the cold season, that to supply the requirements of the market, and to meet the deficiency of native production, they were imported from Egypt; means were employed, of course, for keeping them as fresh as possible during the journey. Another famous place for the winter rose trade was Pæstum, and the surrounding lowlands, bordering on the Gulf of Salerno, *biferi rosaria Pæsti*, as Virgil calls those gardens, because they bloomed for a second time in the late autumn.

We must not suppose that all the villas of the Roman Campagna were absolutely identical in stiffness, of the type

I have attempted to describe; and that in every one of
them nature was constrained into uncongenial forms. I
have excavated and examined one, at least, from which art
had been thoroughly banished, and everything left to the
free play of nature.   The author and inspirer of this magnificent park is the over-calumniated young Emperor Nero,
the Hausmann of ancient Rome.   The place selected by
him is one of the wildest gorges of the Simbruine spurs of
the Apennines, a little above the modern town of Subiaco.
Through this gorge the icy stream of the Anio forces its
way, leaping by three graceful falls into the valley below.
By damming it three times, with dams more than two hundred feet high, he created three mountain lakes, where he
could indulge in the sport of trout fishing and in cold bathing, his passion for hydropathy being well known.   These
sheets of water were overshadowed by enormous oaks and
beeches, and overhanging rocks, in the interstices of which
grew arborescent ferns.   The two hunting lodges, on either
side of the glen, were connected by a bridge spanning the
abyss at a prodigious height.   One of these lodges, discovered three years ago, directly under the famous Sacro-Speco,
the abbey founded by St. Benedict, makes us wonder at its
extreme simplicity.   But what perfection in that simplicity!
What exquisite wall paintings! what exquisite mosaic pavement, and marble ornamentation!   We found, in the course
of the excavations, only one marble statue, and that lacks
a head; but this statue, headless as it is, is perhaps the
only purely Greek work which has come to light since I
began to take an interest in excavations.   It represents a
youthful male figure, nude, in a leaning posture, perhaps
engaged in athletic exercises.   The Secretary of State for
Public Instruction, to whom the care of national monuments
belongs, has accepted our suggestion of leaving the statue

in the Benedictine abbey close by; and henceforth visitors will surely be struck by the appearance of this wonderful specimen of Greek art under the mediæval cloisters of an abbey, hidden in one of the wildest cañons of the central Apennines.

Trajan, who was fond of warlike and hunting sports, moved a step farther in the direction chosen by Nero; he built another lodge, on the very summit of the pass leading from Nero's villa to the source of the Anio, at a height of 3,200 feet above the sea. Words cannot properly describe the natural attractions of the place selected by the imperial sportsman for his summer residence. Limestone peaks 7,000 feet high, marked occasionally with snow even in the heart of summer; green valleys, resorted to as a summer pasture-ground by flocks of cattle from the Campagna; dense oak and beech forests, the haunts of bears and wolves; mountain streams teeming with trout, — in fact all the characteristics and beauties of a modern Alpine summer resort, with the addition of a magnificent marble palace, furnished with the treasures of the world.

Hadrian, the successor of Trajan, inherited his passion and love for travel, for mountains, and for fine natural scenery; only he went much higher. If the Torre del Filosofo, the striking ruin near the top of Mount Etnà, did really belong to a lodge built by Hadrian, we have in it an instance of a Roman summer palace 3,631 feet higher than the Rigi Kulm, and 3,277 feet higher than Mount Washington.

A very interesting chapter might be written on the destruction of the villas of the Campagna, during the appalling vicissitudes which shook and nearly annihilated the Peninsula, in the fifth and sixth centuries of our era. I do not belong to the school which condemns the barbaric hosts, and holds them responsible for the material destruction of Rome and its immediate surroundings. The barbarians took gold, silver, bronze, jewelry, whatever could be easily moved and carried away; they may have set fire to a few monuments in the excitement of battle, or out of spite; in their ignorance and in their hatred of the Latin name, they may have knocked down from their pedestals statues of emperors and gods; but it would be folly to throw upon them the blame and the shame of the destruction of substantial marble, stone, and brick buildings. They did not have time to indulge in that sort of sport; they did not possess the proper tools to accomplish such Titanic deeds; they did not care to commit acts of vandalism from which they could reap no benefit. Rome has been destroyed by its own inhabitants; and, if I dared to deviate from the subject of this chapter, I could easily prove how perfectly true is the statement, announced in the Preface, that during the glorious *cinquecento* more harm was done, more destruction was accomplished, more monuments were overthrown, than in the course of the preceding ten centuries.

As regards the Campagna, however, there is no doubt that the barbarians were the *indirect* cause of its abandonment and devastation in the fifth and sixth centuries after Christ. In that age not only had the patrician families lost nearly all the fortune necessary to keep up those costly establishments, because the *latifundia*, which they possessed in the various provinces of the empire, had already fallen into the hands of the invader; but the insecurity of the Campagna, even during the interval of peace between two successive incursions, had become so great, that no one any longer dared to leave, even for a short time, the shelter of the town walls. Moreover, by the cessation of the supply

of water, the most important source of life, health, and
wealth had been withdrawn from the Campagna.   And
finally, we have the positive evidence of an eye-witness, the
Byzantine historian Procopius, that during the numberless
sieges of Rome by the Goths and Vandals, the districts
surrounding their camps were given up occasionally to
merciless devastation.   In the account of the Gothic war,
Procopius describes one of these camps established by the
barbarians among the arcades of the great aqueducts, at
the sixth milestone of the Via Latina, between the picturesque tower, known by the name of Torre Fiscale, and

The Torre Fiscale, showing the site fortified by the Goths.

the modern race-course at the Capannelle. Here the two main aqueducts of the Claudia and of the Marcia cross each other twice, leaving, between the first and the second crossing, an oval space, two thousand feet long by six hundred wide, encircled by lofty arches, and presenting the aspect of an amphitheatre. This enclosure the Goths fortified by walling up the arches with huge stones; and they established themselves within, with all possible comfort. They numbered seven thousand men, not including the outposts. Here they remained many months, waiting for the proper occasion to storm the city. In the mean time they spent their leisure hours in setting fire to neighboring villas, in uprooting trees, in violating tombs, and in destroying farms, until an outbreak of pestilence obliged them to leave their fortified camp and disperse. Commendatore de Rossi has collected important evidence on the accuracy and truthfulness of the account by Procopius of this episode of the Gothic war. In 1853 he saw many tombs in the course of excavation in the modern road to Albano, and within half a mile of the Torre Fiscale. These tombs were built with the spoils of more ancient ones, and contained skeletons covered with rich clothes woven with golden thread. Other skeletons were bound around the loins and the breast with bands saturated with blood. "I at once recalled," Commendatore de Rossi says, "the account of Procopius, and thought myself in the presence of Roman or Gothic warriors, whose wounds had been hurriedly dressed, and who had been slain during that murderous campaign." This supposition was confirmed by discoveries made near and on the same spot in 1876, and described by the same distinguished archæologist.

In spite of the devastation of the Campagna, which closely followed the fall of the empire; in spite of its pres-

ent state of abandonment and solitude ; in spite of the
works of improvement begun by our national government,
which threaten to change altogether the aspect of this venerable district, there are still, there always will be, nooks
and corners which will enable one to form a vivid idea
of its ancient beauty. Take, for instance, the Casino del

The Casino del Ligorio, Vatican Gardens.

Ligorio and its surroundings, in the Vatican gardens. It
is a perfect image of an ancient country-house. Take,
also, the Villa Barberini, at Castel Gandolfo, which I consider not only the very finest I have ever seen, but also the
one which comes nearer than any other to the type of an
ancient *suburbanum*. It is true that its general plan and
outline follow precisely the plan and the outline of the
glorious villa of Domitian, which that emperor built on the

west slope of the Lake of Albano, uniting in one body
his own with the villa of Clodius and Pompey the Great.
But the ancient ruins, the foundation walls of the huge
terraces, the nymphæa, and other remains are so completely concealed and screened by a thick growth of ivy,
ferns, and other evergreens, that one feels, more than
sees, the antiquity of the place. By a singular coincidence, no tree, no shrub, no flower, no bird, that is not
purely classic, seems to be allowed to live in this magnificent domain. In looking at the groups of aged ilexes,
pines, firs, cypresses, corbezzoli, laurels, myrtles, and pome-
granates, which shade the lawns in graceful and picturesque clusters, one is led to remember the frescoes representing the villa of Livia. No flower is allowed to diversify
the emerald green of the lawns, except the classic rose and
violet. And to make the illusion more perfect, flocks of
peacocks have selected the groves of this villa for their
abode, and increase the variety of the scene with the brilliancy of their plumage. As to the view which one commands from the Villa Barberini, there is perhaps more classic history contained in the district stretching far away,
from the foot of the Alban hills to the Mediterranean, from
the promontory of Circe to Mount Soracte, from Ostia to
the Tiber, than in all other districts of Italy together. Another particular worth mentioning is this: it was a well-
known custom of Roman patricians to build the last resting-place of the family within the precinct of the paternal
villa, — a pious and touching practice, almost completely
abandoned and forgotten by modern generations! It has
not been forgotten, however, in this Villa Barberini at Castel Gandolfo, and the family tomb has been raised in the
lovely pine forest which borders the domain on the side of
the Lake of Albano.

The number of ancient family crypts and mausoleums scattered all over the Campagna is really astonishing; and whereas it helps us to form an idea of the number of ancient villas, within the precincts of which those tombs were raised, it enables us, in many cases, to identify the name of the family to which the property belongs; because we seldom find a tomb, without finding, at the same time, epitaphs and inscriptions relating its history. Among the many thousand tombs which have been discovered in modern times in the Campagna, and among the many hundred which have been discovered by myself, or in my presence, one has always attracted and captivated my sympathy more than any other, — the tomb of a beautiful, fascinating girl of the highest aristocracy, whose premature death has been so sadly and touchingly described by Pliny the younger, in the sixteenth letter of the sixth book. I refer to the sepulchre of Minicia Marcella, daughter of Minicius Fundanus, brought to light by military engineers, on the very top of the Monte Mario, the highest summit in the vicinity of Rome, when they were laying the foundations and digging the moat of the new fortress, which commands the approach to Rome from the upper valley of the Tiber. The family crypt of the Minicii presented the appearance of a room, twenty-six feet square, of modest architecture, with brick pavement, door, steps, and posts of common stone, and walls simply whitewashed. When the stillness and solitude of the place was first broken, and we stepped over the threshold which had never been violated since the burial of the girl, seventeen centuries and a half ago, I saw six marble sarcophagi, without inscriptions, set up in couples against three sides of the cell. Near the wall facing the entrance there stood a marble cippus, or cinerary urn, inscribed with the name of Statoria Marcella, the mother of our heroine.

The cippus, or cinerary urn, contained the ashes of this lady. A fine piece of marble, exquisitely carved and ornamented, stood in the centre of the room. The inscription engraved upon it reads as follows : —

D . M . MINICIÆ . MARCELLÆ . FVNDANI . F . VIX . A . XII . M . XI . D . VII.

" To the soul of Minicia Marcella, daughter of Fundanus ; died at the age of twelve years, eleven months, and seven days." C. Minicius Fundanus, father of the girl, was consul from the first of May to the first of September, in the year 107 ; and governor of Asia Minor in 124. Being a cultivated gentleman, he enjoyed the intimacy of many distinguished contemporaries, — of the Emperor Hadrian, of Pliny the younger, and especially of Plutarch, who speaks of him in his book on " Equanimity," and introduces him, as a leading personage, in his dialogue " De Cohibenda Ira," — " How to check Anger." There is no doubt that Fundanus and Statoria were the parents of the young girl whose tomb we discovered on the Monte Mario : as a proof, we have the beautiful letter of Pliny, above alluded to, addressed to their common friend Marcellinus, of which letter I will give a few extracts : " I write to you with my soul deeply saddened and distressed, on account of the death of the younger daughter of our Fundanus, a bright, lovable, attractive girl, worthy not only of a longer life, but I might almost say of immortality. Although she had not yet completed her thirteenth year, she united the wisdom and the gravity of a matron to the simplicity and gentleness of a girl, the modesty and sweetness of a virgin. With what tranquillity, patience, and strength of mind she supported her fatal disease, followed the advice of the attending physicians, consoled her father and elder sister, and maintained the declining strength of her body with the vigor of her mind! Already she was betrothed to a worthy young gentleman; the day of the marriage had been settled, the invitations issued. I cannot express to you in words the sense of grief I experienced, when I heard Fundanus order that all the money which had been put aside for the trousseau, and settled on for the marriage, should be devoted to the ceremony of the cremation of the poor body." Pliny then urges his friend Marcellinus to hasten his return, that he may comfort Fundanus in his terrible affliction and bereavement, and concludes his letter with the following exquisite sentence: " As it happens that the wounded body dreads, at first, the hand of the surgeon, later endures it, and finally seeks it with anxiety, so the soul, depressed or bent down with sorrow or grief, rebels, at first, against words of comfort, later hears them with resignation, and lastly seeks them as the sweetest balsam for a wounded heart."

CHAPTER XI.

IN a manuscript volume of the Vatican library, belonging to the Syriac collection and numbered 145, a short description of Rome has been found, written, A. D. 546, by Zacharias, a Byzantine historian and Bishop of Mytilene in the island of Lesbos. From his account we gather that, towards the middle of the sixth century of our era, there were in Rome eighty statues of gilt bronze representing gods, thirty-seven hundred and eighty-five bronze statues of miscellaneous subjects, and twenty-five bronze statues which, according to tradition, had been removed from Jerusalem by Vespasian : in all thirty-eight hundred and ninety works of art in bronze, exhibited in public places. Of this immense and invaluable collection a small portion only has come down to us ; in fact, the list of ancient bronzes in modern Rome is so short that, as regards number, the contents of our museums cannot compare favorably with those of the National Museum in Naples. Our list comprises, first of all, the Capitoline group, namely, the Bronze Wolf, the equestrian statue of M. Aurelius, the colossal Head of Domitian, the Camillus or Sacrificing Youth, the Boy extracting a Thorn, and the Hercules from the Forum Boarium. Many errors connected with the origin and the discovery of these famous bronzes have been circulated, and are still believed by many. The equestrian statue is said to have been found between the Lateran and the Basilica of S. Croce in Gerusalemme, in a vineyard adjoining the Scala Santa; the She-Wolf, to have been found under the northwest spur of the Palatine hill, near the so-called Arco degli Argentieri, at S. Giorgio in Velabro; the colossal Head of Domitian to have been found, in 1487, near the Basilica of Constantine on the Sacra Via, and so on. The truth is that these celebrated works were never lost and rediscovered; but, as I have already stated in Chapter I., from the fall of the empire downwards, they have been kept together and preserved in and around the Pope's palace at the Lateran, until Sixtus IV. and Paul III. caused them to be removed to the Capitol.

Of the equestrian statue of M. Aurelius we have records from the tenth century. In the year 966, Peter, prefect of Rome, was executed for rebellion against Pope John XIII., being hung by the hair from the horse; and at its feet was flung the corpse of the Anti-pope Boniface, son of Ferrucio, in the year 974. We hear again of the group in 1347, during the festivities which followed the election of Rienzi to the tribuneship, when, for nearly a whole day, wine was made to flow from one nostril of the horse, water from the other. This constant connection of the equestrian group with the Lateran, from time immemorial, makes us believe that it was never removed there from the Forum, as commonly asserted, but that it must have belonged to the imperial residence of the Lateran from the time of Marcus Aurelius, who was born and educated in the house of the Annii, close by.

As regards the She-Wolf, the positive evidence of its being kept at the Lateran dates from the beginning of the ninth century. Benedict, a monk from Mount Soracte, who wrote a Chronicon in the tenth century, speaks of the institution of a supreme court of justice " in the Lateran

palace, in the place called *the Wolf*, viz., the mother of the
Romans." Trials and executions " at the Wolf " are recorded from time to time until 1450. Paolo di Liello
speaks of two highwaymen, whose hands, cut by the executioner, were hung at the Wolf. It was removed to the
Conservatori palace on the Capitol in 1473, together with
the colossal Head and the Camillus.

The ancient bronzes in the Vatican museum are less
important in number and in interest than those of the Capitol; in fact, only two are worth mentioning, — the Pine-
cone, in the Giardino della Pigna, and the Hercules, discovered in the autumn of 1864 under the foundations of
the palazzo Pio di Carpi, on the site of the theatre of
Pompey the Great.

The Pine-cone, eleven feet high, is generally described
as the pinnacle of Hadrian's mausoleum (now Castel S.
Angelo), in the ruins of which it is said to have been
found. The truth is that the Pine-cone has always been
the central ornament of a large fountain, or basin, or
pond, the water flowing in innumerable jets *per foramina
nucum ;* that is to say, from each of the spikes. Pope Symmachus, who did so much toward the embellishment of
sacred edifices in Rome (between 498 and 514), removed
the Pine-cone from its ancient place, most probably from
Agrippa's artificial lake in the Campus Martius, and used it
for adorning the magnificent fountain which he had built in
the centre of the so-called " Paradise " of S. Peter's, viz., in
the centre of the square portico in front of the basilica.
Considering the decadence, the poverty, and the semi-bar-
baric taste of the age in which Symmachus lived, his fountain must be considered as a real masterpiece. Cencius
Camerarius, who became in process of time Pope Honorius
III., wrote in 1190 the following description of the foun-

THE PINE-CONE AND THE PEACOCKS

In the Vatican Gardens.

tain : " In the ' Paradise ' of S. Peter there is a basin built by Pope Symmachus, surrounded by columns of porphyry, which support a dome of gilt metal ; of gilt metal also are the dolphins and the flowers, from the mouth and the petals of which the water flows. In the centre of the piece stands the Pine-cone." The two lovely bronze peacocks now preserved in the Giardino della Pigna are supposed to have come from the same fountain. M. Lacour-Gayet has recently discovered a remarkable document connected with the Cone, — the very signature of the artist who modelled and cast it, engraved twice around the lower edge of the piece :

P · CINCIVS · P · L · CALVIVS · FECIT

" This is the work of Publius Cincius Calvius, freedman of Publius Cincius."

The other bronze of the Vatican, the colossal Hercules, discovered twenty-three years ago near the piazza di Campo dei Fiori, under the foundations of Pompey's theatre, is remarkable more from having been an oracular statue than from its beauty. Very few persons are acquainted with the most striking feature of this Hercules. I mean, very few persons know of the existence of a hole in the back of the head, thirty-eight centimetres in diameter, through which a full-grown youth could easily make his way into the colossus. The experiment was actually made by a young mason, named Pietro Roega, in November, 1864, in the presence of Commendatore Tenerani and other eminent personages ; and the sound of his voice, in answering the questions addressed to him, was really impressive and almost supernatural. Hercules, like Æsculapius, Apollo, and the Fortune, was undoubtedly an oracular god, as shown by the existence of many temples and sanctuaries in which *re-*

sponsa or oracles were given in his name. Such were the temple of Bura, in Achaia, described by Pausanias; the temple of Gades in Bæ-tica, described by Silius Italicus; the temple in the Cynosargos, at Athens, described by Suidas; and such was most probably our Roman temple of Hercules, near the Circus Flaminius, to which the colossal statue found in 1864 is supposed to belong.

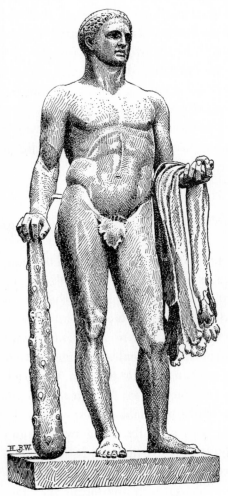

The Mastai Hercules. In the Vatican.

How happens it that so very few, among the many thousand bronze statues of ancient Rome, have escaped destruction? The answer has already been given by Fea, in his "Istoria della rovina di Roma;" by Gibbon, in his "Decline and Fall of the Roman Empire;" by Dyer, in the last chapters of his "History of the City of Rome."

During the long agony of the capital of the world, an agony which lasted nearly seven centuries, from Constantine's age to the final burning of the city by Robert Guiscard and his Normans, in May, 1084, no one, except a few lime-burners, paid any attention to marbles; works of bronze and other metals were sought for, stolen, stripped, and melted with an almost incredible amount of labor and patience, on account of their marketable value and facility of transportation. In justice to the barbarians, upon whom is often cast the blame of spoliations committed by the Romans themselves, we must acknowledge that the emperors set the bad example of stealing bronze and other valuables from public places, especially from pagan temples and shrines, after the recognition of Christianity as the religion of the state. The first inroad upon this class of works of art was undoubtedly made by Constantine, when he transferred the seat of the empire to Byzantium : at any rate, under him began the wanton practice of changing the heads of bronze and marble statues, in order that they might be dedicated to new personages with no cost and no trouble.

The next important step towards the destruction of the artistic treasures of Rome was made A. D. 383, by Gratianus, when he ordered, by imperial decree, the abolition and confiscation of the privileges and the patrimony of all pagan places of worship, on the ground that it was not becoming a Christian government and a Christian state officially to supply the infidels with the means of persevering in their errors. In 391, the edict of Gratianus was confirmed by his brother Valentinian II., and this measure so roused the indignation of the pagan majority in the Senate-House, ready to break into open rebellion, that the emperor decided to strike the final blow; and before that memorable year was over, another decree prohibited forever superstitious sacrifices in Rome and in Italy, even if offered under a private name, at private cost, and within the threshold of a private house.

The masterpieces of Greek and Italo-Greek art, to which divine honors had been offered for centuries, were removed from their temples, and exhibited in public places, in the baths, in the forums, in the theatres, as simple objects of curiosity. There is no doubt, however, that on this occasion, when suddenly exposed to the hatred and violence of a Christian populace, who had so long and so bitterly suffered from the hatred and violence of the pagan aristocracy, the works of art must have suffered a certain amount of damage. The Hercules of the Vatican, for instance, still bears the evidence of an ignoble attack, which must have taken place when the gates of the temple were shut behind it.

In 408, Alaric was induced to withdraw from Rome, on the payment of an exorbitant ransom, one of the items of which was five thousand pounds weight of gold. In order to meet this demand, the Romans were compelled to strip the bronze statues of their heavy gilding. Two years later, on the 24th day of August, 410, Alaric and his hordes stormed the town, and plundered it for three consecutive days, carrying off an incredible amount of articles of value. According to Procopius, the Jewish spoils from Jerusalem, which Titus and Vespasian had dedicated in the temple of Peace, and which are so beautifully represented in the bas-reliefs of the triumphal arch of Titus on the Sacred Way, were among the booty. Traditions, however, differ with regard to the fate of this precious and venerable collection of metals from Zion. The writers of the Talmud, for instance, believe the seven-branched candlestick to have been thrown into the Tiber, and describe the bed of the river as paved with solid bronze from Rome to Ostia. The Jewish colony of Rome, acting under the influence of this tradition, is said by De Brosses to have applied to the

Pope for a permit to excavate the whole bed, and recover the candlestick ; a request which of course met with a refusal. Others think that when Alaric, the plunderer, died in Southern Italy, near Cosenza, his followers buried him and his treasures in the bed of the river Busentinus, first diverting the course of the waters, and then letting them flow again over the tomb. I wonder whether this story is based upon a practice actually followed by the barbarians in the burial of their great chiefs and leaders, or whether it is simply a revised edition of the true story of Decebalus, king of the Dacians. On the approach of the Roman army, led to victory by Trajan, Decebalus caused the Sargetia, now Istrig, to be turned out of its regular course, and buried an enormous mass of gold, silver, and jewelry in a kind of cave which had been built for that purpose in the middle of the dry bed. The river was then restored to its natural channel, and all the men who had been employed in this extraordinary work were slain by Decebalus, in order that the secret might be safe from indiscreet disclosure. The secret, however, was revealed to Trajan by the king's intimate confidant and adviser, Beryx ; and the Romans found in the cave money and valuables enough to defray all the expenses of that costly war. According to Fabretti (" De Columna Traiana," c. 8), some Wallachian fishermen, plunging and diving into the Istrig, towards the middle of the sixteenth century, discovered a considerable portion of the treasure, which had somehow escaped the search of the Roman emperor.

To go back to the Jewish treasure in Rome, it seems certain that the whole of it cannot have been carried off by Alaric, since part was plundered by Genseric, as we shall presently see. In June, 455, the third day after the murder of Petronius Maximus, who had succeeded Valentinian

III., the Vandals, with whom mingled Bedouins and Africans, entered Rome by the Porta Portese, and plundered it at leisure during a whole fortnight. On this occasion the palace of the Cæsars was completely robbed, not only of its precious statues, but even of its commonest brass utensils. Genseric appears to have devoted himself particularly to the plunder of the temple of Jupiter Capitolinus : its statues were carried off to adorn the African residence of the Vandal king, and half the roof was stripped of its tiles of gilt bronze. That portion of the Jewish spoils which had escaped the previous attempt of Alaric, was apparently landed safely at Carthage, where, eighty years later, it was discovered again by Belisarius, and removed to Constantinople. On the 1st of January of the following year, 456, the Senate decreed that a bronze statue should be raised in Trajan's Forum, in honor of Sidonius Apollinaris, the son-in-law of the Emperor Avitus. Although the decree of the Senate must be understood in the sense that a new head, representing within a certain approximation the likeness of Apollinaris, was to be put on a statue already existing, still the fact proves that, in spite of all these inroads and plunders, works in metal were still left in Rome, not only in private palaces and villas, but also in public places, such as the forum of Trajan. Nearly half a century later, in 500, Theodoric the Great appointed a magistrate (or count, as he was called at the time), whose duty it was to take care of the statues ; and although Cassiodorius evidently exaggerates in comparing these to a population of bronze and marble (*populus copiosissimus statuarum, greges abundantissimi equorum*, viz., of equestrian statues), the new office was not a sinecure. The gilding which covered Roman statues seems to have been a motive to theft, or at least to mutilation. As to the metal employed in public buildings, especially in their roofs, an edict of Majorianus, dated 457, which forbids the application of the materials from ancient structures to new purposes, under a fine of fifty pounds of gold, betrays the fact that classical edifices were already regarded in Rome as mere quarries of stone and mines of metal.

On July 11, 472, Rome was captured, for the third time, by Ricimer and his German hordes, and plundered again, except in the district of the Janiculum and the Vatican.

In 537, during the siege of Rome by Vitiges, the mausoleum of Hadrian, which had been long since fortified, was furiously assaulted, and the statues which adorned its forty-eight intercolumniations, for the most part masterpieces of Grecian art, were hurled down upon the heads of the assailants.

On December 17, 546, the Goths, under the leadership of their king, Totila, stormed Rome by treachery, and did more damage to its monuments and works of art than had been done before by the Vandals.

In the following year, Belisarius repaired the line of Aurelian's walls between the Porta Pinciana and the Porta Maggiore : the work was completed in less than a month, undoubtedly at the expense of the neighboring monuments.[1]

It does not enter into my present purpose to follow, chapter by chapter, the history of the destruction of Rome. Two incidents only remain to be noted. First, the erection of a monumental column in honor of Phocas, the usurper

---

[1] Between the third and the fourth tower on the right of the Porta S. Lorenzo, Belisarius enclosed in his hasty fortifications a nymphæum of a private garden, ornamented with mosaics and niches. The statues belonging to these niches were actually walled up in the thickness of the masonry. I discovered them in January, 1883, on the occasion of the opening of the new Porta Tiburtina.

of the throne of the East, and the murderer of Mauritius; because, from the inscription engraved on the pedestal, we learn that the column itself was surmounted and crowned with a statue in gilt bronze. A statue in gilt bronze could not have been modelled and cast in Rome in 608: it was merely a statue cast centuries before, of which, I am inclined to believe, not even the head had been changed. The second incident worth noticing is the grant from the Emperor Heraclius to Pope Honorius of the first of the gilt bronze tiles forming the roof of Hadrian's temple of Venus and Rome. The grant had been requested in behalf of the basilica of S. Peter: it led to the destruction of Hadrian's masterpiece.

At length, in 663, Rome suffered, for the last time, the misfortune of an imperial visit. Constans II., compelled by the guilty conscience of a fratricide to wander from sanctuary to sanctuary, undertook the pilgrimage to Rome in the spring of that year, and was met by Pope Vitalianus and the few inhabitants near the sixth milestone of the Appian Way. The short and friendly visit of this Christian emperor proved absolutely fatal: he laid his hand on everything which, after the repeated sieges of the Vandals, Goths, and Lombards, had been left for plunder. " In the twelve days which Constans spent at Rome, he carried off as many bronze statues as he could lay hands on ; and though the Pantheon seemed to possess a double claim to protection, as having been presented by Phocas to the pope, and as having been converted into a Christian church, yet Constans was mean and sacrilegious enough to carry off the tiles of gilt bronze which covered it. . . . After perpetrating these acts, which were at least as bad as robberies, and attending mass at the tomb of S. Peter, Constans carried off his booty to Syracuse ; . . .

his plunder ultimately fell into the hands of the Saracens." [1]

A remarkably interesting discovery has recently been made in connection with this visit of Constans to Rome. It is certain that the emperor, between his acts of doubtful devotion in churches and basilicas, found time enough to visit the pagan monuments and ruins. These visits were recorded by one of his attendants, as a Cook's tourist would do to-day, by scratching the name of the emperor on the most prominent place of each building which the party chanced to dishonor with its presence. Here is the fac-simile of the record scratched on the " Janus quadrifrons " in the Forum Boarium : —

KωNCTANTINOC⫶εΔεKεNINOC

Another signature has been discovered and read on the very top of Trajan's column. I have no doubt that a careful examination of the principal monuments of Rome — of the Colosseum, for instance, of the Pantheon, of the Antonine column, etc. — would lead to the discovery of other such *graffiti,* and would enable us to follow step by step the wanderings of the last emperor who saw Rome before its final destruction by the Normans.

After such a marvellous succession of robberies and spoliations, there is no reason to wonder at the scarcity of antique bronzes in Rome ; in fact, our wonder is excited more at the fortune which has preserved the few we do possess. The explanation of the mystery is this. Every bronze found in Rome since the Renaissance (I speak of this later period, because our knowledge of earlier discoveries is too imperfect and fragmentary to be valued) had been carefully

[1] Dyer, p. 355.

concealed or buried, evidently under the apprehension of a great and imminent danger. The secret of the hiding-place was never revealed, either because of the murder or death of those who knew it, or else on account of the destruction of the building under which the treasure had been buried. To mention only those discoveries which have taken place in my lifetime, I will name first of all the treasure-trove of the Vicolo delle Palme in Trastevere. In 1849, a few weeks before the storming of Rome by the French army of General Oudinot, under the house No. 17 in the above-mentioned passage, a most remarkable collection of works of art was discovered by mere accident. It included the Apoxyomenos of Lysippus, now in the Braccio Nuovo, — a marble copy from the bronze original, which stood in front of the baths of Agrippa ; the bronze Horse, now in the Palazzo de' Conservatori, described by Emil Braun as " an unique work, masterpiece, and a genuine Grecian antique ; " a bronze foot, with a beautifully orna-mented shoe, which may possibly have belonged to the rider of the Horse ; a bronze Bull, and many other fragments of less importance. Here we have the evidence of a collection of works in metal, stolen from different places,[1] and con-cealed in that remote corner of Trastevere, in readiness for shipment from the quay of the Tiber, close by. Whether the deed was accomplished by a barbarian of the hordes of Genseric, who entered and left Rome precisely at this quar-ter, or by a Jew of the transtiberine community, the fact is that the treasure was never removed from its hiding-place until its accidental discovery in 1849.

[1] It has been proved by Canina that the Horse belongs to the famous group representing the horsemen of Alex-ander the Great, killed at the battle of Granicus. The equestrian statues, modelled and cast by Lysippus, had been removed to Rome by Metellus Macedonicus, and dedicated in his por-tico, *maximum ornamentum eius loci*, as Paterculus says.

The colossal Hercules of the Vatican (Ercole Mastai), discovered August 8, 1864, under the foundations of Pompey's theatre, had been not only concealed, but actually buried, with the utmost care, in a kind of coffin built of solid masonry, and veneered with marble.

In 1881, when the foundations of the English chapel were being laid, at the corner of the Via del Babuino and the Via del Gesù - Maria, a collection of bronze imperial busts was found, piled up and concealed in a subterranean passage. A similar discovery was made two years before, at the corner of the Via Nazionale and the Via di S. Eufemia, when a remarkable set of bronzes was found by Madame Ristori, hidden under the foundations of her palace.

The discovery of the two magnificent statues of athletes, which form the special subject of this chapter, took place in circumstances absolutely identical. In the spring of 1884, an application was made to the national government and to the municipality of Rome for the institution of a " National Dramatic Society," and for the grant of a plot of ground, upon which the society's theatre could be built. Both requests having been granted by the state and city authorities, the society took possession of a beautiful site, on the western slope of the Quirinal hill, between the Colonna Gardens and the Palazzo Campanari, on condition that whatever should be found in clearing it should become the property of the state. The work of excavation had not even begun, when I received a letter from an old digger of antiquities, warning me to watch carefully the building of the new theatre, on account of some rare bronzes which he thought were buried there at a great depth. The surmise was not based on any real knowledge ; the spot had never been explored before ; and no human being could foretell the chances or the results of such an excavation. Strange to say, the prophecy of my humble correspondent, Signor Giuseppe Gagliardi, proved to be correct beyond expectation : the two bronze statues discovered there in March and April, 1885, must be classed among the finest masterpieces ever brought to light from the soil of Rome.

The slope of the Quirinal hill, upon which the society is building, was occupied in ancient times by three different edifices : by the temple which the Emperor Aurelian dedicated to the sun, A. D. 273, after his victories in the East ; by the shrine dedicated to Semo Sancus, an archaic, little-known Sabine god ; and, lastly, by a portico built in the reign of Constantine, and known in works on the topography of Rome as the Porticus Constantini. The limits of these three buildings were so imperfectly known that we could not tell how large a portion of each would be uncovered, in clearing the site for the new theatre. The result of the excavations has shown that the lower portion of the ground was occupied by a private house of modest appearance, the existence of which was altogether unknown ; the upper portion was occupied by the towering substructure of the temple of the Sun.

The house being built on a steep slope, its apartments rose, of course, gradually one above another, in steps or terraces, from the level of Constantine's portico to the level of the platform of the temple, — a difference of nearly fifty feet. The apartments were beautifully decorated with fresco-paintings, mosaic and marble floors, and marble staircases ; but everything was in absolute disorder, as if a sudden catastrophe had destroyed the house. This catastrophe (whatever it may have been, sinking of the foundations, fire, earthquake) must have taken place at the end of the second or at the beginning of the third century, since no coin later than Commodus was found among the ruins.

It must, besides, have been sudden and unexpected, because all the works of art the house contained shared its fate, and were buried under its ruins. Of these works, which show the exquisite taste and finish characteristic of the golden era of Græco-Roman art, I will mention one only, a lovely *tazza,* or basin of a fountain, exquisitely carved out of a single block of *nero antico.* The tazza, four feet six inches in diameter, is fluted all around, the rim being ornamented with twelve beautiful lion-heads in full relief, through the mouths of which the water fell in graceful jets into the basin below. This house and all its artistic treasures belonged to a rather obscure personage, a freedman named Cnæus Sergius Crater.

The way we discover the names of owners of the buildings we are excavating in Rome is very simple and matter of fact, and differs from the practice followed at Pompeii. At Pompeii the property cannot be identified unless a signet ring, or a bronze stamp, or a *graffito,* betraying the secret, is discovered. In Rome, this is done by means of the lead-pipes which carry and distribute the water through the fountains and bathing apartments of the house. Water, in the capital of the empire, was the property of the crown: it was conceded to private families and individuals on the condition that the name of the " concessionaire " should be engraved on the pipes through which the water was brought from the nearest crown-reservoir, — a practice absolutely necessary for distinguishing any particular pipe out of the many, many thousand running in every direction and under every street. The legend of that discovered in the house above described reads thus : —

CNSERGCRATER · · ·

Of the temple of the Sun, the huge foundations of which

tower high above the house of Sergius, I must content myself with a concise account. The immense building was
raised by Aurelian — on the edge of the perpendicular cliff
of the Quirinal, facing the Campus Martius — for two purposes: first, to commemorate his conquest of the kingdom
of Palmyra and the capture of Queen Zenobia; secondly,
to provide the populace of Rome with an easy and unob-
structed ascent from the plain of the Campus Martius to
the top of the hill. This second purpose was accomplished
by means of two gigantic staircases, the foundations of
which are still to be seen in the Colonna gardens, in a good
state of preservation. These staircases are perhaps better
known as having supplied the material for the steps leading from the piazza to the church of the Aracœli on the
Capitol.[1]

The temple itself was built by Aurelian and his architects
when under the influence of impressions received in their
journey through the East; more especially affected by the
two great sanctuaries of the Sun, which they had seen at
Ba'albek and at Palmyra. Our Roman temple was raised
in the centre of an artificial platform, supported by massive
foundations, ninety-two feet high. The desire of the con-
structors to surpass, if possible, the magnificence of the East
is shown by the colossal size of every architectural piece of
their work. Each of the forty-four columns of the peristyle measured seven feet eight inches in diameter, sixty-
five feet in height; the area of the temenos was 464 feet

[1] The steps of the Aracœli, one hundred and twenty-four in number and
all of white marble, are wrongly described in guide-books as belonging to
the temple of Quirinus. They were
removed from the temple of the Sun
in the year 1348, by decree of the
Senate and People of Rome. The
new staircase was begun on the 25th
of October of that year, under the direction of Lorenzo Simone Andreozzi,
master mason. The cost of the work,
amounting to five thousand florins, was
raised by voluntary contributions as a
votive offering to the Madonna.

by 320. To give an intelligible idea of the size of the blocks employed in this building, I will mention the fact that the marble fountain formerly in the Piazza del Popolo, and now in the public gardens on the Janiculum, near the church of S. Pietro in Montorio, is cut out of the base of one of the columns from Aurelian's temple. As an instance of that practical tendency of the Romans which enabled them to seize every advantage offered by edifices of this kind, and to use even such buildings as were ostensibly erected for purposes of display, for any material purpose, I may cite the account of Vopiscus, Aurelian's biographer, in which he relates that the extensive vaults under the portico of the temple were used as a store and tasting-rooms for the wines which the crown offered for sale.

The temple of the Sun seems to have been destroyed at a very early date, save the southwest corner, which bravely withstood the destructive action of man and nature as late as the pontificate of Sixtus V. (1585–1590). This colossal ruin, known in the Middle Ages as the Torre di Mesa, or as the Frontispizio di Nerone, was one of the most important landmarks in this district of Rome. On the following page is a view of it, from a drawing made by Stefano du Perac in 1575, twenty years before its final destruction by Sixtus V.

Only three blocks have escaped destruction, and may be seen under the ilexes which shade the upper terrace of the Colonna gardens. One belongs to the lovely frieze of the temple; one to the capital of a pilaster; the third, belonging to the corner of the entablature, measures 1490 cubic feet, and weighs upwards of one hundred tons. This is the block described and illustrated on page 241.

To come back to the building of the Teatro Drammatico. After clearing away the remains of the house of Sergius,

The Temple of the Sun in the XVIth century.   After a drawing by Stefano du Perac (1575).

above described, we met with a fragment of the Servian walls, and behind it, the southwest corner of the foundations, or, to speak more precisely, of those of the platform upon which stood the temple and its surroundings. The foundations are built of concrete, six feet in thickness, and cross each other at right angles, according to the lines of the colonnades above. The space between these walls was not empty. I mean it was not used as a vault, or cellar, or crypt, but was entirely filled up with

BRONZE STATUE OF AN ATHLETE.
Discovered 1885.

clay and loose earth. This circumstance makes more curious and interesting the discovery which I am going to relate.

On Saturday, February 7, 1885, toward sunset, a workman engaged in clearing away the rubbish which filled up the space between the first and the second foundation walls, discovered the forearm of a bronze statue, which was lying on its back, at a depth of seventeen feet below the level of the platform of the temple. The news was kept secret by the contractor of the works until the following day; and when the government officials met on the spot the statue had been already removed from its place of concealment, and consequently we were not able to study and take notice of the circumstances of the discovery, which, however minute and uninteresting they may appear at first sight, sometimes throw an unexpected light on problems otherwise very hard to deal with.

This noble figure is seven feet four inches high, two feet wide at the shoulders, and represents a nude athlete, or at least a man of the athletic type, in the full development of his strength, whose features are evidently modelled from nature; in other words, it is a portrait statue. Some adepts of that modern archæological school which attempts the identification of everything have started the idea that the statue may represent one of the Macedonian kings, — I do not now remember which; but there seems to be hardly any foundation for such a statement. The figure stands on the left leg, the right being extended a little forwards. The right arm is bent behind the back and rests on the hip, as is the case with the Vatican Meleager and the Farnese Hercules. The left arm is raised high above the head, and was supported by a rod or a lance, the traces of which

are to be seen all along the forearm.   On the breast of the
figure the letters

L · VIS · L · XXIIX

were engraved at a very late period ; that is to say, many
years, centuries perhaps, after the removal of the statue
from Greece to Rome.   These letters have given rise to
much speculation.   They have even been read and explained as follows : L(ucius) VIS(ullius) L(uctavit) XXIIX.,
— " Lucius Visullius fought in the arena twenty-eight
times ! "   I need not dwell on such absurdities ; the truth
being that nobody — not even the great Mommsen — has
been able to give a satisfactory explanation of the mysterious signs.

The excitement created by this extraordinary discovery
had scarcely abated, when, about a month later, a second
bronze statue was dug up, under the same circumstances as
related above.   The discovery took place between the second and third foundation walls, at a depth of eighteen feet
below the level of the platform.   Being notified at once,
we assembled this time on the spot and were present
when only the head of the figure appeared above the
ground, and consequently we could follow and study the
minutest details of the discovery.   On the opposite page
is a drawing from a photograph taken at the moment of
the discovery.

The most important piece of evidence collected in wit-
nessing and following the removal of the earth in which
the masterpiece lay buried is that the statue had not been
thrown in there, or buried in haste, but had been concealed
and treated with the utmost care.   The figure, being in a
sitting posture, had been placed on a stone capital of the
Doric order, as upon a stool ; and the trench, which had

been opened through the lower foundations of the temple
of the Sun, to conceal the statue, had been filled up with
sifted earth, in order to save the surface of the bronze from
any possible injury.

Site of the discovery of the Sitting Boxer.

I have witnessed, in my long career in the active field of
archæology, many discoveries; I have experienced surprise
after surprise; I have sometimes and most unexpectedly
met with real masterpieces;[1] but I have never felt such

[1] To convey an idea of the riches
which our Roman soil is still capable
of yielding, after so many centuries
of uninterrupted excavations, I quote
some figures from the municipal statistics. From January 1, 1872, to December 31, 1885, works of art and objects of *virtu* were found in building the

an extraordinary impression as the one created by the sight of this magnificent specimen of a semi - barbaric athlete, coming slowly out of the ground, as if awakening from a long repose after his gallant fights. (See Frontispiece.) His body is bent slightly forward; his elbows rest on his knees; his attitude is that of a boxer (*pankratiastes*) exhausted by the numerous blows received, the traces of which are visible all over his body. The face, of the type of Hercules, is turned towards the left; the mouth is half open; the lips seem to quiver, as if speaking to some one; in fact, there is no doubt that the statue belongs to a group. Every detail is absolutely realistic: the nose is swollen from the effects of the last blow received; the ears resemble a flat and shapeless piece of leather; the neck, the shoulders, the breast, are seamed with scars. The modelling of the muscles of the arms and of the back is simply wonderful. The gallant champion is panting from sheer fatigue, but he is ready to start up again at the first call. The details of the fur-lined boxing-gloves are also interesting, and one wonders how any human being, no matter how strong and powerful, could stand the blows from such weapons as these gloves, made of four or five thicknesses of leather and fortified with brass buckles.

This bronze was at first thought to belong to the best period of Græco-Roman sculpture; the majority of connoisseurs and archæologists are now in favor of a purely Greek origin. This latter opinion, to which I fully subscribe, is confirmed to a certain degree by a circumstance which loses

new quarters as follows: 192 marble statues, 266 busts and heads, 152 bas-reliefs, 77 columns, 2,360 lamps, 1,824 inscriptions, 405 bronzes, 711 cameos, intaglios, and precious stones, 47 objects in gold, 39 objects in silver, 36,679 coins in gold, silver, and bronze, etc.

none of its importance because it is small. Under the middle toe of the left foot I have discovered the existence of a big A, which was not engraved after the casting (as is the case with the signs on the breast of the standing athlete), but cast at the same time with the figure. The letter is not a Latin A, but a Greek Alpha, and of a rather early shape, its height and width being absolutely the same. This minute circumstance proves, if I am not mistaken, that the work was not cast in Rome, but in Greece, and cast at a comparatively early period.

I have no doubt that the building in which the two statues were exhibited in Rome, and from which they were removed under the apprehension of danger, to be buried so carefully and at such a depth, was the baths of Constantine, separated from the temple of the Sun by a narrow street. Statues of athletes were the special ornament of Roman thermæ, and those of Constantine must have possessed their share of this class of works in metal and marble. No doubt many more statues may be found if a proper search is made under the foundations of the temple ; the work, however, is difficult, costly, and not exempt from danger, on account of the modern buildings under which the exploration would have to be extended.

The third bronze statue, discovered in Rome in the spring of 1885, comes from the bed of the Tiber, from that mighty reservoir of antiquities which seems to be inexhaustible. It was found in making the foundations of the middle pier for the new bridge (Ponte Garibaldi alla Regola), which spans the river between the Ponte Sisto and the island of S. Bartolomeo.

The statue was found in an almost perpendicular position, head downwards, sixteen feet below the bottom of the river,

and twenty-six below the surface of the waters. The merry
god is represented in the full bloom of youth, and has a decidedly feminine type, especially in the arrangement of the
long, curling hair, which is parted in the middle and fastened with a band at the forehead. The band is grace-
fully inlaid with copper and silver. The eyeballs are made
of a soft yellowish stone called palombino.

This figure, compared with the two superb masterpieces
from Constantine's baths, seems altogether too tame, and
need not be described at length. It is, nevertheless, a
Græco-Roman work of the first century of the Christian
era, — a fact proved, first, by the stiffness, and, as we Ital-
ians say, by the *maniera,* or conventionality of the attitude
and outline of the figure; secondly, by the impression of
a coin on the calf of the left leg. Our best numismatists
think that this coin must have been an imperial gold piece,
probably of the time of Nero.

The lower portion of the body has evidently suffered
from the effects of fire; but under what circumstances, by
whom, at what period, this valuable work of art was hurled
into midstream, it is impossible to determine. Its discovery, at all events, affords us a compensation for the many
losses which the gigantic work of the embankment of the
river makes us suffer. One of these losses, the greatest
perhaps of all, is the destruction, or, to speak more exactly,
the deformation of the ancient bridge connecting the island
of S. Bartolomeo with Trastevere, to which bridge two
modern arches will be added on each side, as the bed of the
Tiber must be widened there. The bridge represented was
built twenty-one centuries ago by Lucius Cestius, and restored, A. D. 380, by the Emperor Gratianus, with blocks

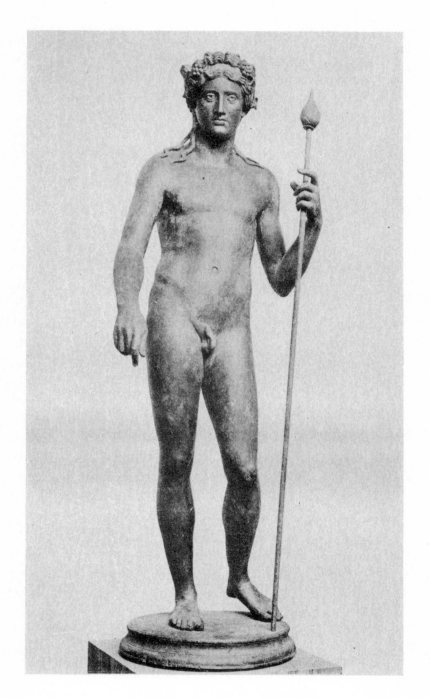

BRONZE STATUE OF BACCHUS.

Found in the bed of the Tiber.

of travertine stolen from the theatre of Marcellus, close by,
— a circumstance which shows to what degree of poverty
and humiliation Rome, the queen of the world, had de-
scended, at the end of the fourth century of the Christian
era.

Bridge built by Lucius Cestius.

INDEX.

Latin personal names are, in general, entered under the *cognomen*, except in cases where some other part of the name has come into general use.

DATE DUE